Interviewing America's Top Interviewers

INTERVIEWING AMERICA'S TOP INTERVIEWERS

Nineteen Top Interviewers
Tell All About What They Do

BY
Jack Huber
AND
Dean Diggins

A Birch Lane Press Book
Published by Carol Publishing Group

A Birch Lane Press Book
Published by Carol Publishing Group
Birch Lane Press is a registered trademark of Carol Communications, Inc.

Editorial Offices: 600 Madison Avenue, New York, N.Y. 10022
Sales & Distribution Offices: 120 Enterprise Avenue, Secaucus, N.J. 07094
In Canada: Musson Book Company, a division of General Publishing Co., Ltd.,
Don Mills, Ontario   M3B 2T6

Queries regarding rights and permissions should be addressed to Carol Publishing Group, 600 Madison Avenue, New York, N.Y. 10022

Carol Publishing Group books are available at special discounts for bulk purchases, for sales promotions, fund raising, or educational purposes. Special editions can be created to specifications. For details contact: Special Sales Department, Carol Publishing Group, 120 Enterprise Avenue, Secaucus, N.J. 07094

Manufactured in the United States of America

10 9 8 7 6 5 4 3 2 1

Library of Congress Cataloging-in-Publication Data

Huber, Jack T.
   Interviewing America's top interviewers / by Jack Huber and Dean
   Diggins.
      p. cm.
   "A Birch Lane Press book."
   ISBN1-55972-063-8 :
      1. Interviewing in television.   2. Journalists—United States—
   Interviews.   3. Celebrities—United States—Interviews.
   4. Interviewing in journalism.   5. Talk shows.   I. Diggins, Dean.
   II. Title.
   PN4784.I6H8   1990
   791.45'028'9022—dc20   90-25282
                                                              CIP

To the memory of
ROBERT JEBB
Publisher, Newspaperman, Poet,
Novelist, Translator, Painter, Guitarist

Contents

Foreword

THIS BOOK BEGAN at a small dinner party given by Mrs. Sheppard Strudwick, the widow of the film and stage actor. Sylvia Westerman, previously unknown to us, was one of the six other guests. We walked her home and told her about our plans to write a book on interviewing, unaware that she had spent most of her professional life in television news production. A few days later we interviewed her, and she arranged for us to see Mike Wallace, Roger Mudd, and Wally Pfister, president of Executive Television Workshop, whom we also interviewed. Wally Pfister called Ted Koppel for us.

Leaving a benefit movie to go to a dinner party, we walked with writer and broadcast executive Tom Morgan to his garage and again talked about our book. We were unaware that Tom had spent years interviewing for magazines and knew a great many people in the media; he generously offered us an interview and countless introductions.

And so it went.

The next-to-last question in each of our interviews was, Whom should we interview? The people we saw told us whom to pursue, thus our selection came in large part from these highly successful interviewers. Our last question was, How do we get to them? In many cases, these people asked us to use their names or made calls or wrote letters for us.

Setting up appointments was anywhere from easy (after Sylvia Westerman called Mike Wallace, we were in his office in a day or so), to difficult (it took us eleven months to get to Barbara Walters, in spite of an array of introductions), to impossible (even with Mike Wallace's introduction the secretary to the assistant to Johnny Carson said flatly that Mr. Carson did not give interviews).

The machinery of arranging the interviews through publicity people, secretaries, assistants to secretaries, and so on, was horrendous. Secretaries naturally protect their bosses, especially if the bosses are extraordinarily busy (Phil Donahue's press secretary was a tiger). Assistants sometimes told us they would return our calls and did not (most did, however). In general, our rule was to keep trying, never showing any annoyance (watchdogs are sometimes powerful, and when offended, they can prevent one from ever seeing their wards).

Although the writing of this book was a collaborative effort, the interviews (except that with Studs Terkel) were conducted by Jack Huber. Thus, when used in the text of this book, the "I" refers to Jack Huber.

With rare exceptions, we edited little of what our interviewees gave us. Our interviewees jumped around as most of us do, especially when asked open-ended questions, which almost all of ours were. Thus, for the sake of clarity, we sometimes found it necessary to put more order into the answers we received. We were careful not to disturb the beauty and color of the language.

We have a great many people to thank for their help on this book.

We are extremely grateful to the nineteen people we interviewed, who are the foundation of the book.

The following people made telephone calls to arrange interviews for us: Phil Donahue, Edith (Mrs. Don) Edwards, George S. Franklin, Jr., William Maxwell, Wally Pfister, Nicholas Pileggi, Gillian Poole, Mrs. Harold Rome, Dr. Linda Scheffler, Phil Scheffler, Frankie (Mrs. William) Schuman, Connie Stone, and Sylvia Westerman.

These people offered to write or actually wrote letters of introduction for us: Marie Brenner, Byron Dobell, Arlene Francis, Sherrye Henry, Judy Licht, and Bill Moyers.

The following made suggestions about interviewees and offered the use of their names to arrange interviews: Amyas Ames, Ken Auletta, Marie Brenner, Byron Dobell, Phil Donahue, Arlene Francis, Sherrye Henry, Jay Iselin, Mary Rockefeller Morgan, Thomas B. Morgan, John Oakes, Diane Sawyer, William Small, Mike Wallace, Barbara Walters, and Sylvia Westerman.

John Chancellor, Woody Doudt, and Anne Morrow Lindbergh suggested and lent us books which were invaluable

to us. Alden Whitman and Craig Wilson gave us information
about the history of interviewing. Other suggestions were
made by Chris and John Carmichael, Byron Dobell, Patricia
Kaufman, Edward Langlois, Kristina Lindbergh, Connie Roo-
sevelt, Beth Wilson, and Sandra Woodworth.

Suggestions about interviewees and tactics were generously
made by Dr. Vera Kwochka, Jack Marshall, Stephen Morrow,
and Helena Franklin Rosier.

Assistance was given by Suzanne Siegel of the Hunter College Library and the staffs of the library at the University of
New Hampshire at Durham, the Portsmouth (N.H.) Library,
and the Rice Library in Kittery, Maine.

Jeanne and Robert Jebb, Emily and William Maxwell,
Richard Hall, and Sylvia Westerman spent hours reading, listening to us read, and offering suggestions about the manuscript. Leonard Koenen suggested the title of this book.

And, of course, Mrs. Sheppard Strudwick invited us to the
dinner party where this book was born.

Interviewing America's Top Interviewers

Introduction

In PREPARING THIS book, we spoke with nineteen journalists and writers who gave us extraordinary interviews. These people spend a major part of their professional lives asking questions. Their television programs, radio shows, newspaper and magazine articles, and nonfiction books come primarily from interviews.

Many of the people in this book have themselves been interviewed countless times and have been subjected to the kinds of questions they ask others. They are asked about their private lives, their marriages, their salaries, their feelings about the famous people they have interviewed. The odd thing is that they are seldom asked about what they do—interviewing.

These busy people, many of whom resist being interviewed, gave us anywhere from forty-five minutes (Phil Donahue) to three hours (Oriana Fallaci) to talk about interviewing and how they do it. We report here what they said to us and what our interactions with them were like, along with a profile of their lives as interviewers.

We heard again and again from the interviewers that, in general, people want to talk, and that the trick is to turn on the tap. These writers and journalists know how to turn on the tap.

What they told us, eloquently and colorfully, with examples from major national and world events, was how they get people—from the man on the street to China's Deng Xiaoping —to talk.

The people we saw reach audiences of thousands to many millions, sometimes with a single exposure. Most of them have won prestigious prizes, not once, but repeatedly—Pulitzer Prizes, Emmys, Peabody Journalism Awards, and on and on. Many of them have achieved celebrity status. The power of these journalists staggers the mind.

What is the nature of this power? Three of the noted media

interviewers we saw have commented on the extent of their power and what it means to them.

Bill Moyers has written: "My mail suggests to me that people of all persuasions watch me on TV.... That's power. The stewardship of air time is critical. It's not the ability to change the course of things directly, but you can change a person's view of the world. You can affect the quality of his day."

Diane Sawyer recognizes her power but places a different value on it: "I love the breathtaking way we walk into people's lives and ask them anything we want and then leave. For a moment you have available to you the whole universe of a person's life—the pain and suffering and the joy and the struggle. You can learn from it and take it with you, and then come back the next day with somebody else."

On the other hand, Robert MacNeil revealed to us that he is appalled by the power of television interviewers.

With unusual emphasis in his voice, he told us:

> One of the things that intrigues me about the interviewer today is what he has become, the range of impertinence he is allowed in the society.... Television has created this animal who is permitted by society, encouraged, and very well paid, to be everybody's kind of—what's the word I'm looking for—an extension of them, you know, a surrogate.
>
> And the license is extraordinary. A television interviewer, especially if he has some kind of national audience and is well known, has a license to ask virtually anybody in the world to let him or her come in and ask them anything. Incredible! I mean, really incredible!

The interviewers represented in this book are the surrogates who think for us, listen for us, ask the questions we might ask if we were on the spot. They, of course, do not have total freedom—they are limited by time (as on radio or television) or number of pages (as in an article or book) and the concern for what will interest their audience. But in a showdown, these interviewers decide what topics we should know about: they pick the interviewees and they choose the questions.

By now, not only can well-known interviewers get almost anyone they want to sit for them, but the interviewee can expect to bare his or her soul if the interviewer has his way.

While this has long been true, the wide exposure of television has given interviewers even more power. It amounts to this: the larger the audience an interviewer can promise a prospective interviewee, the more seductive the offer to be interviewed.

For this book we had broad and specific interests. The broad interests were: What in their backgrounds prepared these men and women for the influential positions they hold? How do they describe what they do? What are they looking for? Why do their approaches to interviewing differ so greatly?

Our specific interests mirrored what we believe a great many people want to know. Questions such as: How does Barbara Walters get wary, famous, overly interviewed people to say in front of millions of people things they apparently never intended to say? For *Thy Neighbor's Wife*, how did Gay Talese entice people not only to reveal their sexual activities, but also to consent to the use of their names? How does Oriana Fallaci get away with screaming at and insulting world leaders during her interviews?

What surprised us more than anything else was the enormous range of answers we received to our questions.

The pithy answers were, we believe, in part a function of our questions. They were broad enough to allow people to take off in many directions. In addition, our experience taught us to be quiet when these people spoke about their work. Once we had asked a decent question, all we had to do was listen enthusiastically and give an occasional understanding nod to keep the interview going.

The following is a sampling of the types of questions we asked our subjects:

What makes a *really* good interview? (This was always stated exactly this way, and was our first and most productive question. Our interviewees usually talked on and on, answering some of the subsequent questions along the way.)

How would you describe to someone who isn't familiar with your work how you use interviews?

What kind of person makes a good interviewer?

Is there a talent for interviewing? (The usual answer was yes, and while the question invited merely a yes or no—generally frowned on in interviewing—our interviewees went on to describe what they felt the talent was.)

How do you prepare for an interview?

How do you record interviews?

What is it you're after in interviews?

What would an interviewer do that would make you cringe?

We ended each interview by asking who else the subject felt we should interview and how we could get to him or her.

We relearned something about questions: in general, the broader the question, the more revealing, personal, and colorful the answer.

We got almost no "automatic pilot" responses (the kind that politicians are said to give if they can get away with it). This may be because, as we have said, these individuals are seldom asked about what they do and perhaps found in our questions some issues and ideas they have not asked themselves. We sometimes got the gold-mine response which they themselves dream of: "I hadn't thought about that before."

Despite great differences in their answers, there were some fairly clear agreements. Most agreed that a good interviewer is naturally curious, is persistent in going after interviews, loves asking questions, and listens intently. These qualities, they told us, "come with the territory," and perhaps cannot be taught (although there was some disagreement about this).

All agreed that a good interviewer prepares carefully for a talk with his or her subject. He must know something about the topic which is going to be discussed. (Tom Morgan tells us how J. Robert Oppenheimer reneged on an interview until Morgan read prescribed articles—"four feet high!" he said—on nuclear physics.) He must know something about the person he is going to interview. (As discussed later in the book, Roger Mudd's intimate knowledge of Edward Kennedy and the Kennedy clan was certainly crucial to his dramatic and fateful interview with the senator.) An expert prepares a list of questions, knowing perfectly well that most of the questions will be scrapped when she gets face to face in the interview. (Barbara Walters, for example, prepares scores of questions for an interview with someone like Elizabeth Taylor, some of which are from anyone she can corner long enough to ask: What do you want to know about Elizabeth Taylor? She then is ready to go in any direction the interview takes her.)

Good interviewers shift gears with the subject's responses. They know that, as a good serve in tennis does not insure that the ball will come back where it is expected, an interviewer has little idea of how her expertly prepared questions will be answered. Journalists use the following scenario to illustrate bad interviewing: the President of the United States says, "Tomorrow we're going to declare war on the Soviet Union," and the interviewer, blindly following a sequential list of prearranged questions, responds by asking, "And are you and the First Lady happy in your marriage?"

The differences we found among interviewers reflect not only their unique personalities, but also the fact that they conduct different types of interviews, with different goals, different signature styles, different time limits, different settings.

60 Minutes interviewers, for example, were originally conceived of as "predators looking for fresh prey," while Barbara Walters wants answers for the questions people on the street have about the famous people she interviews. Robert MacNeil desires on the *MacNeil/Lehrer NewsHour* to present various sides of an event currently in the news, while Studs Terkel strives to find out how "ordinary" people feel about an issue that is central to their lives, such as working (the subject of one of his popular books derived solely from interviews).

Do politeness and civility work better than hostility and prosecution in an interview? Nick Pileggi says, "The adversarial approach is good for the soul but bad for the story." On the other hand, as you will see, Oriana Fallaci's adversarial approach is also good for the story.

We were surprised by the disagreement among print interviewers about using a tape recorder versus taking notes. Some found that a tape recorder sets people on edge; others found that interviewees forget about it almost immediately (this is what we find). Everyone agrees, however, that the time it takes to listen to and transcribe tape recordings is overwhelming. At times, the deadline for a manuscript is over by the time one goes through all this. Notes, on the other hand, can be full of errors. The solution for some interviewers is to use both. We used only the tape recorder and did our own transcriptions. It's true: the task is overwhelming, but worth every minute if subjects use the sort of colorful language typical of the group we interviewed.

The people we spoke with used surprising analogies to describe their interviewing. Diane Sawyer thinks of a good interview as "a dance at its best," Ken Auletta uses sexual and baseball imagery (he talks of the foreplay of the interview, for example), Oriana Fallaci thinks of an interview as a theater piece, while Mike Wallace and Tom Morgan see interviewing as a battle.

Interviewers are, of course, affected by the amount of time they have for an interview. A chronic lack of time is the common complaint of these interviewers. Some, like Phil Donahue, are allowed only a few minutes with interviewees. *Nightline* and *The MacNeil/Lehrer NewsHour* generally allow Ted Koppel and Robert MacNeil a bit more time (but Koppel must deal with the constant interruption caused by commercials). At the midpoint of the spectrum is Oriana Fallaci, who often has two or three multi-hour interviews with world leaders and is sometimes asked back by an interviewee who wants to continue the "conversation." At the other end of the spectrum is Susan Sheehan, who spends years talking with, even living with, someone she later writes about in *The New Yorker*.

A live interview is very different from a taped one that can be edited. In a live one, the interviewer is always under pressure to produce the dramatic question and response. In a taped interview, poorly framed questions and boring answers can be deleted before the public sees, hears, or reads them.

There was some disdain shown for what some interviewers called show-biz interviewing, that is, interviewing that tends to elicit mere entertainment, not information. The contempt was shown, however, only by those who clearly would be considered "news people"; those whose interviews might be considered entertaining did not mention the topic. When this topic does arise among interviewers with whom we have talked elsewhere, the conclusion is pretty clear: Journalists should be free to present material as they like, ask the questions they like and in the way they like, so long, of course, as they can find a forum.

The headiest topic approached by any of the people in this book concerns whether, through their interviewing, they get the truth. Susan Sheehan selected journalism requiring years of interviewing one person because she feels she gets the truth this way. Most interviewers felt that the truth does not usually come out in short interviews (presidential press conferences illustrate this observation). Tom Morgan, who tends to interview individuals for days or weeks (but not years, as do Susan Sheehan, Gay Talese, and Nick Pileggi), feels that he never gets at the truth. In answer to this dilemma, Ken Auletta said to us, "No one is a snapshot. We're all complicated people. I think it was Christopher Morley who said that truth is a liquid, not a solid."

As long ago as 1875, before radio, magazines, books, and television could command such vast audiences, and interviewers had not reached the level of power they have today, Mark Twain found interviewing an interesting enough topic to write about. In "An Encounter With an Interviewer" he chided journalists about interviewing, which was, even then, "all the rage" and was used with "any man who has become notorious."

Informational or show biz, adversarial or civil, live or taped, interviewing is still "all the rage" and is surely here to stay. There is every indication that interviewers, rather than losing power, will only gain more and more power through their stock in trade—asking questions. In this book you will read how some of the famous interviewers do it, how they got to be where they are, and what it is like to be in their shoes.

I

Confronting, Prosecuting

INTERVIEWS AS A MODE of presentation of information and entertainment could be said to have begun when a few journalists illustrated just how fascinating a person could be when asked the right questions. At the top of the list are Mike Wallace in the United States and Oriana Fallaci in Europe and the United States.

These two journalists also showed the viewing and reading public that the person *asking* the right questions can be just as interesting as the person answering them. The popularity of Wallace and Fallaci derives not only from their producing good stories but from their adversarial style of interviewing. Journalists have tried to copy their wild styles, but no one has really succeeded in equaling either one of them in size of audience or longevity.

As two of the most charismatic people in the business of interviewing, they have picked up power along with their popularity. Mike Wallace remarked, "When L.B.J. acknowledged that when he lost Walter Cronkite, he lost the [Vietnam] war, and certainly his own presidency, I think we began to understand, for better or worse...that we were part of the story, not just reporting the story."

What Fallaci drags out of world leaders sometimes makes them quake in their boots. In her six-hour interview with Oriana Fallaci, Indira Gandhi made disparaging remarks about President Zulfikar Ali Bhutto of Pakistan; Bhutto read the report of the interview, called Fallaci, and asked her to interview him ("How could you go to her and not to me?" she reports his asking). In his interview, he turned the tables and criticized Gandhi. Then he reflected on what he had said, traced Fallaci to the Intercontinental Hotel in Addis Ababa ("I don't know how these people in power trace you wherever you

11

are"), and told her that she must take out everything he had said about "Indira." Fallaci made a characteristic reply, "You must be joking, Mr. President." Apparently alarmed, Bhutto said, "Listen, the lives of 600 million people are in your hands," to which Fallaci replied, "My hands are too small to hold the 600 million people." She proceeded to publish the interview as he had given it to her.

Wallace and Fallaci have at least one trait in common: their ability to confront and prosecute interviewees and get away with it. Wallace and Fallaci may be threatened, their inter-viewees may walk out on them, but they are still here.

Tom Wicker of the *New York Times*, discussing the dramatic year of 1968, commented, "The American press in general entered the Vietnam War trusting the U.S. government....The ethic of the U.S. press at that time was not one of digging far behind the story and what the official spokesmen were saying. I think it was the war in Vietnam that began to change that ethic. As a result of that, more than any other single episode, the American press has become more adversarial, more likely to look behind the surface of the story—and the spokesmen's version of it."

While it is probably an exaggeration to say that the American press did not start to look beneath the surface of a story until 1968, it is worth noting that Wallace and Fallaci began long before that. Mike Wallace started his adversarial approach—confronting and prosecuting—on *Night Beat* on October 9, 1956. (That jumps the gun by twelve years.) Oriana Fallaci, a citizen of Italy, whose government officials have perhaps always been suspected of not revealing the unblemished truth, and where the press started aggressively badgering interviewees sooner than the American press did, began as a special correspondent for *Europa* magazine in the mid-1950s where she "cajoled, badgered, and charmed her subjects." Wallace and Fallaci have both been confronting and prosecuting for a long time; they are old pros.

In the course of our interviews we found that Fallaci is generally admired by her colleagues. This may be because of the consistently high status of her interviewees and her extrac-tion of extremely interesting information about world leaders. Wallace, on the other hand, is accused by more than a handful of his colleagues of being more show biz than informational, producing more heat than light (at least in his earlier days on *Night Beat* and *60 Minutes*). How much light he has shed over the years depends, of course, on what light one is seeking; the heat is clear (as it is with Fallaci).

There is no question that people have found Wallace entertaining. In an article on the history of *60 Minutes*, a *New York Times* reporter wrote, "At the end of [the] 1976 season, '60 Minutes' [with Mike Wallace as 'star'] became a hit show, and that changed everything. It suddenly became apparent that a hit prime-time news program was a property of unimagined worth, infinitely more valuable than a hit entertainment show."

Fallaci also is extremely popular. She has an audience all over Europe.

What accounts for the way Wallace and Fallaci conduct interviews? From their comments a few general statements can be made. They confront and get away with it. At a minimum, they are willing not to be liked, and at a maximum, they have the courage to go the limit and risk the consequences.

Oriana Fallaci

Writer

"If I could interview God, provided that he existed, I would not be intimidated by him. I would have so many questions. 'Given the fact that you are a bastard, because you have invented a life that dies, why did you give us death? Since we are born, why should we die? So let's begin with that: why did you do that?' So I'm never intimidated."

THE FEISTY WOMAN who has been called "perhaps the most adept political interviewer in the contemporary world" bristles when she is identified as an interviewer. In fact, when, after considerable delay, she was deciding when to see me (or maybe *whether* to see me), it occurred to her that being included in our book would further identify her in Americans' minds as an interviewer. I had to assure her that I would make it clear that she wishes to be thought of as a writer.

Over the years, she has developed a brand of interviewing that is unique to her. It resembles the most rabble-rousing of interviewing decried by the journalistic elite—she accuses, insults, defies, and sometimes risks her life in outrageous behavior during interviews. However, those who might otherwise be her detractors know that she gets astounding information from world leaders and obviously has a deep sense of political purpose. Theatrical, like the most raucous of contemporary interviewers, she is at the same time highly respected by her colleagues, and sometimes sought after by world figures who wish to be interviewed by her.

In Europe, Oriana Fallaci is a celebrity; in the United States, she is merely well known. Her books, published first in Italian and then translated into various languages, sell hundreds of thousands of copies and garner literary prizes. She covers various subjects, but in almost everything she writes there is a political thrust. Her series on the Vietnam War, *Nothing and So Be It*, for which she spent considerable time in the thick of the war, won the Italian equivalent of the Pulitzer Prize. She has written about space technology in *If the Sun Dies*, about abortion in *Letter to a Child Never Born*, and about the life and death of her lover, the Greek patriot Alexandros Panagoulis, in *A Man*.

Fallaci has collected her most famous interviews in two books, *The Egotists: Sixteen Amazing Interviews*, about entertainers, novelists, and royalty (her celebrity interviews), and *Interview With History*, which consists of her most talked-about interviews with world political figures, including Henry Kissinger, Indira Gandhi, and Golda Meir.

Fallaci has been interviewed often. For an interview in *Playboy*, the editors of the magazine thought it would be a good idea to match her with an interviewer noted for toughness and confrontation. They selected Robert Scheer, who is known for those qualities. He reported later that in his time with Fallaci he experienced "more hours of tension than occurred in [his] three marriages" and concluded, "This was the first assignment I've done for *Playboy* over a ten-year period for which I was underpaid." My experience in interviewing Fallaci was totally different from this.

At the time of my introduction to her through William Small, former president of NBC News, she was writing what she feels is her *chef d'oeuvre*, a mammoth novel. I wrote to her at her home, as Bill Small suggested, and promptly received a letter in which she wrote that she was in the process of finishing her new novel, and that I should contact her in two month's time, when "the nightmare should be over."

I phoned in two months, there were a few more delays, and finally she called and asked me to come to her Upper East side Manhattan town house on a Tuesday at six PM. She asked, "Will two hours be enough?" "I generally ask for forty-five minutes," I replied. "We'll see," she said. We were together for almost three hours.

I am still not sure why she consented to see me, and I forgot to ask her. (I suspect it was the power of her friendship with Bill Small.) About halfway through our interview, she said:

■ I don't give interviews. It is something like four years since I've given an interview. Maybe more. The last interview I gave was to the French TV after I interviewed a man whom I adored—Deng Xiaoping. Since then I've never given an interview. And I shall not in the future. Today I called my office and there were three requests for interviews—one from Paris, one from Holland, one from Bulgaria. I have said to my publisher that when the book comes out, I'm not going to do publicity. I'm not going to promote. The book is beautiful. Why should I explain it?

Once I accepted an interview by phone with a Dutchman. "What is your preferred color?" I said, "Sir, the rainbow!" and pooh! I put the phone down. So they want to interview me, and I don't want to see them. In the best of cases, if everything goes well, I make them a precious gift. Because I give them material that's written; it's written, it's done. Tonight I've written a story. I've talked to you about ideas; the ideas came to me and I said them.

I've done this with you. If I'm wrong about you, it means my perceptiveness is gone because I feel you're not going to betray me. The type of person like you, you don't even have such an interest.

We both did our part to make our interview a pleasant, civilized event. Partly because it was evening, partly because I was visiting her home, and partly because she is European, I brought a large bouquet of flowers. She seemed touched. She ushered me to her large, lushly furnished second-floor sitting room. A silver wine cooler and two crystal wine goblets sat on the oversized coffee table. She offered me a huge, overstuffed chair, left the room, came back with some Italian white wine, and placed it in the cooler. The wine was not Gallo's. She sat on a sofa across from me, but fairly close, and I began.

I left intoxicated (I have explained elsewhere that I am

highly enthusiastic), not with the good wine (I watched how much I drank), but with the intimate encounter with this fiery, powerful woman. She said of herself, "I'm not a typical woman; I'm very virile." On reflection I understood how she extracts the information she does from the world leaders who ordinarily guard what they say. She is a femme fatale. The real thing.

Much later, I told Byron Dobell, the former editor of *American Heritage*, that I had interviewed Oriana Fallaci. He seemed amused and said, "That must have been interesting. I'll bet that by the end of the interview you would have told her anything she wanted to know despite the fact that you were the interviewer." He was right.

She talked without much stimulus from me other than my rapt attention. However, she admitted that she had taken over, and would stop with comments like, "Okay, you want to go more on technicalities, don't you?" to which I would reply, "No, I love what you say," and she would go on. "I will talk at random and you take what you want." Why would I stop someone who spoke directly to the point of my interview (she had caught that clearly) and in a colorful way? She had taken control of the interview, and I had let her; I felt I was in good hands, getting exactly what I wanted. At one point she said:

■ Interviewing is like driving a car. The interview is in the hands of the person who puts the questions. Except with me. If you were interviewing me [I was supposed to be interviewing her], the interview would be in my hands, because I'm the driver. I cannot forget it. You send me the best interviewer—I'm going to drive.

I was interviewed by Dick Cavett. And Dick adores me, because he's as lazy as I am. I'm lazy, would you believe it? It's my guilt that makes me work. By instinct I would be lazy. All intelligent people are lazy. And Dick said to me, "I was very worried about interviewing you. I don't know where to start." I said, "Don't mind; I start." And I gave a lecture like I'm doing with you. He didn't have to ask one question.

Her frankness can be devastating, as one can see in her interviews. With me she would be frank about her disdain for interviews, seem to realize that she might have offended me, and try to smooth things out.

Oriana Fallaci is petite—five feet, one inch tall and 105 pounds. It would be hard to imagine anyone not finding her sexy, though what it is about her that gives this feeling is not obvious. I felt she was acutely aware that she was with a man, and she seemed to like that (she said later that she likes men better than women). Her liveliness and energy overwhelmed me. She speaks, as others have said of her, "in italics and exclamation points." She makes outrageous sounds, like a wildcat, a vampire; her enthusiasms and disgusts are expressed with outlandish guttural sounds. Her salty language adds to the flavor of what she says. The tapes were hell to transcribe (her Italian accent is strong and she spoke in English, obviously in deference to me), and I lost some of what she said.

Her strong political stance was built into her background. She was born in Florence, Italy, in 1930, of Spanish and Italian descent. She grew up with a highly active political father. He was a cabinetmaker and poor, but he was a socialist politician and a resistance leader in World War II, frequently in prison for anti-Fascist activities when Fallaci was a child. She found her niche in life fairly early.

■   When I was sixteen, I finished school, two years in
    advance, and I went to the university for medicine. I
    wanted to study the brain. Every time I see a book on
    the brain, I buy it! And if I had the money, which I
    didn't then, I would become a psychiatrist, but I had to
    go to work.

Her uncle, the founder of the magazine *Epoca*, suggested to her that she offset her school expenses by taking a job as a reporter for a newspaper in her off hours. She fell in love with words; in addition, journalism paid well, and she dropped medicine.

Her career as journalist naturally required interviewing,

and she quickly showed an extraordinary knack for it. She told a *Newsweek* reporter, "Sometimes I blush, not only for them, but also for myself. I always feel I am undressing them."

No interviewer but Fallaci stated the fact that the type of interview she gave me is a gift from the interviewee to the interviewer. Here is her gift:

■ I want to make a little preface to what we are doing. Do not forget that my interviews are far from my mind. I mean Alpha Centauri is nearer than interviews are from my life for years now. Because each time I write a book it takes years. *A Man* took three years. In the end this will be three years. My pregnancies are those of an elephant, three years.

I must also say that I don't love interviews anymore. They don't interest me. We can discuss that later. And making interviews is not easy at all, and people think it's easy. It's stupid to think it's easy. But for me, compared with the difficulties of what I'm doing now, it's outrageously easy. When you have to deal with forty-three characters that you have to put together with a plot, it all has to come out of your imagination. That's so crazy that an interview becomes like smoking a cigarette.

And so I look at each interview with a little disdain. You understand? [I felt she realized that she might have offended me.] That's...that's...I don't want to diminish that kind of work, but for me that's the reality. [She stopped and waited for me to say something. I explained the rationale for our book more fully and said I would ask questions.]

Okay. Ask me questions. [I did not rush in with a question.] Okay. There are no rules. There are no rules because in a very minor way, it is an act of creation. It's journalism. Journalism is not the creation that literature is, of course, but to some degree it is creation. When you come to the field of creation, you come to the field of art, and then, really, there are no rules. I mean, Leonardo, Raffaelo, Michelangelo, could tell their pupils, "Keep the brush this way, use the colors this way, mix the yellow and the green and remember that when you do like this you have to do like that." But those pupils were not artists. They had not this creativity in themselves. The poor guys could go on for years and they couldn't do it. When you come to the field of art, it reflects the personality, the individuality, of the person who performs one art or another.

When I visit the universities, they say to me, "I want to be Oriana Fallaci." I say, "That's idiotic. What is your name?" "My name is Mary (or John) Wilson." I say, "I don't want to be Mary or John Wilson. And you cannot be me." But they want to make the interview like me. I say, "You cannot make the interview like me." "What does it take to make interviews like you?"

"It takes a woman of my age, born in a certain place, in a certain time, who had a certain life. You must be one meter, fifty-seven centimeters as I am, and to have blue eyes, and have walked around Florence when you were a child, to have seen the Ponte Vecchio and Michelangelo and Giotto, etcetera, etcetera, etcetera. And you must have known the world. You must have had a father like mine and a mother like mine and professors at school like mine and all the difficulties and tragedies of my life, all my loves, at the same time. My brain will never be yours and vice versa. My brain and what is stored in it gives birth not only to certain behaviors but to certain ways of approaching not only people but facts."

And it corresponds to the moment of your life. Today I would never make the interview as I made them twenty years ago, not even three years ago. I'm a different person, changing. I change my attitude toward life, my judgment. I am at this point in my life more cynical, at the same time more merciful, full of pity, and I understand much more.

Hah! I was already much more generous when I interviewed Khomeini, because I was older. I was very ungenerous in the very beginning, and I've done interviews that I would never do the same again. No!

[She screams.] Of course not! I was blinded by my predilections. I'm much more relaxed now.

Most journalism worries me. And interviewing is a very equivocal thing. It's a trap, because it has all the earmarks of honesty and can be the most dishonest thing on earth. Each time you read an interview, you should get a copy of the tape to see how things really went.

Generally I do not like TV journalists, because TV journalism produces mindless interviewers. In one interview, I was asked about Alekos [her murdered lover, Alexandros Panagoulis]: "Why was he a Communist?" I replied, "You don't even know what you're talking about! Alekos was an anti-Communist. He was an anarchist. Do you know the difference between a Communist and an anarchist? Oh, my God! You cannot insult philosophy like this. Who prepared this question?" I found out that they have a team of people who prepare the questions— one who reads the books, another one who reports to someone else, and so on. So you go to these people, these veeerrrry famous interviewers. But if you call them interviewers, I don't. They are like my secretary— "Write this letter"—and she writes this letter. And they do the same. And maybe they have a cute face and they're telegenic. So why be interested in these interviews? Aren't you bending to a fashion? [By this time in the interview, I did not think she felt she was going to offend me.]

I was always driven by passion, by beliefs, by truth, *not* by that attitude of the policeman who has a uniform on: "I'll settle you right now because I'm the press."

I never enter the private life, unless the interviewee wants to enter. And when these journalists come and put the very private question, I could kill them. They think that everything is permitted to them. It is not true! Everything is not permitted. Some things are permitted, and many others are not.

It's a funny thing about me. People are intimidated by me. I'm so polite when I go to these people. I'm so

polite always. It's very funny; they are intimidated
before I arrive. And then I enter the room. If they don't
know me from before, they know my face very well.
They are surprised. I'm very short and very thin. And
they always say the same thing, "I thought you were very
big and very tall." If they're stupid, they get relaxed. I'm
very sweet; I'm not hypocritical, like journalists, most of
them. Secretly I feel guilty for entering the soul of this
person, because my interview is an interview of the soul.
And I feel guilty, too, when I give interviews, because I
don't like the others to do that to me.

It happened even with Khomeini. Khomeini was very
intelligent. Khomeini would never look in your eyes, but
he did very often with me. And then there was that clash
between him and me, because he got angry, rightly so.
But I didn't throw the chador [the full-length veil that
Khomeini ordered all women to wear] away—that's what
journalists say, but I didn't throw it away. I just took it
off, this chador. I didn't want it anymore, to hell with it;
I did it very quietly. They say I threw the chador in his
face! Now, come! Could I do that? He's an old man and
I'm his guest, and I'm going to throw a chador in his
face? I took it off coldly, very insolently. Then I said,
"Mr. Khomeini, I refuse this. Why did I put on this
thing for you? I don't want it." I let it fall with
contempt. He got very angry, silently, got up like a cat.
This old man jumped up like a cat, and left. And the
interpreter said, "He's gone." And I said, "Like hell he's
gone. He's not gone because I have to finish the
interview." Then he said, "You must get up." I said, "No,
I'm not going to get up." "You must; it's over." "It's not
over." "You have to come back." "I come from the other
part of the world, and he promised me an interview, and
damn it, he's going to finish the bloody interview." So he
said, "You have to get up." I said, "You don't touch me,
because your religion doesn't permit you to touch me,
and if you touch me I'll begin to yell and scream. You let
me sit here alone." And I was two hours and a half
sitting there. At a certain moment I was desperate

because I wanted to make pee-pee, but if I got up I'd spoil everything. Finally, Khomeini's son went to Khomeini and came back, saying, "Listen, we do it tomorrow." I said, "You swear on the Koran." "What do you mean?" I said, "You swear on the Koran." Otherwise I wouldn't get up. They gave me the interview on one condition, and I said, "I don't accept conditions." They said, "You have to accept this condition, and the condition is that you don't pronounce the word 'chador,' and you don't speak about women." I said, "I don't accept the condition."

The next day Khomeini comes and he sits up on the carpet, and I say, "Mr. Khomeini, they said to me there was a condition, and I don't accept conditions. They said to me that I should not pronounce the word 'chador' and the word 'women.' Therefore, let's start from the chador again and from the women again. Now, about women and the chador..." Khomeini looked at me with such sympathy; there was so much in those eyes! They looked in mine and I looked at him, and there was overall respect. And we spoke about the chador and we spoke about women.

That's very different from saying, "When are you going to divorce?" to someone who just got married a minute ago. See what I mean?

So who does this? I can do it, because I am who I am. Mary Wilson cannot do it; she will do something else, will fly to the moon, but she will not do that.

So where do you find the rules? I can tell you how I begin and how I end, but I cannot make rules for an interview like that. Mine are moral rules. It is to have the guts to put in the very beginning the very difficult questions, because journalists are cowards very often. And since they are cowards, they start with, "Do you love your mother? Does your mother love you? Do you like summer or winter?" When they are at the door, ready to escape, they say, "Did you steal the money last night? Si o no?"

So you've got to put the right questions. With Khomeini, I said, "Mr. Khomeini, we all know that you are a tyrant, that you are the new king of Iran, that you have taken the place of the shah. You are the new shah of Iran. Given this fact, I wish to ask you..."

I wanted Khomeini to know that I considered him the new shah of Iran, a tyrant, the new king. Maybe I will change in the course of the interview. He was smart, certainly. He said to me, "No, we are not the new shah of Iran, we are not the new king. Your approach is wrong. As Aristotle said..." and he started speaking about Aristotle and it was very beautiful, and I wrote it. When he went into the stupidity and the bullshit about women and his fanatics, I wrote that also. So there are rules, but they are moral rules.

I never publish what is said without the tape recorder. Without the tape recorder, people don't measure the words; they open themselves. Since my interviews are with people with power, which means responsibility, they measure their words with me and I respect that—they should measure their words. And if they say something to me while we are at lunch, or at dinner, or accompanying me to the hotel with their car, and I publish that— it's a betrayal. You've got to be very, very, very moral and very honest to be a journalist and to be an interviewer.

I think it's profoundly dishonest to take a phrase out of context. I never do that. Since I don't do it, I'm obliged to write very long interviews, outrageously long. Sometimes they have to be published in sections, like the books in the 1800s. And it's very difficult for me to sell them because they said, "We have to reduce it." "If you reduce mine, you don't buy it." "We'll give you $15,000." "You can give me $20,000 and I won't give it to you. And if you steal it, I'll sue you." And so if I also add my own comments to my interviews, which sometimes are better than theirs, I would write a book for every interview. That is why I summarize what I say in my published interviews.

Sometimes I say nothing during the interview, or I say, "Yes," "No," "Tell me more." Sometimes I have discussions, real discussions, if they like. Sometimes they want to know what I think, and I say, "My friend, we have no time." And they reply, "I give you the time, okay?" They see me again—one, two, three more times, so each of my interviews could be a book. Usually they last four, five, six, ten hours.

I'm not interested in fighting. I'm interested in discussing and writing a good piece of literature, which it can be, even if it's an interview.

There is only one case in which I was not honest. I am ashamed of it and I put ashes on my head. It's the case of my interview with Lech Walesa, who's a stupid man and I made him sound intelligent. He's a very little man; I made him sound like a great man. I knew immediately that Walesa was no good, but those are the mistakes you make when you don't follow your instincts, your heart, and your brain, which are all the same thing. At that moment, if I wrote that Lech Walesa was a bloody idiot, I'd do such political damage. And I made him sound exquisite. But he's a little man who understood nothing, who made tremendous mistakes, who got drunk with power—I say this on tape—and who didn't know how to administer his power. Here and there he was very poetic. He said some beautiful things. I'd have to think a week and I might never find such beautiful words. But he also said such stupid things, unacceptable things. I corrected him, I censored what he said for his own good, and I feel guilty because I have not left for history the picture of who Walesa is. He is a little man manipulated by the Church. It was a very dramatic choice—a big dilemma. Do I leave a little note in history saying that Walesa was not the hero they say, or do I damage freedom? I had to choose between being myself, which means being a writer, and being a politician, which I am to a certain extent. And I made the second choice, and I feel uncomfortable now. So the ashes are on my head. This is the first time I've revealed this.

I did not have this dilemma with Qaddafi, whom I hated so blindly. First of all, he made me wait, locking me in a room for three hours, and I wanted to leave. "I'm not going to do the interview with you; to hell with

you. You've locked me in this room; you have no right.
I'm not interested in seeing you. I'm not!" I told you I
was very polite, but I told you there are exceptions.

In this case I said, "People give up their dignity to
make an interview. I don't, ever! I cannot do an
interview with a bastard who keeps me in a room for
three hours." At least I can say to him, "To hell with
you! I don't want to see you anymore." "Please, Miss
Fallaci, come, come, please. Please, please, please,
please." "Okay, let's start. Come on, sit down. Let's try
it."

But it takes a lot of guts. You can get killed.

But I am not intimidated by anybody. If I could
interview God, provided that he existed, I would not be
intimidated by him. I would have so many questions.
"Given the fact that you are a bastard, because you have
invented a life that dies, why did you give us death?
Since we are born, why should we die? So let's begin
from that: why did you do that?" So I'm never
intimidated.

When I interviewed Haile Selassie, they said to me,
"Don't say the word 'death.'" He was very old and almost
dying. He had said that death was too much in his life.
The interview was not an interview; it was bad. He was
sitting on his throne—so nasty, so evil—and he was
saying nothing. I needed the vendetta, the revenge, like
the Sicilian who goes Boom! Boom! So I said, *"La morte,
vôtre Majesté? Vous êtes très vieux—quand vous allez mourir,
vous avez peur de mourir?"* ("You're very old and you're
afraid of dying, aren't you?") It was *so* evil of me. At that
point, this man got crazy. He started yelling, "Who is
this woman? Get her out!" At that point, I loved him.
That was what interested me—that he was afraid of
death.

My interviews are *pièces de théâtre*, because they are
written by a writer. I'm not a journalist, I'm a writer. I
am a writer who has done journalism all her life, not a
journalist who has become a writer. So my approach is
that of a writer, of a novelist, of a playwright. And when

I go to do an interview, I really see it as a playwright.
Something happens which tells me, by instinct, where
the play must go.

When I began interviewing, not many people did
interviews, and I am responsible for a couple of things.
First, because of my popularity, I caused a proliferation
of women journalists, and women journalists sometimes
are even worse than male journalists, if that's possible.
It's very difficult to be worse than a male journalist, but
sometimes they succeed. Everybody wanted to be this
Oriana. Second, I developed interviews to such a level
that I made some journalists fall in love with
interviews—"If she can do it, I can do it." And I caused
an inflation of interviews, like inflation of the lira, and
now everyone does interviews. They have discovered
that, as badly as they do interviews, they are much easier
to do than writing. You go to the person with a tape
recorder and even if you're not too bright, you can put
questions together. Then all you have to do is just copy
what the person said. You take the "flower" of others
and you sell it as your own. With an interview, you never
have the blank page in the typewriter staring at you. Ah,
when I am writing, each time I put a blank page in the
typewriter, I have a heart attack; it scares me. With an
interview, you'd never have that blank page. And also
because we have this marvelous machine, it's all written
here. When you put your page into the typewriter, you
don't say, "Mamma mia! I've got to fill it!" because it's
already written. So it's easy to do interviews.

You ask why it's so easy for me—Oriana Fallaci?

The amount of intelligence necessary to understand a
person and a situation—I do have it, no doubt about it.

The amount of imagination it takes to put certain
questions—I do have it, no doubt about it.

The amount of courage it takes to put those
questions—I have it, no doubt about it.

The will to work, because I'm a tremendous worker—
I do have it, no doubt about it.

And given the fact that the moment you push the

button of that machine, the blank page is already written—eh! It's easy.

Of course, it's not easy in another way, because at my level, when I go to interview people in power, it takes intelligence and guts, and maybe the guts come first.

The interview with Henry Kissinger is the worst interview I've ever done in my whole life. It was not an interview; it was the beginning of an interview, which stopped every five minutes—Nixon calling him on the phone—"Mr. President. Yes, Mr. President." Have you ever seen the sergeant who stands in front of the general? He answered the phone like that sergeant. The interview was continually interrupted by this bastard Nixon. It was not an interview. I started being interested when he told me the reason for his success. [In her interview of Kissinger, Fallaci quotes him as saying, "I've always acted alone....Americans like the cowboy who leads the wagon train by riding ahead alone on his horse, the cowboy who rides all alone into the town, the village, with his horse, and nothing else...."]

At that point I forgot journalism! This man who thinks he is a cowboy...and I said, "Ooh, la, la!" [Whistles] He must have terrible fantasies when he dreams; he sees himself like Julius Caesar crossing the Rubicon. But Nixon called him again and interrupted everything. So that's the case with Kissinger, which was an interview that was not an interview.

When was I impressed with someone? Okay—Deng Xiaoping of China. He has one eye—they had beat him during the cultural revolution. He was sitting in this chair and he said, "Chong chong chong chong chong," and the girl translator—she was fantastic—said, "The president says he is sitting on the chair where Mao Zedong was sitting and you're sitting on the chair where Nixon was sitting." And I said, "These bloody chairs should be purified." She was like a sheep—translating everything—and she translated, "Good, it is time that the two bloody chairs be purified," and he started laughing. I fell in love with him.

It was like being in a theater. There were sixty, seventy people there, and I didn't want them. I said, "Mr. Deng, who are they? I don't want these people." "That's my government." "I don't want them. Tell everybody that I don't want them."

Then I saw two journalists. "Who are *they*? No, no, no, no, no. I came from New York not to give them my interview. Out! If they don't get out, I don't talk. Mr. Deng, I'm sorry. I don't start." So he said, "Out!" and they all went out. And so he loved me; he fell in love with me.

I didn't put many questions to Deng, because he was worse than me—when he opened his mouth, nobody could stop him. It took an atomic bomb to stop him. I was fascinated by his humility, intelligence, simplicity, humanity. It was the very first time in my life that I was interviewing a man of power who behaved like a man of the subway. Usually they're very pompous.

At one point, he started yelling because I had asked a question he didn't like. He said, "Would you do that to your father?"

I said, "Sure."

"Did you ever do that to your father?"

"Yeah."

"Did he slap you? Your father should slap you."

"Do you want to slap me? Do it! I'll write it down here."

And he said, "Ahhhhhhhh!"

Deng had said he would give me two hours, and at the end of two and a half hours, I felt I needed more time—the interview was not over. So I said to myself, "How do I ask to see him again?" As I was looking for the words, he said, "*Ching chong foo chong kiau,*" and the translator said, "Deng wants to know if you would honor him with a second interview. Please don't say no."

At that point, I lost my mind. I jumped, I fell on him, I kissed him. [She ran across the room to me and demonstrated. I loved it.] The guards all jumped at me

because they thought I was going to kill him. It was the
commedia dell'arte italiana.

When you are with Deng, you feel that you don't have
another occasion, and you're very tense. You feel like a
boxer in the ring because the bell is going to go "Dong,"
and you're out. Time gives a tremendous limitation.

I have more rapport with some people than with
others, and they want to stay with me. They give me all
those hours. In a few cases, I didn't have it. For
instance, I didn't have it with Bhutto.

I was with Indira Gandhi for six hours and then she
finally said, "Now listen, it's my government—they've
been waiting for two hours. I'm so sorry to leave you. I'll
get you a taxi." And we walked together in this
incredible palace for ten or fifteen minutes, and she had
my arm like this. [She demonstrates on her arm.] She
said to me [she whispers], "How can I govern with all
these bloody idiots all around me?" I never wrote that.
Yes, you can write it. It was very funny seeing this
woman telling the guards to call a taxi for me. As we
stood, she whispered, "See how stupid they are?" There
was a very special rapport between us.

Indira was a relationship. Deng was a relationship.
Makarios [archbishop of the Eastern Orthodox church]
was a relationship. When Makarios left me at the door of
the Plaza [Hotel in New York], he whispered to me,
"What a pity you're a woman." I said, "What a pity
you're a priest."

When I interview somebody, I want two things. I don't
know which is more important. I want to leave a piece of
history and I want to write a good piece, well-written. I
care so much about writing that I could sell my soul for
it, like Doctor Faust. But I also want to leave a piece of
truth. History is always written by those who win; you
never know how the others felt. For example, Nero, the
Emperor Nero, was a great man—interesting and of
great intellect, a little like Trudeau when he was the
prime minister of Canada. History has been written by

the winners, by those terrible Christians, and they have
slandered Nero. I am obsessed by Nero, and I cannot
stand the slander—that he was stupid, that he was crazy.
If I had interviewed Nero, I promise you that you would
know Nero.

But now, no more. I don't care. My former Italian
teacher in high school, who is now a writer and novelist,
said to me, "How are you, Oriana?"

"I'm tired."

And he said, "Of course, you're tired. You've been
living for two hundred years."

I think I've been living for more than two hundred
years. And I have seen more at my age than I should
have seen. I think it's dangerous with me—the lack of
curiosity. Everywhere I go, I see the same things. I'm
sick and tired of going to the wars, because it's all the
same stuff. People don't surprise me anymore. I seem to
know it all. It can be interesting to verify what I know,
but the fact is, rather than discover, I now verify. It's
terrible.

Mike Wallace

Interviewer, CBS's 60 Minutes

WITH ACCOMPANYING COMMENTS BY DON HEWITT,
PHIL SCHEFFLER, AND SYLVIA WESTERMAN

> "Mike is interviewing this bad-ass accountant, and there are
> like forty million people watching this broadcast. And only
> Mike would say to a guy whom he interviews, 'Just between
> you and me....' Now this guy forgets; he thinks it *is* between
> him and Mike."—*Don Hewitt on Mike Wallace*

THE FIRST PERSON from Mars, at his first dinner party,
listening carefully to what American television is all about,
may well ask, "What is a Mike Wallace?" The name is part of
American media history, a name that has been a lodestone in
American television for more than forty years, a name that was
mentioned—with both praise and criticism—more than any
other by his colleagues whom we interviewed. This man has
won more media prizes than you can shake a stick at and is the
mainstay of the most popular news program in television
history, a man for whom CBS broke tradition when they
granted him another contract after the usual retirement age of
sixty-five.

As Wallace himself says, "The executives at CBS were not
about to retire the goose that kept delivering such golden
eggs."

What is a Mike Wallace?

For starters, Mike Wallace is the television interviewer who is
known to millions of people as hard hitting and aggressive;
reviewers have used the words "browbeating," "relentless,"
"theatrical," "fiery," "coaxing," "needling," "audacious," "ruth-

33

less." He is the prototype of the harsh, piercing interviewer whom not even the wiliest of celebrities—presidents, crooks, politicians—can get around. Wallace himself apparently likes the image of toughness; when an interviewer asked what Wallace would choose as his epitaph, he replied, "Tough, but fair."

There is no question about the tough part. Friends have granted him interviews, and he has cut them to shreds in front of millions of people. He once risked a woman's life in order to interview her. On the other hand, he has been known to cut short an interview because he was moved to tears by what the interviewee revealed.

Three questions about him come to mind: Why do people, many of them shrewd, consent to talk to him in front of millions of viewers when they know they are almost sure to be clobbered? For example, what was the reason for the shrewdest of the shrewd, Roy Cohn, already bombarded by negative publicity, consenting to an interview when he undoubtedly knew that Wallace would raise issues Cohn wanted desperately to hide? And why, once Wallace gets an interview, do people open up as they do? Finally, what does Wallace do that gives people the feeling that the interview is "just between you and me"?

For the first question—why do people consent to see him when they can anticipate tough questions—the obvious answer is that some people want to be seen regardless of the consequences, they want publicity no matter what kind, and they think they can leave unscathed, can outfox him. As Sylvia Westerman, a former CBS vice president who worked behind the scenes at CBS for sixteen years and was a self-proclaimed Mike Wallace watcher, said to me, "Internally, we thought that some pompous asses thought they could stop him—the high and mighty and the crooks. We used to say that somebody could make six figures a year simply telling people what to do when Mike Wallace calls and requests an interview. They're walking into a buzz saw and they know it. DANGER, it says across the front."

But why do interviewees open up? Why aren't people more careful?

In Wallace's presence, I got a hint of the answers.

After our interview I left feeling a little drunk. I liked him excessively, given the amount of time I was with him. I was charmed, emotionally seduced (I admit, however, that I am given to excesses of feelings about people).

But with Mike Wallace, there was something else. I liked *me*. What he did—with or without design—was make me feel good about myself. In an aborted forty-five minutes (we were twice interrupted), he managed to tell me, in the most convincing way, what a good interviewer I was (and, by implication, what he thinks makes a good interviewer).

■ When an interviewer comes in well prepared, like you are, someone you respect, like your politeness here [I had left when we were interrupted, despite his urging me to keep my seat, once when the telephone rang, and again when his producers, Don Hewitt and Phil Scheffler, came in], the interviewee wants to give, becomes interested, and you can see it in the body language. Look at the way I'm sitting [he was far forward with his elbows on the desk]. It makes you want to give to the interviewer. Then there's that moment when the eyes meet, and you're in real contact.

No matter how much experience one has had as an interviewer (I have been at it for close to forty years), a compliment like that one is heady stuff.

I felt that he was describing the way he looks at himself. If he believes he is a good interviewer (and he surely does, I suspect), then as he described a good interviewer, he painted a portrait of himself.

But there is much more to it than that. He is a charmer. He begins by playing on his flute and then the snake comes out of its basket. He gets people—all types of people—to like him, and they ultimately like themselves because of the way he treats them, regardless of his toughness.

In our interview, he made contact. He was thoroughly present and totally focused. He seemed to know what he was doing at every moment. And despite the interruptions, he was fully attentive. If he acts this way with the people he himself interviews—and I suspect he does—he could charm the pants off almost anyone.

Phil Scheffler, his senior producer, gave this example of Wallace's ability to attend, to focus:

☐   We did a broadcast about Scientology, and he went to interview the president of Scientology, who was there with his lawyer, of course. But in addition, the man we were interviewing insisted on having three of his own cameras recording the interview. He also had about one hundred people from the church sitting in back of Mike so they could witness the interview. This, of course, was on his turf. And Mike was able to ignore all of this—all the other cameras, all of the people behind him, the open hostility of this man and his lawyers.

He has no fear of appearing stupid, silly, or uninformed. He doesn't care what the subject thinks of him. Mike has no ego about that. If an interviewer listens very carefully, he has to submerge his own ego to the person he's talking to.

One of the things about a good interview in journalism is the willingness to ask embarrassing questions. We're not accustomed in our ordinary lives to ask questions like, Are you getting along with your wife? How come you're divorced? Did you ever perjure yourself? But in journalism it's just the opposite: you have to be prepared to do that. That's all part of submerging your own personality, which Mike can do. It means having to ignore the desire to have the other person like you. We're careful about the way we deal with others in the normal course of our lives because we want to be liked. Journalists can't think about that. Obviously, they would like the other person to like them, but that's not one of the controlling forces in the interview. And to the extent that it is, it interferes with the content of the interview. You must be prepared at the end of the interview, as Mike is, to end with the subject not liking you an awful lot; maybe even being mad at you—maybe mad enough to sue you, or hit you.

Obviously, you don't like that, but it happens.

Stand off to one side and watch him do an interview. You can see in his eyes how hard he is working. He listens to the answers so hard you can practically hear his brain turning over.

He really has an enormous curiosity. He wants to hear what you have to say, and he won't accept easy answers. If you give an offhand answer to him, and this is true whether I'm just talking to him about a story we're working on or we're discussing the affairs of the day, he's not satisfied with easy answers or slipshod behavior. He keeps pressing and pressing, pressing and pressing; he wants to hear more and more and more and more all the time.

Don Hewitt, executive producer of *60 Minutes*, gave this account of one of Wallace's interviews:

☐   Mike is interviewing this bad-ass accountant, and there are like forty million people watching this broadcast. And only Mike would say to a guy whom he interviews, 'Just between you and me....' Now this guy forgets; he thinks it *is* between him and Mike. Mike has a way of doing that.

Mike Wallace was born Myron Leon Wallace in 1918 in Brookline, Massachusetts, where he attended public school. In high school, he did only tolerably well (B – average) but involved himself in the dramatic club, the school newspaper, and public speaking. He thought he would become an English teacher, but at college he found what he really wanted to do. He got a job as radio announcer at the college radio station and, according to his account, he was "trapped."

He graduated from college, the University of Michigan in Ann Arbor, in 1939, and it took him ten years to hit his stride. During that time, he was a continuity writer, an announcer, and a radio actor and had done a stint in the U.S. Navy.

It was not long after his service days that he finally made his first of three big successes. He began a TV talk show, *Mike and Buff*, with his then wife, actress Buff Cobb, to whom he gave a crash course in interviewing, bombarding her with such exercises as, "I'm Jack Benny, ask me ten questions!" The show hit it big in Chicago and even bigger in New York, but the Wallaces divorced, and that was the end of the show.

After a respite, he hit it big a second time. He joined a program, *Night Beat*, that would turn him into the Mike Wallace of today—the focused, tough snake charmer.

Early in his career, he "discovered how much he enjoyed the parry and riposte of interviewing." From the parry (look it up in the dictionary: warding off blows) and riposte (firing sharp swift responses), it was an easy step to doing interviews on *Night Beat*. This was the program that introduced a new format for television shows, one uniquely suited to Wallace's experience and talent and one which would stamp him. The staff focused on how to "nail this pompous ass or that fatuous blowhard who would be stepping into our lair later that night." He adds, "I must confess, however, that there were times when in the heat of battle we went too far." Prior to this, Wallace says, interview programs had been "verbal minuets," "the bland leading the bland." Under Wallace's questioning, his guests, often distinguished celebrities, like Dame Sybil Thorndike, revealed amazingly personal things about themselves, and the ratings skyrocketed. ABC bought the program and renamed it *The Mike Wallace Interview*. One critic compared the program to a "third-degree setup in a police station." The topics were shocking for the time: communism, desegregation, psychoanalysis. The program had a short life—eighteen months—but the Wallace style had been impressed indelibly both on Wallace and on the public.

For the next ten years, Wallace had some very creditable assignments on television, but it was not until 1968 that he came to his third great success—surely the jackpot. That year Don Hewitt conceived and aired the new CBS program, *60 Minutes*, with Mike Wallace and Harry Reasoner as his regular reporters. The most successful news program in the history of television was born.

Wallace refers to himself and Reasoner in the early years of *60 Minutes* as "tigers on the prowl." They hardly had a chance to "catch their breath before moving out again in search of fresh prey."

Defending the "ambush" journalism of *60 Minutes*, Don
Hewitt told me:

☐   Mike is as fair an interviewer as I know. You know,
    you've heard so much about these ambush interviews;
    that's just not true. What happened was that we very
    carefully tried to get people to appear on *60 Minutes*,
    people that we knew an awful lot about and who were
    wanted or were about to be indicted—they were people
    who had committed some sort of malfeasance. After
    trying every which way to reach them by mail or by
    phone or in person, and failing, we sometimes camped
    outside.
        But other people saw this as excessive: "This is the
    way *60 Minutes* and Mike Wallace do it: you get yourself
    a trenchcoat, you hang outside, and you badger people."
    Well, what happened was that we got tarred by a brush
    that was not of our making. We did not do those kinds
    of things. Other people did them and they became
    caricatures of Mike Wallace. Mike and our style has been
    to talk with people about malfeasances that we know
    about but that they don't know we know about.
        For instance, we kind of went under false pretenses
    into a phony cancer clinic in Murietta, California, and
    nailed the guy who was running the clinic. Gene
    Patterson, of the Tampa–St. Petersburg paper, a
    wonderful guy, said to me, "That's unethical." I said,
    "What's unethical about that?" He said, "You've got no
    right to move in on this guy and sail under false colors."
    I said, "The guy was committing a crime." "Yes, but he
    hadn't been convicted of any crime. What right did you
    have of violating his privacy?" I said, "Wait a minute.
    Are you telling me that people are entitled to privacy to
    commit a crime? If you want to commit a crime, you're
    entitled to privacy?" He said, "Yes, if the guy's not been
    convicted of anything, he's entitled to privacy." "Okay,
    Gene, tell me something. Has your newspaper ever run
    one of those pictures of a guy robbing a bank?" "Yeah."
    "Wasn't he entitled to rob the bank in private? What
    right do you have to watch him rob the bank? He wasn't

convicted of anything. You're invading his privacy.
Taking a picture of the guy robbing a bank is as much
an invasion of privacy, by your definition, as Mike
Wallace walking into a phony cancer clinic and watching
them robbing people of their life savings." You pick and
choose when you do those things. I wish we had more.

We got kind of scared off by all this talk about
ambush and confrontation. I told the staff, "Confrontation is not a dirty word." Confrontation is the best kind
of journalism, as long as you're not confronting for the
sake of confronting. If you're just doing it for the sake
of "Hey, look what we did to this guy," or "Look how we
confronted this guy," that's baby stuff. If this is the only
way to tell a story that's worth telling, of course
confront. Surprise him if you have to. Ambush
journalism. I didn't invent the technique. William
Randolph Hearst and Henry Luce in his early days, and
Roy Howard before I was born—they were doing that.

Wallace's reputation as tiger and predator is well deserved.
He wielded the stiletto, even on his friends. Oddly, the friendships which help him get the interviews in which he stabs
people, are often reestablished. As I observed in person, he is a
charmer.

Wallace has maintained a long friendship with Nancy Reagan, a relationship which would allow for granting favors. Just
before the 1980 presidential convention, Ronald Reagan and
Nancy Reagan granted Wallace an interview. As Wallace admits, "What I did was sit there and ask him every tough
question imaginable...in their own living room. And he
looked at me as though, 'Good Lord, what are you doing?'"

Here is an excerpt from Wallace's interview of his old friend's
husband:

WALLACE: How many blacks are there on your top
    campaign staff, Governor?
REAGAN: I couldn't honestly answer for you. No.
WALLACE: That speaks for itself.
REAGAN: Huh?
WALLACE: I say that speaks for itself.

REAGAN: No, because I can't tell you how many people are on the staff. We've got...

WALLACE: But you can tell black from white.

REAGAN: Oh yes, but I mean we've got a...we've got a mix of volunteers and staff members and...

WALLACE: I'm talking about top campaign staff.

REAGAN: Well, let me put it this way...

WALLACE: Let me not belabor it. I mean...

REAGAN: Yeah.

WALLACE: Apparently there are none.

REAGAN: No, I don't think so, I mean, I'm...I don't...I don't agree with you on that.

The interview did not prevent Nancy Reagan from calling Wallace when her husband was in the hospital after surgery.

Wallace's aggression once gave him more trouble than even he could easily survive. In May 1981, he came well prepared by his producer to his fateful interview with General William C. Westmoreland, former commander, U.S. Military Assistance Command, Vietnam. Westmoreland had met Wallace in 1967 in Vietnam and apparently did not expect what Wallace was to do to him on the air in 1981. "Most of the interview with Westmoreland focused on the step-by-step decisions that were made in 1967 'to suppress and then to alter' [the information that United States troops were facing a much larger enemy than the official estimates indicated]. Seldom has a major figure in American history been put so squarely on the spot in a network interview."

Westmoreland eventually sued CBS for this broadcast, which contained the word "conspiracy" in the introduction. After a series of Alice in Wonderland moves on the part of people on both sides in the suit, Westmoreland dropped the case. In the end, everyone suffered. Wallace was hospitalized for exhaustion and depression during the suit. Again, the Wallace touch is apparent; Westmoreland and his wife sent flowers to Wallace in the hospital.

Wallace seems to think that on at least one occasion he went too far in getting an interviewee—literally placing the life of the subject in danger. In 1972, Dita Beard, a Washington lobbyist working for International Telephone and Telegraph, disappeared suddenly after a columnist published a memo, allegedly written by Beard, indicating that the Nixon administration, through its Justice Department, had gone easy on ITT in return for a promised $400,000 donation to the 1972 Republican convention. Rumor had it that she had gone into hiding, and Wallace's interest was aroused. After some legwork, he found that she had entered a hospital because of a mild heart attack. She was found first by some members of the Senate Judiciary Committee, who went to the hospital room and interrogated her, only to be stopped by her physicians when her heart began to beat irregularly. A few days later, Beard said she was willing to see Wallace, but not on-camera. Off-camera was not enough for *60 Minutes*, so Don Hewitt and Wallace tried to win her over, employing that old journalistic sawhorse—she would have an opportunity to get her story across to the American public—and after a half hour of selling, Wallace and Hewitt succeeded. The hospital would allow no television cameras, so, against the advice of her doctor, they took Mrs. Beard off in kimono and nightgown to an apartment rented by her son. Later, Wallace said he had noted that she was probably not as sick as some people thought; she was, after all, smoking furiously in her hospital room. Mrs. Beard was safely back in her hospital room an hour after the interview, and Wallace and Hewitt returned to New York.

To someone without knowledge of the full range of Wallace's interviews, it might come as a surprise that Wallace can be touched to the point where he will stop an interview and lose potential fireworks.

He once interviewed the mother of a nineteen-year-old Marine Corps deserter who was seeking amnesty, and when he asked her what she would say to the mothers and fathers of people who fought and were wounded or killed, her voice broke and she began to cry. Wallace immediately called a halt to the interview, not only for her benefit, but, he says, because his own feelings were out of control.

Near the end of my interview with Wallace, I asked him how he prepared for interviews.

■ I get all my material on my desk so it's all in front of me. I digest it, then I keep looking. I write down questions, but of course I know I'm not going to use them all. I cross them out. Then I talk to the producer and he suggests questions and we knock it around. Of course, I choose the final questions because I have to be comfortable with them. But a big thing is that there's more than one person feeding into it.

Once he is in an interview, Wallace's face lets the interviewee—and the audience—know what he is feeling: "a frown to express puzzlement, a grimace to convey disagreement, raised eyebrows to indicate skepticism. He is always communicating both to the interviewee and the audience all at once—he lets the interviewee know he is listening intently and lets the audience know exactly how he is feeling about what he is hearing (raised eyebrows communicate, 'I don't believe what this guy is saying and neither should you')."

Part of Wallace's skill may be that like Zelig, the chameleon-like character in the Woody Allen film of that name, Wallace can adapt his psyche and behavior to conform to those of the person he is with. Some of his one-word responses ("Right," "And?" "Yeah?") seem to be in agreement with the interviewee, no matter how outrageous the interviewee's comments. For example, on November 19, 1979, Wallace interviewed the Ayatollah Khomeini shortly after Iran had captured American hostages. Khomeini said that the shah should have been returned to the people of Iran. Wallace simply replied, "Right," and Khomeini continued.

A highly dramatic example of Wallace's ability to ask penetrating questions is apparent in his 1969 interview of a soldier in the infamous My Lai Massacre, in which Vietnamese civilians were murdered at the command of an American lieutenant. Stricken with remorse, the soldier was willing to talk on television to Wallace, and reported emptying four clips from his rifle into the civilians, about sixty-eight in all.

WALLACE: And you killed how many at that time?
SOLDIER: Well, I fired them on automatic, so you can't—you just spray the area in on them, so you really can't know how many you killed, 'cause it comes out so doggoned fast. So I might have killed about ten or fifteen of them.

WALLACE: Men, women, and children?
SOLDIER: Men, women, and children.
WALLACE: And babies?
SOLDIER: And babies.
WALLACE: Uh-huh. How do you shoot babies?
SOLDIER: I don't know. It was just one of them things...
WALLACE: And nothing went through your mind or heart?
SOLDIER: Many a time. Many a time.

Has Wallace changed over the years? In 1985, he told an interviewer that he was "simply not as comfortable with my old style as I used to be." Wallace believes the Westmoreland case changed him profoundly. He saw how it felt to be treated unfairly by the press, and that gave him serious doubts about what he himself had been doing as a journalist. Wallace feels he has matured, become wiser; he says he used to think he was after light more than heat, but admits that it was heat that brought him the attention he received. He feels now he is genuinely after light.

Wallace treasures a quote from George Bernard Shaw in which the playwright responds to complaints that he focused too much on the three subjects that were supposed to be taboo in polite conversation—sex, religion, and politics: it is only "the common and less cultivated people who make a rule that politics and religion are not to be mentioned, and take it for granted that no decent person would attempt to discuss sex." On the other hand, Shaw adds, "The ablest and most highly cultivated people continually discuss religion, politics, and sex. It's hardly an exaggeration to say that they discuss nothing else with full awakened interest." You better believe it, if you are going to be interviewed by Mike Wallace. You may even discuss more troublesome topics than religion, politics, and sex.

II

Presenting the News

In THIS SECTION we have assembled interviews with four of the most respected news journalists in the business—Ted Koppel, John Chancellor, Robert MacNeil, and Roger Mudd. These are very serious fellows.

Two of these men hammered away at something that sticks in their craw: a newsperson doing a star turn. For example, MacNeil sees himself as the surrogate of his viewers, with no interest in showing himself off. Mudd sees himself as a reporter, not a show-business person.

To some of these television men, even the anchor position on television news, the coveted, high-paying maximum-exposure job, is a star turn. If there is a star, a focus, they say, it is the interviewee. What they did not say was that to remain in a top broadcasting job today, the broadcaster may have to be something of a star, or he or she will lose the job. Two of these highly polished, highly respected journalists did lose coveted top-banana jobs to other men who are consistently more prosecutorial and tougher and perhaps possess more "star" quality.

All four television newsmen seem to reject the confrontational, prosecutorial approach to interviewing (they frequently mention Mike Wallace, the most popular bad boy on this issue). But avoiding confrontation in television is not as easy as it may seem. Ratings may be based, at least in part, on a bit of heat. The television newsfolk do, in fact, as you will see here, often turn on "light" with a bit of fireworks. As we noted before, Tom Wicker of the *New York Times* commented that since 1968 the American press "has become more adversarial." If interviewees cannot be trusted to give the press the truth, then how can the press be effective without using confrontational techniques? And the four television men have done, on more than one occasion, just that.

A more subtle issue here is whether or not the news interviewer should take an advocacy role. In general, these men
seem to reject taking sides on issues, but as you will see, if you
read carefully, you may find some inconsistencies.

Nicholas Pileggi is another story. His methods for obtaining
crime and corruption stories for magazines are much more
hidden than those of television journalists. His interviews are
private; his interviewees are often not named. He can almost
never be adversarial or confrontational or his sources will clam
up.

Ted Koppel

Host and Interviewer, *ABC's* Nightline

"...it's perfectly all right for the cat to look at the king, perfectly all right for the journalist to say to the President, the prime minister, or whoever it may be, 'You're not answering my question.'"

Sprinkled liberally through our interviews are admiring comments about Ted Koppel. Mike Wallace, for example, acknowledged, "There's none better. None better." Phil Donahue admitted to me that if he had his way, he would be doing something more like *Nightline*.

Koppel is probably used to unabashed adulation by now. A *New York Times* television critic said of him, "As much as anyone on television, he has become the ringmaster on the great stories of our time." On June 5, 1987, *Time* magazine put Koppel's picture on the cover with the caption, "'Nightline's' Ted Koppel Asks All the Right Questions."

The *Time* article suggested that he was "on a roll" in 1987. Actually, Ted Koppel is still on a roll and has been since 1980, when *Nightline*, a mixture of interviews, discussion and debate, and magazine show, began. Almost from the start of his career (Koppel says he began as the "youngest network correspondent ever"), he has been admired and praised as a serious journalist, but it took *Nightline* to make him a celebrity.

Koppel had the educational background ordinarily reserved for the children of the rich. Actually his parents were wealthy in Germany before Koppel was born, but his father was imprisoned by the Nazis because he was a Jew. His parents fled Nazi Germany for England. His father was invited there to open a factory in Lancashire, but instead was interred for still another year, this time in an English enemy-alien prison camp. In 1940, two years after the family arrived in England, Ted Koppel was born. His parents sent him to a boarding school there where he added French to his already fluent English and German.

In 1953, the Koppels emigrated to New York City, and again he attended private school, completing the four-year curriculum in three years, despite what Koppel admits was his predilection for waiting until the last minute to do things. He once said to Nancy Collins of *New York* magazine:

> I'm not very well organized....I'm always a last-minute person. I'll be sitting in the studio a half-hour before I go on air gobbling up some last piece of information. In college, I was always the guy who would spend the last three days frantically cramming, always doing well enough to squeeze out a B −. When I met Grace Anne [whom he married] in graduate school—and there was that competitiveness, when I had someone I wanted to beat—then I made A's.

Koppel attended Syracuse University and, like others in this book, was a broadcaster at the campus radio station. He got a master's degree in journalism from Stanford University. Failing the Associated Press broadcaster's test, he started a teaching job at his old prep school in Manhattan. That lasted only until he landed "a glorified copyboy" job at the New York radio station WMCA. He did not have to stay long at this either; broadcasting was apparently in the cards.

His early entry into broadcasting resulted from a chance move on his part, which he questioned later. His application for a broadcaster's job at New York's WABC required his turning in two proposed scripts for programs, and it was the scripts that impressed the people doing the hiring. As for Koppel, the prospective broadcaster, they felt he looked too young—sixteen at age twenty-three, he estimates—and they rejected him. However, they offered him a writer's job at double his salary. He apparently surprised even himself by rejecting the job, despite the salary increase and the fact that his family could use the money. Two days later, Koppel's determination paid off: the station hired him as a radio broadcaster, realizing that no one sees a radio broadcaster anyway. That was in 1963. His willingness to forego a good job because it did not suit his wishes was to be repeated later in his career. The radio job began an association with ABC that has continued to this day.

With determination, professionalism, and luck pushing him along, he moved up steadily from radio broadcaster. He began doing general assignment news commentaries, and here he had opportunities to show off what has often since been called his "unflappability." For example, following the Kennedy assassination in Dallas, Koppel was assigned to cover the new President, Lyndon Johnson, as he drove by in Washington. The trouble was that Johnson was delayed, and Koppel had to ad-lib for one and a half hours, a feat that did not go unnoticed.

In 1967, four years after he became a commentator, he made the big shift from radio to television in his new assignment as correspondent in Vietnam. He is often cited admiringly for developing a working knowledge of Vietnamese before he went there.

In 1971, he became chief diplomatic correspondent, which made him a major figure in network television, though he was by no means a celebrity. During his time on this job, his well-known, and sometimes criticized, association with Henry Kissinger, then secretary of state, was established. Of this alliance Koppel has said, "I have never gotten close before or since to someone I cover. It's a mistake. Having said that, I'd defy those who make that accusation [that he had been taken in or seduced by Kissinger] to point to even one story in which my affection for Henry Kissinger colored the story to the detriment of its accuracy."

The professional payoff of this friendship came from the "lectures" on foreign policy and diplomacy that ex-Harvard professor Kissinger gave to newsmen accompanying him on his worldwide shuttle diplomacy junkets. Koppel admits learning not only about foreign policy from Kissinger, but also about listening: "I've learned to listen very carefully. I'm more likely to miss a nuance in the written word than I am in the spoken word. If someone is trying to do a verbal dipsy-doodle around me, I don't miss it very often, because Henry Kissinger is the best dipsy-doodle artist in the world."

Feminists and others as well admire a decision Koppel made in 1976 when his career had really taken off. His wife had entered law school in the fall, and in order to take over household chores and watch over the children, Koppel quit his job as diplomatic correspondent. He resigned at the meeting in which his boss had intended to talk to him about becoming vice president of ABC News or executive producer of the Barbara Walters-Harry Reasoner show.

While all profilists and many feminists praise Koppel's nonsexist "sacrifice," Koppel himself shies away from the credit; he took off only nine months (albeit at a crucial time in his career) and insists he knew he had his old job to return to. Besides, he continued to broadcast from home, went to New York to anchor ABC's Saturday night news (an additional job he had already assumed), and wrote a novel ("It ended up being terrible," he says).

And then Koppel took a fateful vacation. While he was away, the new president of ABC News, Roone Arledge, fired the executive producer of the Saturday night news, without a word to Koppel. When Koppel returned as diplomatic correspondent, he quit the anchor position, but the new president would not accept the resignation. Things improved between them, but Koppel lost the anchor job, while continuing his diplomatic assignment.

Then his career took its big leap. According to Nancy Collins in a 1984 *New York* magazine profile, Koppel always knew that he would be a "big star" at ABC, but at age thirty-nine, and almost seventeen years after he had been hired by the network, he still had not become a celebrity. Apparently, he was not bothered by the wait; he is known for his self-confidence.

Then it happened. During a creative and risky late-night programming move at ABC, instituted by Roone Arledge—a program on a single topic, the Iran hostage crisis—Koppel substituted for the anchor (he had expected to be chosen as anchor, but Arledge had passed him over). Koppel knew he was where he should be: "There was no question about it in my mind. I had put in sixteen and a half years with the network, had done almost every kind of story. If ever I was going to do something new and different, this was it."

Nightline, the new program born of the Iran hostage crisis, was instituted, and Koppel was still not hired to do it. He cites an in-joke that went around at the time: "Here we have this new nighttime broadcast that we're going to put on the network to go up against Carson and the CBS movie. So obviously we will put some funny-looking diplomatic correspondent no one's ever heard of in the job, and he will be an enormous success." The funny-looking diplomatic correspondent was notified on his fortieth birthday that *Nightline* was his.

How does Koppel account for his success?

■ I can't honestly say. A natural curiosity is part of it, and you either have it or you don't.

A good general background is necessary. I mean, I really didn't start this kind of interviewing until I'd been a network correspondent for seventeen years, and before that I had worked in journalism and before that I had been a teacher and before that I had studied political science and history. All of these things somehow provide a reservoir. This is not to say that a twenty-one-year-old can't be a very good interviewer, but if the twenty-one-year-old is a very good interviewer, I would bet you any amount of money that by the time he is thirty-one, he or she is going to be better; by the time they're forty-one they're going to be even better than that, because the life experience and professional experience that they gain can only enhance the attributes that they had when they were twenty-one.

For those who would be Koppel, the question should be asked: What does all this bring you? It brings a salary rumored to be in the seven figures (Koppel is reputedly a disarming but shrewd bargainer), journalism prizes and praise from your peers, and, for Koppel, the feeling that you are doing some-thing worthwhile. In 1984, he said, "In this industry, you realize that being the president of ABC News isn't going to make a hell of a lot of difference fifty years from now any more than being chairman of the board of ABC or even President of the United States is going to make a difference.... Those things just aren't important. What is important is being happy in your life with your family and trying to do a little bit of good. And now I'm in the position where I can do a little bit of good."

By 1987, his mind had changed a mite: "I'm just old enough [forty-seven] that I'm coming to the lamentable conclusion that there's no second time around. There is more to life than what I'm doing now, and I may very well stop it soon." What will Koppel do if he quits what he is doing now? If he knows, he is not telling.

When Kissinger once offered him the job of State Department spokesman, Koppel turned it down, explaining that after that, he could never return to journalism. In 1987, Kissinger, out of power but imagining how he would use Koppel in government, said he would offer Koppel assistant secretary of state for Europe. A close friend believes Koppel would be an "outstanding secretary of state," but Koppel makes no such claims. In his characteristically private manner, his answer even to the question of whether he is a Democrat or Republican is, "I'm a registered independent, because my politics are nobody's business."

I had an introduction to Ted Koppel from Wally Pfister, president of Executive Television Workshop, and Koppel invited me to come to Washington for an interview. I told a few colleagues where I was going, and in addition to the admiration they expressed for him, they asked about something which apparently fascinates many people. In disbelief, I listened to a colleague's serious request that I tell Koppel to change his haircut.

I stuck to business when I saw him, and he told me how you get to be Ted Koppel, at least Ted Koppel, the interviewer.

■   The idea of a good interview is to convey information, but there are many different ways of doing that. Sometimes you convey information by getting a lot of facts; sometimes you convey information by getting the subject of your interview to reveal a lot about himself. Frequently people reveal most about themselves—for example, about sex—by their demeanor, or by the way they are able to control themselves or unable to control themselves.

For example, I did an interview with Lyndon LaRouche [the right-wing cult leader]. I don't think we learned a lot of facts about him or about his movement, but I think we learned something about the man, Lyndon LaRouche, because in that instance I allowed him to ramble at times. He is somebody who has to be allowed to ramble, because it is in his rambling that he conveys some of the distress that is in his personality.

A most useful technique that I can recommend to anybody for almost any kind of interviewing is that you listen. That sounds like a truism, but it's amazing how few people do it. It's amazing how many people come into an interview having already decided what their questions are going to be, having decided on the order of those questions, and then pay absolutely no attention to what the interviewee is saying. Frequently people reveal something about themselves in an interview, but if you don't follow up on it, it will be lost.

Again, if you're talking in the very narrow context of the sort of interviews I do, there is a process that has to take place—the interview has to be self-contained. The viewers who are watching live television interviews are not, for the most part, going to be able to run it back again on a VCR and watch if they missed something. They are not going to have the advantage of whatever it is that you have learned about or from the person you are interviewing before or after the interview. It has to be self-contained.

Whatever editing is going to take place has to take place within that live interview. So that if most of the time you have someone who is rambling or avoiding your question, or perhaps has misunderstood the question, you have an immediate obligation to edit, the kind of thing you might be doing in an editing room with a videotape machine, where you can permit someone to do what you're doing with me right now. That is, just let him talk and later on I'll decide that I want this sentence and that thought, but not that one and not that one. I have to do that on the air. So again, if we're talking in a very narrow sense, on a *Nightline* interview you have to be able to edit and you must be able to listen. One is the function of the other; you can't edit without listening.

In interviewing you need to be able to sublimate your own opinions and sometimes even your own personality.

The biggest mistakes I've made have been not to maintain arm's length, no matter how tempting it may be at times to get a good interview. Sometimes I deliberately don't follow this rule, like if one guest is a lot weaker than another and I feel that the person needs a little propping up. Or I will take one side just to play the devil's advocate—that's all right. It's not all right if you do it because your own views are beginning to predominate and you can't stand what you're hearing; therefore, you've got to get in your own point of view.

Remember that you're a representative of a vast audience. That means that there are going to be people out there who like the person you're interviewing and those who disagree with that person. Therefore, you rarely if ever can let yourself fall into taking an advocacy role.

Interviewing Geraldine Ferraro, I was frustrated by the fact that no one had tried to pin her down on where she stood on matters of great importance had she ever become Vice President. I wanted to talk to her about strategic nuclear weapons and nuclear freeze. And I wanted that so badly, and felt it was so important to do that, that I really wasn't paying attention anymore to what she was saying. I was more concerned with what I was saying than with what she was saying. A bad interview.

The poorest interviewers are the ones who have to show how smart they are. They're trying to convey information themselves to the audience; they don't even need that second person there. They are not interested in the subject matter or the person being interviewed. That conveys itself very, very quickly to an audience.

According to a *New York Times Magazine* profile of Koppel, control is a major concern of his in his interviewing. He seldom if ever allows an interviewee to sit face to face with him. Instead, interviewees hear him through an earpiece but do not see him or the other guests on a screen. His executive producer says, "Ted needs any edge you can give him." Of course, this allows Koppel to see the body movements of his subjects while they do not have the same privilege.

In discussing Koppel with various viewers, we found that some people see him as very tough in his challenges of people—too tough; others feel he is "just right," and some find him relatively easygoing. Koppel seems to think of himself as courteous, fair, not unkind.

■ I've come to the conclusion that when I challenge people, I have to allow them the courtesy of my admitting that I may have misstated what I said before, or I may have missed the point. In other words, to say to someone "You're lying; tell me the truth," would be an extreme way of saying something that I've come to learn that you can do in a much gentler way, but really with the same effect. And that is to put the onus on myself, by saying, "I'm obviously not functioning at full power today, but I missed what you were saying there, because the question that I asked you was this and you said that, and clearly it's my mistake."

Now, what you're saying is, "You gave me the wrong answer. Take another chance. Do it again." But you're saying it in a way that permits that person not to take offense, to use that second opportunity. And you have raised a little red flag for the viewer that says, "Now pay attention. That answer the person gave really was not a good answer. Let's see if he does any better this time around."

I think, in general, it helps to understand that the viewer at home, when he or she is watching a television interview, begins by identifying with the interviewer, begins by saying to himself either consciously or subconsciously, "Here's what I would ask." If you push too hard, or too soon, and maybe the too-soon is even more important than the too-hard, then you lose that sense of identification.

If at any point during the course of the interview, you reach a point where the viewer at home says, "That was a terribly unfair, unkind, impolite, flat out rude way of asking the question," then all of a sudden they've made a transfer of allegiance. Now they're sitting there being the interviewee, and saying, "Boy, if I were the interviewee, I'd sure tell Koppel to take a long walk in a short period." And then you've lost them. And it's very hard to get them back. It's very important during the course of the interview that you keep the audience on your side of the fence. That sometimes means that you have to permit the person you're interviewing to go a little bit further than the audience thinks you should. They evade not just once; they evade two questions; they evade three. You let the person go on, not for thirty seconds, but for forty-five seconds, or a minute, or a minute and a half. The people at home are beginning to push and fidget, depending upon who it is. But there again, how close is the identification with the person you're interviewing?

If it's the President of the United States, people are going to require of you a greater tolerance, a greater level of respect, than if you're interviewing a senator, a congressman, or a baseball player or a movie actor. Therefore, you may have to let the President go on for two or three or four minutes. And then, when you sense that even the most died-in-the-wool supporter of the President is saying, "Stop it! He's not answering your question; he's going on endlessly and he's just giving you all kinds of drivel," then you can ever so gently jump in and say, "Mr. President, that was a fascinating exposition of (whatever the issue he was talking about), but if you'll permit me, "What are you trying to get at?" And you have to be very cautious and very polite, but also firm. You are the one controlling the interview. If you let the other person control the interview, then you've lost.

The wrong way to go into an interview is to say to myself, "I don't care for this person; he is a liar, a scoundrel, a thief, a dictator, a murderer, and I'm going to nail him to the wall." For example, in my interview with deposed President Marcos [of the Philippines], I couldn't help but have a lingering trace of admiration for anyone who refuses to give up.

Here's a guy who had seen himself treated like a pariah and who only a few weeks before was one of the most powerful men in Southeast Asia, certainly one of the richest. I can't help but be intrigued by whatever strength it is that keeps him going, when lesser people among us would just be crushed. There is that Nixonian quality—I think there are people who can't stand Nixon but who admire him—here he is, back again; the guy just will not give up. There's something tremendously admirable about that.

So if I brought anything to that interview, it was the determination that I wasn't going to crap all over him. He deserved the dignity of at least the recognition that he's a fighter, which he was. In that context, I think it's perfectly permissible to say, "What you're saying is fascinating, but..." And when he started talking about the shoes [the two thousand pairs of shoes Mrs. Marcos was found to have stashed away in her closets], I don't think there's anything wrong with expressing the sort of exasperation that people all over America were feeling: "Come on, how many pairs of shoes can you wear?" That was only symbolic of the excesses of that administration, but sometimes you have to grab onto the symbolism.

You have to learn something that I think you only learn with a certain amount of age—not to be afraid of people.

The more important one is, the more imposing that person is, and the less inclined you are to ask him probing questions. There seems to be a kind of arrogance about saying, "Now, wait a second, you're not telling me what I want to hear. Here's what I want to hear. Now tell me…" That requires in interpersonal relations a kind of arrogance which is not really the same thing in interviewing. In interviewing it is a professional requirement.

If you find yourself overawed by your interview subjects, you aren't going to do a good job. You can't be nervous about the interview. The people watching are not nervous because they're sitting at home, or they're lying in bed, and they're saying, "For crying out loud, why don't you ask him such and such? Didn't you hear what he just said? Jump on him! That's obviously not true. Tell him it's not true!" Well, that's easy when you're sitting at home, kind of like watching a quiz show on television. You always know the answer when you're sitting at home. When you've got the lights on you and an audience in front of you and you know that everyone is watching you, then all of a sudden your mind doesn't function quite as keenly as it does when you're relaxed on your own couch. But that is a necessary function of a television interview.

There's a convention that says, It doesn't matter who comes on the program for the time that the interview is being conducted, whoever it is that comes on has conferred upon you, the interviewer, the right to ask penetrating questions. When a program has begun to develop as *Nightline* has, over the course of the last few years, a reputation of a fairly tough program for people who are being interviewed, then that convention becomes broader and broader.

So that it's perfectly all right for the cat to look at the king, perfectly all right for the journalist to say to the President, the prime minister, or whoever he may be, "You're not answering my question." Under any other circumstances, I wouldn't be allowed to do that. Under any other circumstances convention would require that my respect for the office and my respect for the man or woman would be so great that even when they're giving me drivel, I'd have to nod and smile and say, "Thank you very much. Awfully nice of you to take the time to talk to me." When they come on the program, that goes

out the window for those fifteen, twenty, twenty-five
minutes; they have agreed to the rules of the game. The
rules are, "I ask the questions; you give the answers."
And if I don't like the answer, I can tell you, "I don't
like the answers. Let's try again."

Koppel has a particular reputation for being a master at
interrupting. *Washington Post* television critic Tom Shales called
them "judicious-to-delicious interruptions"; and Wally Pfister,
of the Executive Television Workshop, told us, "Koppel interrupts somebody more graciously than anybody I know, and
with all finality."
Koppel had this to say about getting at the truth in certain
types of interviews:

■ Sometimes I know I'm not going to get light. Sometimes
light can only come out of heat. It is really the height of
arrogance, for example, to assume that you're going to
get light when you are able to get a Palestinian to come
on with an Israeli. All you're going to do is to convey to
the audience, "You've heard that these people have a real
hard time exchanging information. You have heard that
these people have a hard time coming to an agreement.
Let me show you tonight why that is."
     In a sense, that is light, but you reach that only by
demonstrating that they just won't talk with each other.
They're talking around each other, at each other, they're
giving out propaganda but it's hardly light, not getting a
lot of information. But you're saying, "Here's why the
problem is as complex as it is."

I asked Koppel if there is a background that he could suggest
to a young person who came to him saying, "I want to do what
you do."

■ I think you have to come to this craft of interviewing
with the sense that there is no such thing as a boring
subject. There really isn't. I don't care what the subject
is, whether it's the plastics industry or the mating habits
of a certain insect, you will always find there are people

out there who have devoted their entire lives to the subject. You have to start with the assumption that they wouldn't have done it unless they were absolutely fascinated with it. Well, if it can fascinate one person, then you can extract a kind of enthusiasm from that person and transfer it to others out there: "I've never really thought about it, but imagine that person who makes lights that light up the highways, think about that—this guy makes thirty-one million dollars doing that." Even if they're not interested in the subject, they're interested in the result. Even if they don't care about how the light works, they do care about the fact that this person has twenty-five thousand people working for him, and that this person has been able to buy a sixty-four-foot cabin cruiser, the result of his invention. And the more you think about it, the more the really common things, the things that we take for granted, whether it's a button, safety pin, a zipper, a tie, or a cuff link, or whatever it is, someone has devoted a lifetime to it. It's because it has either been enormously profitable psychically (they really love the subject), or it's tremendously profitable in terms of money. Either way, you can make that interesting.

If you don't come to the craft of the interview with that predisposition, you're a bad interviewer. Just to assume, Oh, sure, you get me the Pope, you get me Bush, you get me Gorbachev, and I'll do a good interview—that's a loser. It really is. What you're really saying is, Get me someone who is generally perceived to be one of the most interesting people in the world and set a microphone in front of him and say, "Talk," and you'll get an acceptable interview. Some people are so interesting to begin with, or so powerful to begin with, that anything they say will make news. That's not an interview.

Interviewing really involves being able to say, Even if we have just fifteen minutes and we really care about this subject, I'm going to try to convince other people that they should care about this subject. Start with that and you can't go wrong.

You're dealing with a mass audience, an audience that has a wide range of expertise. On any given night, there are more people who know more than you could ever have dreamed about that particular subject, and watching at the same time are people who have never heard of that subject, have never heard of that person, know absolutely nothing about it. Somehow you've got to be able to accommodate both sets of viewers. You have to make sure that you don't leave people behind. You have to make sure, no matter what your own expertise on the subject, that you don't try to dazzle people about how much you know. But make sure that you don't leave people behind, because television is a medium of the lowest common denominator.

John Chancellor

News Commentator, NBC

"The object of an interview is to satisfy, for a journalist, the who, what, when, where, why of a situation."

Iｆ SOME UNIVERSITY does not one day give the distinguished interviewer and potential professor John Chancellor a chair in journalism, I will be surprised. As I interviewed him about his job, he impressed me as a born teacher.

Actually, teaching has been in his mind for a long time. As long ago as 1979, he told an interviewer that he did not have any immediate plans for teaching, but he probably would teach at some point. Four years later, he co-authored, with Walter R. Mears, a writing guide for young journalists, *The News Business*. Three years after that he was credited with "giving a master class in the art of interviewing" when he was selected to moderate a symposium of eight former White House chiefs of staff or their equivalents. The symposium ended up in Samuel Kernall and Samuel L. Popkin's *Chief of Staff: Twenty-Five Years of the American Presidency*. His opening question to the chiefs of staff was "How do you talk a President out of a damn fool idea?" They loved it.

Like some other television interviewers in this book, John Chancellor went from print to television journalism, and as with them, his love affair began early. Born in Chicago in 1927, he caught the fever (he was said to have been "dazzled") at fourteen, working after school for the *Chicago Daily News*.

He left school at age fifteen and had a series of "oddball jobs," followed by a stint in the army, where he worked on the post newspaper and in public relations. On discharge, he started college, but he left after a short time to take a job with the *Chicago Sun-Times*. Here his rise was rapid—from copyboy to feature writer in two years.

Then his career made the crucial switch. In 1950, at twenty-three, he got a job in broadcasting, where he has been, with the exception of two years, all of his adult working life. For twelve years, he worked at various correspondent posts around the world, picking up experience and awards of all kinds. His career then took a dramatic turn about which he was hesitant from the beginning.

NBC made him co-host (with Tom Brokaw) of the *Today* show and Chancellor apparently early on wondered about becoming just another "character" on television. While he became nationally known in the slot, being exposed to four-million people every weekday, the job was not for him. He left after little more than a year, returning to a correspondent position, first in Brussels, then in Washington, D.C.

Out of the blue came the offer of a job never before offered to a working journalist: President Lyndon Johnson invited him to take the post of director of Voice of America. Chancellor accepted, and he remained there for two years.

Returning to broadcasting, he became co-anchor of *NBC Nightly News*, a job much better suited to his talents and personality than the one on the *Today* show. After twelve years, he reached age fifty and took stock of himself. For him, it amounted to this: "I had money and I had fame.... But the last thing I wanted to be was a sixty-five-year-old anchorman. So I decided to take control of my life." Since that time he has been a commentator, writer, and broadcaster for NBC.

Chancellor is tall, imposing, distinguished looking, reminding one of a chief executive officer of a major corporation, an ambassador, a professor with a chair at Yale. After talking with him only a short time, I felt I had known him for years. I left the interview with an impression of him not unlike what his NBC colleagues thought of him as long ago as 1961: "charming, eclectic, gentlemanly, impossibly energetic, an excellent bar companion, a people collector."

At the end of our interview, an incident gave me a hint of the extent of his enthusiasm for what he does. I still had a few more allotted minutes to go and a couple of questions still to ask when Chancellor arose from his desk, obviously obsessed with something but concerned that he might appear rude to me. He walked toward his television set and turned on the 6:00 news, apologizing to me. Big international news was breaking, and he was glued to the set. I left as discretely as I could.

Two days later, I received his only copy of *Chief of Staff* to borrow as long as I needed it. Accompanying the book was a letter thanking me for a "stimulating conversation."

We did not, in fact, have a conversation. Instead, as I said, I got a one-hour education in broadcast journalism:

■ Interviewing is such a fundamental part of what journalists do that it's neither codified nor defined. It is just what we do.

And I don't know that it can be taught. Mainly it comes out of our own curiosity and, I suppose, the knowledge of what we need from an interview to make a news story out of it.

The object of an interview is to satisfy, for a journalist, the who, what, when, where, why of a situation.

There are rules of inquiry. If you're interviewing an eyewitness to an accident—let's start at that level— someone who saw the car crash into the other car, you do it very much the way a lawyer or a policeman would. First: name, address, middle initial (very important in all journalism), and age, if it's at all relevant, because if it's a sixteen-year-old or an eighty-five-year-old, you need to say that in the story—it adds a certain dimension to the believability of the person.

You ask a lot of questions about what they saw, and you go over that several times if you can, because people tend to change their recollections. Or you ask them, "How could you see it because...wasn't there a truck that passed between you and the accident at the time?" "Yes, there was a lot of traffic." Then you start in another way. Or you go to a police officer or a fire chief at the scene of a fire. You are trained to ask a lot of questions about the height and depth of the building, the number of people who work there—a lot of technical things that you are trained to do.

Sometimes we need to use a translator in interviewing. The French go very fast, and although I speak enough French to get around, I don't speak any foreign language well enough to use in journalism. I use my French for many other things, but I always use a translator in interviewing. That means that interviews done in countries where you have to use that kind of translation technique tend to be more shallow and less insightful than interviews done in your own tongue. Interviewing with a translator is one of the most difficult things in the world for most of us, because we don't have what the President and heads of state have when they meet, which are simultaneous translators whispering in their ears. Simultaneous translation is good because you can follow the facial expressions of the person who's talking to you, whereas you can't in consecutive translation.

Most reporters get consecutive translation, however, when they're interviewing in a foreign language, because they can't really afford to have simultaneous translation. But it's very difficult to get to the root of things without the simultaneous translation.

In terms of Washington coverage, sometimes the kind of interviewing you do, say in the White House and the other big departments, is altered by the rules of the interview. We have various rules about quoting. There is "on the record" and "off the record." There is something called "background," where you're not supposed to quote the official you're talking to, but you very often say, "It's attributed in the United States to American officials." Or sometimes, depending upon where the interview is—White House or State Department or Defense Department—there is something that isn't used much anymore. There are two phrases for it, the Lindley Rule, or "deep background."

"Deep background" means the reader or viewer or listener must assume that you know this. Let's just say,

for example, "We sent a planeload of arms to China."
On the record, you say that was said by such and such
official. Off the record, at the other extreme, you can't
even write that a planeload of arms went to China.
That's simply for your own information to help you flesh
out other parts of the story. On "background," you can
say, "An American official said that a planeload of arms
went to China." On "deep background," you can say, "A
planeload of arms went to China." You just have to say
that on your own, as though God had reached down
with a finger drawn by Blake and anointed you with that
information.

We always assume it's all on the record. Our rule is
never to ask, because very often they can say, "Well, let's
put this on background." You just assume it's on the
record unless someone says, "You can't attribute this to
me." Sometimes you have to give in and say, "Yes, I'll
accept that," if you think you can get the information
which you need, increase the knowledge of the story
you're covering.

Now, off the record is a dangerous thing to fool with.
I'll give you a concrete example of that. In the 1980
elections, around the time of the Wisconsin primary
elections, I was in the temporary office we had in
Milwaukee the weekend before the voting, and there
were a number of stories in the press which indicated
that, I think, President Carter had sent a letter to the
Ayatollah with some phrases in it that looked like sort of
a cave-in. The telephone rang and I picked it up and it
was the White House operator asking if I were there,
and I said it was I. "The President would like to talk to
you," and I thought, "I think I know what that's all
about. He's scared about these stories and he's calling
up." And so he came on the telephone and we
exchanged greetings. He said, "John, I have to talk to
you off the record." And so I swallowed hard, and I
said, "Mr. President, we have a rule around here. If we
accept information off the record and we think it's going
to block some of the reporting we would be doing, we're
not allowed by NBC News to accept that information. It

hinders us in our work, and I suspect, sir, that you want
to talk to me about Iran and the hostages. If that's the
case, I'm afraid I cannot take the information." So there
was a long, long pause. Finally, he said, "Well, I'll tell
you anyway." Then he told me that he hadn't sent the
letter.

That's a good example of how some officials in
possession of pieces of information they know you're
after can get your pledge to accept it off the record, and
that means your hands are tied. You cannot use it. If
you find yourself in this situation, and of course all of
us have been burned by that in our earlier years, you
just sort of get a sixth sense about it. "Wait a minute, I
don't want to take this." Then they can say, "I'm sorry, I
can't talk to you." And you can say, "Yes, of course,
you're absolutely right. Thanks very much. Goodbye."

In government work, and increasingly now in covering
other kinds of stories, people have learned to set up
these rules of interviewing. If somebody is going to buy
a baseball team or a tract of land, you find these days
that they're saying, "Well, I can only talk to you off the
record." And in that case the wisest thing for the
interviewer to do is to say, "No, thanks, I'll get it
somewhere else," and you usually can. There's something
self-important about saying, "I'll only talk to you off the
record," that smaller officials sometimes use just for
their ego.

Let me talk about preparation for interviews. If you're
interviewing a president, there are various techniques.
Some people write down all their questions on a yellow
pad seriatim, without dividing them into categories. I
write down the foreign policy questions on one side, the
domestic policy questions on the other, the political
questions at the bottom. And then I try to organize
them in a way that I can provide a flow to them. Often
with presidents you're not alone; you've got two or three
other reporters, and they may be asking the same
questions that you have. I suppose I've gone into
interviews with presidents with thirty, forty, or fifty
different questions. Of those fifty, maybe ten get asked.

As you proceed through journalism, you begin to specialize. Reporters on foreign affairs find themselves asking about decisions taken in previous American administrations or some historical parallels. Reporters covering science know a good deal about the process involved, and their questioning follows that.

A. J. Liebling, who worked for *The New Yorker* for many years, used to tell this story about interviewing a very famous jockey for a profile. In Joe's preparation for the interview he read a good deal about how jockeys ride and how they do their jobs. And so when he sat down for the main interview, with great casualness, as though it wasn't an important question he asked, "How many notches is your left stirrup higher than your right stirrup?" because, as I didn't know, jockeys tend to ride one way. Well, he said that the jockey talked for about twenty minutes, wonderful stuff. At the end of the twenty minutes, the jockey said, "You ask pretty good questions."

And what Joe said later was, "I didn't ask pretty good questions; I didn't know anything about this until I read it a couple of days before, but I thought it would put him at his ease and I thought it would make him think that I knew a little bit about this." By asking an informed, technical question, you make the person being interviewed relax a little bit and say, "Well, this interviewer knows something about what I'm doing."

And I think this is true as a basis for all interviews. You have to do your homework. If you've done your work properly, you can take a mediocre person and ask him to consider things he has not considered before. Elizabeth Taylor is probably a more interesting interview than the lady who cleans the wastebaskets here at NBC, but if you really went to work on that lady, you might make her more interesting than Elizabeth Taylor.

If I'm interviewing in somebody's office, I prefer to use both notebook and tape recorder. The tape recorder is kind of an insurance policy that I get the quotes right. I use a notebook because in a sense it helps me to organize my thoughts or pick up certain phrases that the person being interviewed uses. (You never use the word "interviewee," do you? That's a terrible word.) Sometimes someone will say something very interesting and it will trigger a thought. You just write that down while you're getting the basic interview.

One of the things that I was taught as a young reporter in Chicago is an interviewing technique that I have used all my career. That is the value of *not* asking a question. This is especially useful in any eye-contact interview, whether it's for print or for broadcast; it's not so useful over the telephone. The technique involves asking a series of questions that lead up to an important question that may be vexatious to the subject.

If you have the time, you usually ask several questions before you get to the question that you've come in to ask, which is, let's say, "Alderman, they say you stole the money. Did you steal the money or not?" You try to put him at his ease and impress upon him that you're a decent fellow and that you're not out to get him. You butter him up. And then you say, "I have to ask you this question because it's in the news, and that's why I'm here. Did you steal the money?" And the alderman will say, "No, of course I didn't steal it." He will then proceed to give you a carefully worked out answer about why it would be inconceivable that anyone would say that he had stolen the money.

Now you say nothing. You don't change your expression and you don't look down. You just sit there looking at the alderman. And in about ten seconds of silence, that alderman, nine times out of ten, will start to babble. And when he starts to babble, you'll get much closer to the truth. This applies to almost everybody; they will start filling in the details that hadn't been included in their carefully worked out two-hundred-word answer. I wouldn't try that on a very smart person, like the late Roy Cohn, because he catches on right away, and you can't do it too often, but you can certainly do it once or twice in most interviews. Mike Wallace knows all about that, more than I do, and can judge, sometimes brilliantly, I think, when not to speak.

In some cases, in a hostile interview or a contentious interview, to see that you're upsetting the person with your questions is a signal to go on. I don't know where it's going to lead, but if somebody starts sweating, there's a reason for it, and it's your obligation to follow through. I've seen lots of public officials get nervous when you sort of accidentally stray into something that they didn't think you knew about, and you may not know about it, you may not know what you're talking about.

I got into trouble once interviewing President Gerald Ford on live television. (I just think it's a stunt to interview the President of the United States on live television. You really should tape it, have a look at it, and then put it on.) Anyway, I had some bad research in that interview. It was an allegation in a magazine that within the last few days the President had ordered a secret military mission for some kind of unit of troops in the Caribbean. And I didn't check on it myself; a young researcher checked on it and came back and said, "Yes, that's true." On live television, I asked the President what he could tell me about this secret movement of troops in the Caribbean. And he paused and said, "John, I can't talk about that," which I took to be pay dirt. That was confirmation. Well, all the reporters who were watching this in the press room went crazy. "Secret movements of American troops—the President just said he couldn't talk about it."

Well, you didn't have just one dope, me, on that interview. You had two dopes—me and the President. Because he should have known his job well enough to say, "That's the silliest question I've ever heard; we're not sending any troops anywhere. What have you got on your mind, you jerk?" But he didn't. He was as nervous as anybody is on live television in a situation like that, and he just said, "I can't talk about that."

So we had a difficult evening after the interview sorting that out. If I'd been interviewing him in his office and he'd said, "I can't talk about that," I certainly would have had to press him by saying, "Mr. President, by saying you can't talk about it, you've *confirmed* it,"

really putting him into a corner because that's a volatile
piece of information. But we were on the air, and he said
he couldn't discuss it. Our researcher had made an
assumption on the basis of what somebody had told him
at the Pentagon. We finally tracked down the man at the
Pentagon who said that he hadn't intended to give that
impression at all. And I believe him.

If you think that the person you've interviewed has
made a mistake, the thing to do is to follow it up and
say, "Did you really mean what you just told me?" That's
ethically very important. It's also an enormous safeguard
for the journalist. We're not in business to puzzle and
befuddle the audience. Interviewing has to produce
clear responses. It's your responsibility, because people
get things wrong.

There are all kinds of people in journalism. Some are
bullies and some of them are nice people.

I don't come out as a bully in journalism, but when I
was a young reporter on a newspaper I was awfully
good at working the telephones and going out and
doing the nice-guy interview, getting people to tell me
things because I was a pleasant person to be with.

There's another way, however. In Chicago, around the
time I was there, there was another reporter named
Seymour Hersh, a famous investigative reporter. Sy
Hersh is the toughest man I ever met in my entire life
in an interview. He will say to people he's interviewing,
"How dare you lie to me! I'll have you in jail for that!"
Actually he's a pretty nice fellow, but that works for him
on the kinds of stories for which he does interviews.
And don't lie to Sy Hersh! If he catches you in that, he
gets personally offended and he's back in your office or
on the telephone screaming at you, yelling at you. In the
course of that, he sometimes gets unexpected amounts
of information, whereas I, on the other hand, would say
I get it out of sympathy: "Gee, he's a pretty nice fellow
I'm talking to; he's not going to harm me."

Rudeness is one of the things that bothers me more
than anything else. Using the interview, especially on
television, as a kind of weapon to get somebody to say

something that he doesn't want to say is also, it seems to
me, not a productive or reasonable way. I think it's a bad
kind of interviewing. I also think that being rude to
important government officials on television hurts
journalism.

Our surveys show that we have very high credibility
with the American public. But in the areas in which we
have lower credibility, it comes from issues involving
invasion of privacy, badgering people with questions,
and being rude to public officials.

Now, there's a complicated business. Let's take the
most prominent case, a presidential press conference.
That's seen on prime-time television by an awful lot of
people. And we take our lumps because of that. Now,
television has brought that about, all by itself. Reporters
doing their jobs have to ask tough, probing questions.
Their questions sound, to the uninformed people who
don't know what we're doing, pretty tough and
sometimes verging on disrespect. For instance, at a
presidential press conference I would stand up and say,
"Mr. President, how can you believe that the American
people won't think that just for political reasons you
were doing so and so?" Well, if my mother were sitting
at home, she'd say, "I didn't raise my boy to ask nasty
questions to the President of the United States."

So that in the process of doing our work, when it is
televised, it tends to make us look much tougher than
we really are. Even with Jack Kennedy—the press loved
Jack Kennedy—or Nixon in the first term, or other
popular Presidents, the questions have to be tough and
probing; that's what we get paid for. That's why there are
press conferences. But to uninformed people, it's beating
up on the poor President. And, of course, Presidents
know that and use it.

And then I suppose there's the uninformed interview,
which you've seen and I've seen often on television. I see
it, too, with print reporters when they call me here on
the telephone, when they have obviously not read
enough or learned enough about you or about the story

in which you're involved. So you keep saying to yourself, "Boy, I could have asked better questions than that!" When you find yourself saying, "Why didn't you ask him that?" or "Why didn't she give him the chance to defend himself?" that's a bad interview.

So what goes into a good interview? Homework, courtesy, and a determination to get as much as you can out of the person being interviewed without becoming a bully. I hope that doesn't sound excessively old-fashioned.

Robert MacNeil

Co-Host and Interviewer, PBS's MacNeil/Lehrer NewsHour

"A television interviewer, especially if he has some kind of national audience and is well known, has a license to ask virtually anybody in the world to let him or her come in and ask them anything. Incredible! I mean, really incredible!"

Robert MacNeil, one of the two founders of the *MacNeil/ Lehrer NewsHour* on public television, is obsessed.

The obsession he has had for many years focuses on the power of television and its interviewers in this country. In our interview he made a surprising detour from a question I asked in order to express his alarm:

■ One of the things that intrigues me about the interviewer today is what he has become, the range of impertinence he is allowed in the society. The society has created this television culture. It has created a person for whom I can't find any equivalent in history, except maybe the court jester, who sits at the king's feet and is permitted incredible license to be impertinent, to play the fool, but to be the sort of *idiot savant* some of the time, to say very penetrating things, to be a soothsayer as well as a wit. Television has created this animal who is permitted by the society, encouraged, and very well paid, to be everybody's kind of—what's the word I'm looking for?—an extension of them, you know, a surrogate.

And the license is extraordinary. A television interviewer, especially if he has some kind of national audience and is well known, has a license to ask virtually anybody in the world to let him or her come in and ask them anything. Incredible! I mean, really incredible! They're in a few societies—America, Canada, Australia, Britain, France, and others—not in totalitarian countries except to a degree. It is really incredible.

It was summed up for me in a strange way when it was David Frost who was the interlocutor of Richard Nixon after Nixon had resigned and was pardoned. There was no appeal to a court of law—Nixon was never brought before any bar of justice, because he resigned before an impeachment proceeding was called. And whether his crimes were exaggerated at the time, or whether they were not, whether they were trivial or very serious, at least because of his stature as President, the whole incident was extremely important in the history of this country.

Nixon submitted to no questioning by anybody except to a television performer—for pay. And a television performer who wasn't even a journalist, and certainly wasn't a judge or lawyer, or a jury, or anything else, but a smart man with a certain ability as a television interviewer who prepared himself as well as he could. His persona became the kind of embodiment, personification, of American, or Western, outrage at Richard Nixon. So that Frost had to serve the role of inquisitor, prosecutor, judge, jury, public opinion—the surrogate of all those things, all rolled into one Englishman who could pay Richard Nixon to come on and be, for the most part, extremely self-serving and defensive about the whole operation.

MacNeil knows what he is talking about. His career in television reads like a history of the place of television in American society.

Robert (often called Robin) MacNeil was born in Montreal in 1931. He attended Canadian public schools and then, like proper British boys, boarding school.

MacNeil was not, like some television people, "hooked" on journalism from an early age. He had three chosen careers, each of which he tried before finding that journalism put food on the table and gave him a life-style he liked. He discovered some time later that it is fascinating work.

For about two years he attended naval training school in preparation for a career as an officer. But he found that this was not for him, and tried his second dream, acting.

He got a job acting for the Canadian Broadcasting Company, with some announcing and disc jockey work on the side. He even tried summer stock in New York for a short time. But acting was not it, and at twenty he gave it up and returned to the Canadian Broadcasting Corporation, attending college on the side.

He still was not bitten by the broadcasting bug. He went to London to write plays, but soon gave up.

He fell back into journalism without much enthusiasm, but the wolf was at the door. MacNeil never left journalism.

A series of jobs moved him ever upward—in London he was editor at Reuters, then roving foreign correspondent for NBC. He moved to the network's Washington bureau, then to New York as an anchor at NBC. It was this job that helped to focus him—in a negative way. He told *TV Guide*, "I liked the money. I liked being recognized on the street. But it was a pretty phony business, anchoring, reading an hour of stuff I got five minutes before we went on the air."

He left NBC for the British Broadcasting Corporation's prestigious documentary series, *Panorama*. For this job he traveled back and forth across the Atlantic covering stories on both sides. In addition, he worked on documentaries for the newborn Public Broadcasting Laboratory.

Then an extraordinary series of events occurred in which he had the worst of times and the best of times—and in the end everything gradually fell into place for him.

In 1971, still in England, he was invited to join a new American venture, the birth of public television news in the form of the National Public Affairs Center for Television (NPACT). He took a leave of absence from the BBC and returned to the States to become one of two senior news correspondents, along with Sander (Sandy) Vanocur, for NPACT.

There was, however, a major difficulty: Richard Nixon and

his White House staff were not happy with the way news was being handled by public television. With the apparent ultimate goal of restraining, if not controlling, public television, they began a campaign against Vanocur, and to some extent Mac-Neil. One sore point was Vanocur's liberalism; another was that Vanocur's and MacNeil's salaries were higher than that of the Vice President, Supreme Court justices, and other high government officials. In March 1973, the Corporation for Public Broadcasting, controlled by Nixon appointees, canceled funding for such "controversial" programs as *Washington News in Review*, which MacNeil worked on. It was a tough time for him. "The answer we now know is that we were not paranoid; there *was* a conspiracy and the President himself was directly involved," he wrote in his autobiography, *The Right Place at the Right Time*.

In the meantime, Vanocur had resigned, apparently hurt by the attacks, and was replaced by a newspaperman from Texas, Jim Lehrer. Lehrer and MacNeil devised a new weekly documentary series examining one theme each week—and they had hit upon the forerunner of their current program.

And then Watergate blew up. The Public Broadcasting System decided to use MacNeil and Lehrer to anchor its coverage of the Watergate hearings with no interruptions. Public response to their program was quite good. Money from viewer subscriptions tripled in some cities. As MacNeil wrote, "By a curious turn of fate, public television, one of the victims of the Watergate mentality, had been saved by it."

Still, MacNeil and Lehrer's idea of a nightly national news program was not picked up, and MacNeil, tired of bickering, returned to the BBC in England. But in less than two years he was back in the States. Jay Iselin, the president of WNET in New York, offered MacNeil the money to start a half-hour nightly news program for the station—and the program Mac-Neil and Lehrer dreamed of finally came to fruition.

For the program, the two men invited "talking heads" and let them talk, going after "light" rather than "heat." Their thrust was to avoid the confrontational approach to interviewing and provide viewers with the different sides of an issue; they insisted that they had no interest in changing people's views. The program was an almost immediate success, winning numerous awards and an audience of an estimated four-and-a-half million people. MacNeil loved his job. He had found his niche.

In 1988, the *MacNeil/Lehrer NewsHour* was given a $57 million package of corporate support that will probably carry the program through mid-1993. The grant was the largest financial commitment to a single program in the history of public broadcasting.

In 1989, MacNeil was selected to edit and write an introduction to *The Way We Were: 1963, The Year Kennedy Was Shot.* He undoubtedly was selected not only because he writes well but because at least one experience during that time has become part of journalism lore. From the point of view of interviewing, it illustrates more than any anecdote I know the missed opportunity to ask the right questions at the right time of the right people. (MacNeil would be the first to say this.)

Covering the fateful Dallas motorcade, MacNeil was in a press bus seven vehicles behind President Kennedy's limousine. Suddenly, MacNeil heard something like shots. He jumped off the bus and ran, first following several people running up a knoll who seemed to know what they were doing (they did not) and then some policemen who seemed to know where they were going (they did not). He still did not know who, if anyone, had been shot. On the knoll people were lying on the grass in panic, trying somehow to cover themselves. They could have told him who had been shot, but he did not think to ask.

Seeking a telephone, he entered the first building he thought might have one. It turned out to be the Texas School Book Depository, and he ran in just as a young man was coming out. MacNeil might have asked if the young man knew anything about the shooting. Instead he asked where a phone might be, and the young man pointed to a person talking on a phone, saying, "Better ask him," and left the building. MacNeil found an office with a phone and called his own office. His news, of course, did not include an interview with the assassin Lee Harvey Oswald, who seems surely to have been the young man on his way out of the depository, or interviews with the people lying on the knoll who had witnessed the assassination. As he explained, there is "no time to think in such situations."

MacNeil is unmatched among television interviewers in the

number and quality of books he has produced. The first two
he wrote contained his tirade on the role of television in our
culture, *The People Machine: The Influence of Television on American Politics* and his memoir, largely about journalism, *The Right
Place at the Right Time.* His later books focus on his preoccupa-
tion with words: *The Story of English* (co-authored with Robert
McCrum and William Cran) and *Wordstruck.*

My interview with MacNeil took place at the busy, crowded
offices of PBS in New York. His office is not large, and it faces
another building. MacNeil was easy to interview—polite, serious, low-key but involved, as he is on television. When I left, I
felt I had been with a scholarly intellectual. I wrote to thank
him for the interview and got back a polite and very warm
note. I was unused to receiving replies to the thank-you notes I
wrote to the busy people we saw, but it seemed characteristic of
MacNeil to write a note. Nice man.

In response to my first question, "What makes a really good
interview?" he gave the kind of well-thought-out reply I
expected from him based on what he has written about his
work.

■ Interviews have different purposes—dramatic moments
of confrontation, revelation, prosecutorial accusation, or
confession, as on *60 Minutes*; exploration of deeper
philosophical reaches of somebody's mind grappling
with the moral or political issues of the day, as with Bill
Moyers; getting at the personal attitudes, self-revelations
of some prominent show business personality or public
personality, as with Barbara Walters.

In formula political interviews, it's a bit of a game
between you and the interview subject. He has his
defenses up and he is able to say only what he intends to
say. Most people one finds oneself interviewing have
been interviewed many times, or at least they have
uttered the thoughts they're known for many times.
Most questions produce in them, as they do in me, a sort
of quick random search of the memory computer for the
answer they've thought out long ago, and they push the
button and the tape plays back the answer.

If the interviewer can get past that, and either by

angering or, I would prefer, intriguing, the person, he is
forced to come up with an original answer and say to
himself, "Gee, I hadn't thought of that." That excites
me. We don't often have that opportunity because the
interviews are too short, or they're for a different
purpose.

There is another kind of interview where you want
somebody to tell his story—this is usually the case for
filmed biographies or profiles. A lot of the story has
already been told; it's in print or in other interviews.
And you just want them to regurgitate it another time,
at the length and with the kind of color that's appropriate to the purpose you're going to use it for when you
edit it.

You work on different levels with different people and
different circumstances, and sometimes you are
confident that the force of your own personality will
ingratiate you with the person, break down defenses
gradually, get that person to trust you enough that
you're not going to betray him or her into some terrible
indiscretion, and that you're all right to talk to. Then
they open up, and you can get them to talk along the
lines you want them to talk.

This is the extended, quiet, personality interview for
which you may record many, many, many times the
amount you're going to use. You're listening for those
pieces that James Joyce called "epiphanies."

You can hear where the scissors are going to go in at
either end of it, and you're saying to yourself, "That's a
good bit. That is really revealing. This person is talking
from the heart." Or at least, "This has a tinge of
originality and revelation about it that all that I've read
of what she or he has said before doesn't include."

At the same time, with somebody like Rose Kennedy,
for example, you want them to get beyond what they've
said many times, because the standard story becomes
like those tape-recorded bits where people just
automatically replay what they've said before. "What was
my reaction the day that Jack died?" you know. With her

I had to spend about an hour and a half breaking down her own preparation.

She condescended to be interviewed because her publishers had persuaded her it would be good for her book. She treated me as a person who had come to deliver the flowers or one of the many parts of her preparation for her performance. She called downstairs (she was dressing upstairs), "Where's the one who's going to ask the questions?"

The one who was going to ask the questions was brought upstairs and introduced to her. She was half undressed and being made up—having her eyelashes put on, that kind of thing. It was like a great actress preparing for her performance. She said, "Over there on the bed you'll see the questions and the answers that we've prepared." On the bed was a Dior gown that she was going to wear, a new one for this occasion, and beside the gown were the questions and the answers, all neatly typewritten by her secretary. It was basically how she wanted herself to be thought of and presented: "I'd like you to ask me about my time in London, and how wonderful the Queen was, and how nice they were to us and our children, and what wonderful people the British are," that kind of thing. I had to spend time sitting on a little stool at her feet while the process of making her up and getting her ready continued.

I had to sort of say, "Yes, I'd like to hear what she had to say about that," but I wanted to ask her other questions. And eventually—it took a long time—we got both what she wanted to say and what I wanted her to say. And it ended up extraordinarily moving, I thought—some of it.

Ninety percent of getting people to talk is the interviewer's reputation beforehand. It is a balance between the reputation you have as somebody they can trust, and somebody whose audience they want. Most people accept being interviewed because they want the publicity, not because they want to bare their souls, not because they want to get confessional. Sometimes the interview is an opportunity, they think, to exculpate themselves, but most of the time just an opportunity for aggrandizement or furthering their celebrity status, adding to their commodity value as a lecturer, author, health food expert, or whatever. So it's a balance between what you can do for them—that's most of it—and whether they're a sympathetic enough person to do it. But more important than anything else is the audience that you bring to them.

Other kinds of interviews are designed—often on television—to show off the interviewer. They are a showcase for the interviewer's show business personality, and that can take many forms. A lot of it is a kind of theatrical posturing that sometimes looks like heavy prosecutorial interviewing, and sometimes like a really friendly "Come on, we're just buddies" kind of chat.

Interviews on our nightly program are designed, most of the time, to elicit information from people we know have it, and most of the time want to utter it. I'm not talking about the challenging interview with a public official at a moment of crisis where they have come to say what they want to say to serve their own purpose. The purpose of the interview is to get them to say even more than they want to say, or to challenge the self-serving points of view that they're saying. But most of the time we invite guests on the program because they have a point of view and it's going to be put in juxtaposition with another point of view. Our purpose is to elicit as clearly and sharply as possible that point of view, and challenge it enough so that the intentions of the person are clarified.

When we can arrange it, our reporters pre-interview the guests, and we know pretty well what they are there to say. That doesn't apply to some top government officials who can't be pre-interviewed and won't be. Or some other very busy individuals. But for the most part there are pre-interviews.

A lot of people are helped by pre-interviews. They verbalize what they may not have verbalized until then; it's a bit of a rehearsal for them. Not everybody is

skilled—as is evident from my rambling on and on—at
rapping out televisually appropriate, succinct bites—
terse, pithy observations on the world—even if they
know their own minds very clearly. Most people ramble
on a bit, and it may help them to put their thoughts into
words beforehand. It also helps to relieve nervousness.
We want to calm people down and not create a hostile,
intimidating environment, which is what a television
studio is. If they're nervous, I see no reason for not
telling them what you're going to ask them, if you're not
there to trap them or trick them.

Treat a person as you would like to be treated if you
were jammed into a television studio under a lot of hot
lights. Television has imposed on many people in all
walks of life a kind of imperative to be effective by its
demands—spit it out in thirty seconds, and sound
attractive and dynamic and energetic and sexy and more
useful than you really are—all those things at the same
time. In other words, as imposed on the society at large,
a requirement to be as telegenic as television's own
professional performers are, never to be at a loss for
words, always to have a quick, ready answer to rap out,
and hopefully it will be both dramatic and terse and
human and revealing. Terrible, terrible imposition!

So anything we can do to relax them a bit, I think, is
dandy. And the pre-interview does that.

There's something we haven't talked about—the
difference between a live and taped or edited interview.

Live interviews, which are so much of daily television
really, are a very different animal from taped ones,
where many of them seem to be designed to showcase
the interviewer, rather than to elicit information.

The dynamics of the live interview work very
differently, because both the interviewer and the
interviewee feel compelled to fill in the spaces, and not
to say silly things, not to hesitate, not to do what a
newspaper interviewer or researcher would do, "Let's see
now, just a minute ago you said...Just give me a second,
I want to go back over something." A live interview has
to be a performance, a polished, completed

performance. There mustn't be long pauses; you mustn't lose the sort of performance rhythm and tension and dynamic.

Is there a talent for interviewing? It's something I never thought of. I think some people, whether it's a talent they're born with or part of their upbringing, have it as part of their personality—they enjoy asking questions. It may be a form of social defensiveness. If I wasn't born with it, I certainly discovered very early in life that I enjoyed asking questions. In fact, I was often told, "You shouldn't be asking such probing questions in social settings." The way I was brought up, with somebody you didn't know very well, you asked one or two polite questions but you didn't pursue it too far, too intimately. I have always liked asking questions. It's part of my nature. I like asking more than I like giving answers. In social situations where I don't know people, that is how I carry on a dialogue—by asking questions— unless I'm cornered and get asked questions myself.

Certainly whatever talent somebody is born with, or develops in their upbringing, there are things you can do to enhance those talents.

It is really essential that the interviewer have curiosity. And it can be genuine curiosity, or it can be manufactured curiosity, or trained curiosity, but at some point, it's got to become at least as genuine as the feelings that a very fine actor has when he goes on stage and tries to renew every night the experience that he's playing and to make it real.

I frequently find that if I spend five days a week interviewing, which is essentially what I do, I am not particularly interested in interviewing the person I set out to prepare for. But it has to happen, and it usually does, that the exercise of going through the preparation makes me curious.

We have help in preparing interviews—everybody does—and people suggest questions. And you read material, and at some point, even if it's going through it by rote—"I'm not very interested in this"—if you read enough and get into it enough, you say, "Well, I don't think he's been asked that," or "Could I get him to say this?" or "I wonder if this is a question that he hasn't considered."

When I went to London to interview John LeCarré for the television production of *Tinker, Tailor, Soldier, Spy*, I had already read his books and was intrigued by them, as millions are, and I read every interview I could get my hands on that he had given. I thought that I had found a kind of chink. One thing that he didn't seem to talk about was his attitude toward women, which up to that time was on a largely negative and pejorative note. He hadn't yet written *The Little Drummer Girl*. It just seemed to me that his attitude toward women was a part of his personality that might be very constricted, and I wondered about that. And he said, "You know, I hadn't really thought about that before," and it got him to talk about it and begin to think about it. And he went into a lot of detail about his relations with his mother and his first wife and how that colored his experience; a lot of it was negative.

Somebody who's a talented interviewer is somebody who can listen. That's probably before anything else. And enjoys listening. While he's listening, he's sorting the material and thinking of other openings, if the interviewee gives him a chance. And he's changing the direction of his questions. There's a terror among people who have too little time to prepare thoroughly, or too little time on the air, that creates an opportunity for an awful lot of dumb questioning.

It's very, very hard to listen and have the next question ready if the subject suddenly stops talking, still keeping track of the time and what you're intending to get out of the interview and whether you're getting it. It's a complicated business.

I've learned a great deal from Jim Lehrer. I used to be part of the school of thinking that it was smart in a question to show how much I know about a particular subject and to over-background the question to show off my knowledge. I learned from him that the simpler the question, the more direct. And not to be afraid to say,

"Wait a minute—what does that mean?" or "Why?" or "Say that again." Just not to be afraid to be seen as not understanding or not following. I do a lot more of that now.

I don't have any rules about the way I ask questions. It is in our natures—Jim's and mine—to ask questions reasonably politely.

I think there's an impression growing in television in this country that unless you ask a question in the manner of Perry Mason with a witness in the dock, you're not a tough interviewer. That has led to a school of interviewing I don't happen to like, which is very mannered and postured. The interviewer gives himself a lot of airs as the one who's really the repository of wisdom, and why can't the interviewee match up to it? This is part of the business of making the interviewer the sort of star, the focus of attention, and not the interview subject.

Our philosophy on this program—and I don't want to sound goody-goody about it—is, "We're here every night, we've been here every night for years, thousands of people have passed through our hands, we're known quantities to the audience, we don't need to tell them who we are, and we don't need to show them what we know." We invited these guests before the audience because these people have got something to say, and it seems to us stupid and self-defeating to then get in the way of that person's saying it by constantly interrupting him, challenging him, or generally being show-off.

I believe in Aesop's fable about the North Wind and the Sun being in competition to get the traveler to take off his cloak. The North Wind said, "Oh, I can get him to take off his cloak faster than you can." The North Wind blew and blew, fierce and loud and long, and the traveler just wrapped his cloak tighter around himself. And the Sun came out and shone, and in a few minutes the traveler took the cloak off.

Roger Mudd

Interviewer, PBS's MacNeil/Lehrer NewsHour

"I think to ask a person questions is to flatter the person, because it shows you're interested, and that you want to hear his story. I have lived most of my life with Southerners, and Southerners hesitate to inquire, mostly because it's not socially acceptable and they don't want to appear nosey."

MY INTRODUCTION to Roger Mudd, who has been called "the best Washington broadcast reporter of his generation," came through Sylvia Westerman, an old friend of his. She said I would have an amusing and informative time, but she put me on guard. Mudd, she said, is "never out of the interviewing mode"; he would try his best to interview me, and I had better watch my step if I did not want to leave the interview with his knowing a lot about me and my knowing nothing about him.

Before I even got to see him, I thought I had ruined the chance of an interview. In our telephone conversation to set it up, I explained our purpose, as I always do. I did, however, use an unfortunate word which incited a response that surprised me. I said that I hoped to pick up some of his "tricks" of interviewing, a word I had not used before and have not used since. I was startled when he snapped back, "I don't use tricks. Mike Wallace uses tricks." In later boning up for my interview with Mudd, I read that after his famous interview with Ted Kennedy, Mudd replied to critics, who said he focused too much on Kennedy's private life, that the interview had been "conceived and undertaken by honorable men and women" with "no tricks, no deceits, no contrivances."

From his tone with me, I was sure he would call off our interview. I was wrong. I had thought I would go to Washington, but he made a date to see me in New York early in the morning after a late night broadcast he had come from Washington to do.

When I arrived in his suite in an East Side hotel, he was the hospitable Southern gentleman. He helped me off with my trench coat (my uniform for interviewing television people), and left the room to hang it up for me. (Only the other Southerner, Marie Brenner, had done that.) He returned and sat down by the coffee table when I began setting up my tape recorder.

Mudd sat quietly for no more than a couple of seconds, and then, as if he could not hold back any longer, he asked, "By the way, what's your background?" In a flash, I looked up at him and pointed an accusing finger. Laughing, I said, "I *knew* you were going to do this. Sylvia told me. I'm prepared for you! Sylvia told me the story of the dinner party she gave for you and Mrs. Mudd and the new president of *The New Yorker*. He was dying to meet Roger Mudd, a hero of his. And he left the dinner party saying to his lady friend, 'Damn! I never got to ask Roger Mudd one question.'" Mudd laughed, and said, "Maybe that's defensive on my part."

He referred to me as "Doctor," while the other television people I interviewed had always called me by my first name immediately. When I told this to a friend of Mudd's, the friend interpreted the gesture as reflecting Mudd's respect for academics, a field which Mudd almost entered.

Roger Mudd grew up in Washington, D.C., where he was born in 1928. While he admits to not doing very well in lower school, his intelligence was hardly the problem. He received a B.A. and then an M.A. in American history and literature, writing his thesis on intellectuals in government. He seems to have been interested in intellectuals from early adulthood, and one wonders how much Mudd's own "intellectualism"—he has been called "erudite"—interfered with his having the charisma of a top news anchor, a position around which his career revolved.

After graduate school, he intended to get a Ph.D. in contemporary history and focus on the press and intellectuals in power. However, he thought he should first get some press experience, and this decision put him into the media rather than on the academic track. He found a job first as a newspaper reporter, then as news director of a radio station. Finally, he was hired in television to cover Congress. It was not long before he was a television "star."

Accolades became the mode for Mudd as early as the 1970s. He was extravagantly praised in the press; his *Selling of the Pentagon* in 1971, for example, was cited in *Variety* as "a journalistic job...so astounding that the most frequent question asked by the industry and plain viewers is, 'How did it get on the air?'" *Selling of the Pentagon* won the George Polk Award for outstanding achievement in journalism. Mudd received Emmys for his reporting of the shooting of Alabama Governor George Wallace (1973), for *The Senate and the Watergate Affair* (1973), for *Watergate: The White House Transcripts* (1974), and for his reporting of the resignation of Vice President Spiro Agnew (1974). And his interview with Ted Kennedy won him the 1979 George Foster Peabody Award for meritorious service to broadcasting.

Then, in 1980, an unforeseen event occurred. Mudd's bosses at CBS gave Dan Rather the cherished position as anchor of the *CBS Evening News* when Walter Cronkite gave up the job, although Mudd had been Cronkite's regular replacement and everyone thought he would inherit the star role. After nearly twenty years at CBS, Mudd left in "an act of choler," according to the *New York Times*, and did not return for the eight remaining weeks of his contract. Mudd released this statement: "I've regarded myself as a news reporter and not as a newsmaker or celebrity," apparently criticizing Dan Rather, again according to the *Times*. Mudd told a *Time* magazine reporter, "One of the problems with broadcast journalists is that we have been convinced, sometimes against our better judgment, that we are not reporters but show business people. I've tried not to live my life that way."

NBC created the job of chief Washington correspondent for Mudd. He also was promised first refusal on John Chancellor's anchor position on the *NBC Nightly News*, the network's most prestigious news post, whenever Chancellor left the job. But again things did not work out that way. When Chancellor changed jobs, Mudd did not replace him as the sole anchor, as promised. Instead, when Tom Brokaw, who was on the *Today* show, threatened defection to ABC unless he got a chance with the *Nightly News*, Mudd offered to share the anchor position with him, and that is what Mudd and Brokaw tried.

The arrangement did not go well in almost any way. Brokaw complained to *New York* magazine, "I *ran* the *Today* show...I mean it was all my baby....Here I've had to adjust my rhythms to this other person." As if that were not bad enough, the ratings did not rise as expected. The *New York* writer added, "NBC News insiders...wonder why Mudd doesn't get out of the office more. He is the best Washington broadcast reporter of his generation and many people question why he isn't prowling the Hill or the back corridors of the Senate and putting his brand of personal reporting on the air." He was dropped as co-anchor and named NBC's chief political correspondent after a long dispute during which he was not on the air at all. However, he had a contract which supposedly paid him $1 million a year, still to run for several years.

That same year he took on *American Almanac*, a weekly network sketch of Americana, but it did not fare well. NBC renamed the program *1986* and added Connie Chung as co-host. In December 1986, the program was cancelled.

The next month, NBC and Roger Mudd, after what were said to be bitter exchanges, agreed to sever their relationship, and in 1987, Mudd went to public television, where he has remained. His career has gone "full circle," as the *New York Times* noted; he is now chief Congressional correspondent for *The MacNeil/Lehrer NewsHour*, "the beat that built his journalistic reputation back in the 1960s at CBS News."

Mudd is a maverick. As early as 1981, *Current Biography* made this summary statement about Roger Mudd:

> The imperturbability that Mudd projects in his broadcasts correctly suggests a man who stands outside the mold of the intense, competitive journalistic workaholic. Trying to keep his work in balance with his personal life, he has been willing to make professional sacrifices here and there as the price for steadfastly maintaining his base in Washington, close to his family and his home in McLean, Virginia.

Mudd is known by many of his colleagues as a mimic, humorous, bright, a serious journalist who makes a powerful impression on his friends. I unfortunately did not witness what at least one mutual friend of ours sees as his skillful mimicry, but I saw the other qualities. All in all, he makes a powerful impression. Handsome and comic enough to be in show business, and having been called a "star" for years, no one would call him "show business." He is a serious fellow, as our interview illustrates.

■ For many people it's hard to ask questions of a person when he walks into the room; you don't want to offend him, and you don't want to appear inquisitive. So an awful lot of people in social situations, at dinner parties at Sylvia's or whatever, don't ask questions and they go away having spent the evening with you and not really knowing anything about you except what you have said on your own.

There's a running joke between my wife and me. Our children call and my wife says, "Daniel called last night," and she sums up what he said. I ask, "Did he say that he was going to...?" "I didn't ask him that." Then I ask, "Well, when will he...?" "I didn't ask him that."

The only device I deliberately use is I try never to ask a question that can be answered with a yes or no. It forces the subject to answer it in his own words. That's an easy device, but an awful lot of people don't do it. [I suggested that sometimes we hit it lucky with a yes-no question.] Lucky because somebody feels generous. But most people, particularly people who are not professionals, are a little nervous about being interviewed and so aren't terribly loquacious.

I'm not sure about training; it seems to me that you're genetically put together in a way that makes you curious or not curious, and makes you want to ask questions because you're interested in what people carry around inside of them.

I think if there's training to be done, it's the emphasis on preparation and being totally immersed in the subject. For example, knowing as much about Robert

Penn Warren as Robert Penn Warren does, knowing
everything he said on record, knowing his history,
talking to Eudora Welty and Eleanor Clark and
everybody else before you go up to Connecticut to talk
to him.

You can train that in a person. If a person is well
prepared, then the questions flow naturally. He will then
not have to be so hung up on the next question, and,
"Oh, God, will I forget what I am going to ask?"

I think the greatest single failing, particularly on
television interviewing, is that the interviewer has a set
of questions prepared ahead of time and is determined
to get through that list of questions. In the process of
worrying about getting through the questions, he doesn't
listen to the answer that he's eliciting. And therefore he
fails to ask the perfect follow-up question, which comes
right out of the answer. The reason most people have
that list of questions is that they're not really prepared.

"Really, the Ted Kennedy interview stands as the best one
I've ever done," Mudd replied when I asked for transcripts of
his favorite interviews.

Based on Mudd's relations with the Kennedy family, Ted
Kennedy had every reason to believe he was safe when he
submitted to a prime-time interview at a time when he was
moving toward candidacy for the presidency of the United
States. One event in particular stands out. Covering a presidential nomination campaign, Mudd was at the Ambassador
Hotel in Los Angeles when Robert Kennedy was assassinated.
Quickly, Mudd found Ethel Kennedy and, with her, elbowed
his way through the crowd to take her to her dying husband. "It
was because of Roger, who led me through the crowd, that
Bobby and I got to say good-bye to each other," she said
afterward.

Ted Kennedy invited Mudd to ask him any question. It was
at a time when the tragedy at Chappaquiddick was still a major
topic, Kennedy's marriage was widely known to be rocky, and
he was accused of marital infidelities. The interview was a
chance for Kennedy to clear things up.

"When I did the interview, I didn't have any questions at all written down," Mudd said, "because I knew nearly as much about him and Chappaquiddick and what happened as he did—not really as much as he did, but I was into it, as you would say. CBS had given me time to become totally immersed in the subject, so it wasn't a matter of 'You've got a day and a half.'"

During the interview, Kennedy became visibly uncomfortable and irritated when Mudd went straight ahead with touchy topics. Given the opportunity to display his presidential caliber, Kennedy instead "appeared vague, nervous, and inarticulate, often answering questions with platitudes and incomplete sentences," reported *Current Biography*.

A rundown of the most sensitive questions Mudd asked gives some flavor of his style:

—What's the present state of your marriage, Senator?

—Well, what—what happens, Senator, if some heckler stands up at a rally, a Kennedy rally, and says, you know, in a loud voice, red-faced, he's angry at you, and he says, "Kennedy, you know you were drinking, you lied, and you covered up!" What—what are you going to tell him in a situation like that?

—Do you think, Senator, that—that anybody will ever fully believe your explanation of Chappaquiddick?

—You've said that—that the physical trauma of that accident bears really no relationship to the pressures that are brought on by decision of public policy that—that you are required to make as Senator. They're really separate. But what guarantee does a citizen have, or what assurance does a citizen have, that in the future you would not again act, as you said, irresponsibly or inexplicably when your own career came in conflict with the public's right to know?

—Why do you want to be President?

As noted above, Kennedy answered these very pointed questions with platitudes and incomplete sentences.

"The ice was beginning to get so thin and I was having to pick my way," Mudd told me, "and I finally got in my mind to ask about Kennedy's marital problems. He knew he couldn't lie about it, because there was so much in public print that it was not in good shape." What people saw on television was an edited interview; Mudd could have edited out Kennedy's most embarrassing statements, but he did not. Here, from *CBS Reports* (November 4, 1979), is one of the last interchanges, perhaps the most damning to Kennedy's presidential hopes:

MUDD: What—what is it about a—a so-called couch question that makes you feel uncomfortable? Is it—do—do you not like to talk about yourself in public? Is—does it—is it unmanly or what? I—I'm asking you for a serious answer.

KENNEDY: Well, I don't—I mean, I think it's really left to—to—to others. I don't—I suppose I just don't like to talk about myself just generally. I'd rather talk why I'm in public life, is because of my care and concern about—about using the—whatever influence or—that I have to—to—to move the—the process towards meeting the—the goals which I care very deeply about. And I think that's what's—what's important.

MUDD: I could—

KENNEDY: I suppose the—the rest of it is just a natural indica—natural reflection of one's desire to maintain as much privacy as—as one can, which is a fairly natural phenomenon, I would ima—imagine, of people.

MUDD: But I—I could go to ninety-eight Senators with a camera and set up for an interview, and ninety-seven of them would start every sentence "I—I—I." It is a characteristic of politicians that they like to talk about themselves. And my question is, why aren't you that way?

KENNEDY (laughing): Why don't you ask them about why they like to talk about themselves?

MUDD: But I mean, you are an exception to that rule. There's a—an enormous amount of vanity in the Senate, in the Congress, and you're always promoting yourself, generally speaking. And my question is why can't I break through and get you to talk about yourself in an intimate way?

KENNEDY: Well, I—I don't really have much more—
(laughs)—to add to the earlier answer. I—
MUDD: Well, let me try to break through once more.
(Kennedy laughs). What—what are you going to do,
Senator, during the campaign, with the published
reports that link you to women other than your wife?
How do you deal with that issue?
KENNEDY: Well, in what—in—in what respect?
MUDD: Well, I—
KENNEDY: I mean, I don't have a—I mean, I—I'm
married. I've—care very deeply about my wife and my
children. And we've—we have a rather special set of
circumstances which is perhaps somewhat unique, but
we're—I think we're making very substantial progress.
Joan's—would help and assist, and it's been, I think, of
enormous both love for her and—and—and for my
family. So, I don't think I'd respond to scurrilous kind
of gossip, but I—I don't know what el—else you'd—
you'd expect.

This *CBS Reports* interview marked what many observers
regarded as the beginning of the end of Kennedy's 1980
presidential candidacy. It is said that Mudd's relations with the
Kennedy family have never been the same since that interview.
As a longtime Washington correspondent, Mudd has given
considerable thought to the ins and outs of interviewing the
President in Washington. He brought up the subject without
my asking him specifically about it.

■ The difficulty about interviewing a President is that you
are kind of a guest in the Nation's House, and he is our
leader and you can't cross over. And you have to be very,
very careful of being disrespectful, which was Dan
Rather's mistake. Rather stood up in some Nixon press
conference down in Texas. There was applause when
Rather stood up; Rather was known as an antagonist of
Nixon. Nixon said, "Are you running for something, Mr.
Rather?" And Rather said, "No, Mr. President, are you?"
That was, I thought, a serious mistake, because it

revealed a lack of perspective on the presidency,
whatever you think of the occupant.

But an interview with the President is probably the
toughest interview. What makes it doubly difficult is that
while you're interviewing the President, there have got
to be fifteen or twenty people in the room, Secret
Service, Press Secretary...and they're all looking at their
watches and they've given you [the press] thirty minutes
and no more. And you can hear them shuffling, and
you just sort of feel that if you really ask the worst
question in the world, they'll shoot you or something.
The physical presence of those people is intimidating.

Mudd's playing with humor mixed with what has been called
his "piercing" interviewing and his "wry, dispassionate style"
produced an incident that Mudd obviously regrets.

■ I think a major flub I've made was in the Gary Hart
interview [during the presidential primary session of
1984]. I'd been out on the road with Gary Hart and
knew the general perception that he was in fact trying to
come on as Jack Kennedy—hatless, coatless in the raw
weather, hands jammed down into the jacket, buttoned
like this [he demonstrates]. It was well known in
Washington, so I asked him a question about that. And
he did not like it at all.

The televised sequence went like this:

MUDD: Why—a lot of people want to know, Senator, why
do you imitate John Kennedy so much?
HART: I don't.
MUDD: What do you do?
HART: I am Gary Hart.
MUDD: Well, I mean all the notions with the necktie and
the chopping of the air and your hand in the pocket. All
those people—people all over the country say he—all
he's doing is imitating John Kennedy.
HART: No, reporters say that. People around the country
say, "We like this candidate and we want to support

him." I have spoken the way I have spoken all my life, and I think there are plenty of people who will verify that. I'm not imitating anyone. The American people can spot a phony, and I think they are supporting someone they think is genuine and authentic.

Mudd did not leave the subject of imitation for long; he was intent on getting something from Hart. Near the end of the interview that is what happened:

MUDD: And a final question. Would you do your Teddy
   Kennedy imitation for me now?
HART: No.
MUDD: I've heard it's hilarious.
HART: I don't think it is.

As Mudd told me of the episode (we did not have the transcript in front of us), I became confused and said, "Edward Kennedy or...?" Mudd jumped at this:

▮ You see, that was my mistake. You didn't quite know
   whether I had said Teddy or Jack. The fact is that he
   does a marvelous imitation of *Teddy* Kennedy. People
   thought I was asking him to imitate our martyred
   President, dead in the grave, sealed in a coffin.
      I kind of knew he wouldn't, but I was trying to lighten
   up the interview and attempt to get some kind of push
   coming back to me. He was furious, because the
   question revealed that in fact he does do an imitation of
   Teddy Kennedy; it's a famous imitation. He didn't like it
   that I had revealed that.
      Other people didn't like it; many people, including my
   boss, thought I was asking him to imitate our martyred
   President. That was a serious mistake. I was not trying
   to embarrass him publicly; I was trying to make the
   interview light and unrehearsed. I think probably the
   basic mistake was asking him to perform, which is in
   effect demeaning.
      Do you know about the "reverse question?" So much
   of the tone of interviewing on *60 Minutes* and other

interview programs, unless they're live, is never quite like it was during the interview because of the editing. One of the hidden tricks is the old reverse question, which has now gone out of style. I'm sure you're familiar with that. I guess *60 Minutes* uses two cameras, but it costs an awful lot to have two. It has to be over here looking at me and over there looking at you, and that costs a lot of money.

So in the old days, and still most of the time now, there'll be one camera and it will be looking at you. And I'll ask you a series of questions and we'll record you answering. But after you've gone, we take a camera and point it at me, and I'll reask the questions so that they can be intercut back in the studio and it will look like a two-camera interview. It will aid in the editing.

But there's a certain dishonesty in that. It was basically for budget reasons in the beginning but then it got abused. The interviewer, whether it was Roger Mudd or Mike Wallace or whoever, would take advantage of that reverse question to sharpen up the questions.

So when *The Selling of the Pentagon* was done, there were some abuses. I did the interview with the then Secretary of Defense. In the editing of the interview, there were some answers taken from question fourteen and tacked onto the answer for question six. It made the flow better and the information was better laid out, but it wasn't the way it was, so the then president of CBS put out a policy book on interviewing and the techniques of editing. You couldn't use reverse questions. The answer had to flow logically from the question asked. You could eliminate chunks of the interview, but you couldn't turn it upside down. My point is that frequently the reality of the interview is not exactly transferred to the television screen because of editing and because of the cameras.

What happens now—and I know you're aware of this also—is what's called the Kissinger rule: many officials in Washington refuse to be interviewed unless it's live, because what's happened is that film crews come in and set up lights and bring their cameras in to Dr. Kissinger, who makes a lot of money and whose time is very valuable. They'll spend an hour doing the whole thing and they'll take it [the film] back and nine seconds will appear on the nightly news.

Another thing about editing is the problem of dead air. I've never been much afraid of dead air. When you're taping, dead air can always be eliminated later in the editing. It's embarrassing if you're live, doing *Meet the Press* or something, and suddenly you have a brain freeze. Sometimes that happens. Sometimes you're so intent on listening to the answer that in fact you forget what's next, and occasionally you do have notes and little mnemonics on what you want to remind yourself to cover.

But I've had moments on *Meet the Press* or whatever, where I have just frozen, and that's why you have a partner who is waiting to pick up. When that happens, there's suddenly an eight-hundred-pound rock on your chest. Oooph! You feel foolish that you can't, you know, we all want to be thought of as on top of things...rapid fire...but that's not the way it always is.

I have no reason to insist that journalistic interviews be kept separate from entertainment interviews. The problem is that entertainment interviews are so mindless, really. Generally speaking, they consist of a guest working one-liners and going for laughs, and the host saying, "Where are you appearing next?" "Well, I'll be in Las Vegas in the last week in June and then we're going to San Diego..." or whatever. And what it constitutes is not information but just promo about the star, so that the entertainment interview is just a guest shot and it doesn't give you much information. It's an opportunity for the guest to come on and be funny or dramatic or beautiful. It doesn't give you an awful lot of nitty-gritty, does it?

But so much of interviewing on television is hit-and-miss, fly-by-night, slam-bam-thank-you-ma'am, and go on to get the twelve-second quote and get out of there, that the art of interviewing on television, at least in daily news coverage, has been lost because the daily news programs are not much interested in really strong

interviews. So what you do in the daily grind of
television journalism is ask a few questions until you get
a twelve-second bite, and you're not interested any more.
    So that means you have a whole generation of
television journalists who are not really trained or
interested in doing good interviewing work because
there's no market for it anymore. And so there's no skill
at it.

Nicholas Pileggi

Reporter, New York; Author of Nonfiction Books

> "Here you are, coming from this big-shot magazine or newspaper, and you're going to quote and expose interviewees, so you've got to be their best friend in the world. You're joining them in seeing how best to present their story to the public. You're on their side. That's why I think the adversarial approach is good for the soul but bad for the story."

AFTER YEARS as a fairly well known "old-fashioned street reporter," Nick Pileggi met a hustler and hit the jackpot.

His best-selling 1987 book *Wise Guy: Life in a Mafia Family* is based on interviews of a "hood," "a full-time working racketeer, an articulate hoodlum from organized crime, the kind of rara avis that should please social anthropologists as much as cops." *Wise Guy* was made into the widely praised film, *Good-Fellas*, for which Pileggi and Martin Scorsese wrote the screenplay.

Pileggi has interviewed criminals of all kinds, cops, detectives, FBI men, drug enforcement officers, lawyers—all those involved with crime and corruption, and the politics behind crime and corruption. His first book, *Blye, Private Eye*, was based on a year spent with Irwin Blye, a private detective. Some of his magazine pieces are under option to movie producers.

For *Wise Guy*, he interviewed the central figure, Henry Hill, whom he referred to in our interview, for two years under the complex and secret conditions of the Federal Witness Protection Program. Meetings took place only where Hill's safety could be guaranteed. Hill arranged for Pileggi to interview

101

both his wife and his girlfriend; others helped Pileggi see a host of other people.

> I went to a lot of places and I talked to a lot of people, a lot of guys who worked along with Hill—at least those who are still alive. Some of them were pressured by cops who are friends of mine to talk to me, some by other friends of mine, some by their lawyers. I've been a reporter since 1956. I knew the big mob lawyers when they were little mob lawyers. You begin to build up credibility; they know I keep my word.

> I would fly to these places, and we'd—Hill and I— spend a couple of days together....Sometimes I'd see him for weeks in a row, and then I wouldn't see him for a couple of months while I distilled all the stuff. But we were able to talk on the phone almost every day.

One interviewer asked Pileggi if he and Henry Hill, the wise guy, are friends after all the time they spent together.

> I don't think so....We came out of it with an acquaintance. Henry doesn't have friends. None of these guys has friends. I am not going to delude myself into thinking that Henry and I are pals. I've seen what happens to Henry's "friends."

Naturally, Pileggi has been asked if he ever worries that his life might be in danger.

> Not much. Crime reporters are about as likely to get shot as court stenographers. We get to things long after they've happened. We're primarily messengers, irrelevant to criminals' lives.

Pileggi grew up the son of a shoestore owner in the Bensonhurst and Bedford-Stuyvesant sections of Brooklyn. He graduated from Long Island University as an English major, but at the time had no interest in writing. For his last two years of college, he was a copyboy for the Associated Press.

> Once I saw what being a reporter was like, I was hooked....You were always where everyone wanted to be.

You were always seeing what was happening—crossing the police lines, seeing the bodies or the fire. You were the messenger. You would go back and tell everybody what it was like. I found that fascinating as a kid.

Pileggi's notions of doing graduate work and going into teaching were aborted by the offer of a reporter's job for the Associated Press's New York bureau; he stayed in the job for twelve years. "Reporter," however, meant doing the leg work, being the "messenger"—collecting information and relaying it to the writers—in and around East and West Side Manhattan "police shacks." "It was a great time," he says.

He did not actually write professionally until he was thirty, when he began doing pieces for *Esquire* and other magazines. The then editor of *Esquire*, Byron Dobell, introduced me to Pileggi as one of the best interviewers he knows.

In 1968 Pileggi became a contributing editor for the newly founded *New York* magazine. "The stories I do are not global in any sense. They're New York stories, about politics, crime, and corruption." He has won numerous awards for his writing.

For my interview with Pileggi, I arrived at the office of *New York* magazine at 8:45 AM, fifteen minutes early. The security guard took my name, and I asked if Mr. Pileggi was in yet. "Oh, yeah. He's been in for a long time. Comes early always, guess he works better that way." I went up to the third floor, announced myself at the desk, and in about one minute Pileggi came out from his office, smiled, and said, "Come in," calling me by my first name.

He is tall, athletically built, and graying at the temples and has powerful hands with manicured fingernails. His working space is an open cubicle that is part of a huge office; he pulled up a secretary's chair for me to sit near him. I had the feeling while interviewing him that everyone could hear me and was checking up on my style.

Pileggi looks like my idea of a detective. I wondered whether he could get around the seedy side of New York City as well as he does if he did not look the way he does. When I thanked him for seeing me, he replied, "My pleasure."

Unlike Bill Moyers, who was unsure about whether he wanted to analyze his interviewing technique, Pileggi said, as

we shall see, that it is not really anything worth analyzing. He
believes it is a matter of intuition. He did, however, talk a lot
about his interviewing style.

■   There are two kinds of interviews, I think.
    There are people who want to be interviewed because
they're trying to sell something, like a movie star. I've
never interviewed any of them, never done a profile of a
movie star or anyone like that, or someone who's used to
being interviewed. They develop calluses all over the
edges. So you wind up getting what is pretty much a
dead interview. I find it with politicians, for instance.
They have been interviewed so many times, they know
all the answers. They know the way they want the story
to move; they're quite often more skilled at it than the
interviewer. So they can pretty much dictate the way the
story is going to appear. They know exactly what to say
and when to say it, and I just find that so tiring that I
just don't do it. I don't do politicians.
    When I did my book, I was sent all around the
country to be interviewed. But I began to see it happen
to me. You begin to know that there are certain stories
that work in talking about your book in three minutes,
ten minutes, thirty minutes, whatever. You're able to get
through it no matter what they ask you. You give them
the answers you want to give them.
    So people who are doing interviews should be told
that when they interview people who are calloused, who
are just going through it, it's hard to break through.
    The people I wind up interviewing are the people
who don't often talk to the press, or anybody—cops, FBI
men, federal agents of all kinds—who get to know you
over the years. They know they can trust you and can
tell you a little bit. Then you just begin to pick up the
pieces, a little bit from this one and a little bit from that
one. I find that no one talks to the other, none of these
people, say, in law enforcement. FBI men rarely talk to
detectives, and the FBI men don't talk to the drug
enforcement agents, and the drug enforcement agents
don't tell everything they know to the prosecutors

because prosecutors are going to make trouble for them.
Prosecutors don't tell the FBI and the federal agents
anything because they don't want them to screw
anything up.

So when you've been doing it as long as I have, you
begin to build some personal friendships among the
various segments of the community. You become the
catalyst to some degree. I go with little tales of news to
each of these people. They find out for me what the PA
[prosecuting attorney] is doing. The PA finds out what
the FBI is doing.

You wind up having to be very careful. You have to
remember just about everything you've been told and be
able to not tip your hand or not make any of the people
you speak to worried that you talk too much. They're
very paranoid, these men and women, and they should
be.

You smile and are polite, dress decently, show up with
a tie and jacket. I mean, I act like my parents told me to
act when you're in the presence of relatives. Respectful.
And no matter whom you're interviewing, you act that
way. I'm not a threat. I don't have a tape recorder, don't
come in with that. I always believe in asking if I can call
back and check any stuff, and they always say,
"Absolutely," which gives me a second or third shot, on
the phone at least. And I always say, "If you think of
anything, call me. Here's my number." I always have a
card I give them.

And if they have a secretary, give the card to the
secretary as well. It gives you access again.

And always leave great friends, pals, and if there's
anything he says that you have knowledge of...I mean,
if he loves golf...you can see things on people's desks
and what they like, that may smooth the way.

So you start to talk to a guy, and he says, "Who do you
know?" He's feeling you out. He uses some nicknames
and I know the nicknames. So we know the same
gangsters, we know who the people are. It turns out he
doesn't know their last names. He knows, you know,
Johnny and Frankie Wagon. "What's their name,

Wagon?" he asks. I say, "Vatico." "Vatico, yeah. I think that's...of course, it is." So again you have to have the background and the knowledge when you go in to those interviews. If I don't know all those names, he loses interest. He goes home and that's it.

These guys aren't going to hand it to you. These guys don't give you anything. There's no free lunch. But it will indicate to him that you've done your homework, you know more, and you might pick up a little more.

So you start talking with the guy. Let him talk, let him go on. Be as friendly and supportive as possible during the interview. You really want to hear what he says; you're truly interested. That's important—that you're interested. And it allows him to talk.

Let them talk. I think one of the things with interviewing is, for me, that I let them talk. I do what you do—nod in agreement. I'm not agreeing, I just nod. "Yes, I hear you." They think of that as agreement, and that helps them.

In the end, you offer them space in a paper or magazine. They're going to get their name in the paper. "Now, the fight on organized crime today, indeed, in the nation, is being carried on by...."—fill in the blank. That's the only strength I've got. And I sort of play it.

I try not to say anything, or say as little as possible. It's their shot. And try to be as friendly and open as possible. I am providing them with a platform. That's all I'm doing. I know the story is going to go in this general direction.

That's the way you're going to get them to tell you what you couldn't get them to tell you if you pushed. You're sitting and talking to them and they're under a lot of pressure. Here you are, coming from this big-shot magazine or newspaper, and you're going to quote and expose them, so you've got to be their best friend in the world. You're joining them in seeing how best to present their story to the public. You're on their side. That's why I think the adversarial approach is good for the soul but bad for the story.

I've been to interviews where the interviewers actually argue. The guy will say, "Well, you know, so we popped him," as the cops say. "You know this guy who pulled a gun on me, boy, we took him in there and we gave him...." meaning that they beat the defendant. And the interviewer says, "You're not supposed to beat prisoners. What kind of thing is that?"

All of a sudden here you are listening to a crooked cop who beats witnesses. But don't argue with him at that point. Write the story later. But you're hearing it right from the guy, and he thinks you are in agreement with him. Let him.

I find more and more that young journalists who grew up at a period when you were allowed to speak up are apt to say, "Well, that's outrageous. I think we should sell all our interests in South Africa." Using that feeling, that kind of tradition, which is a noble one, in an interviewing session, can be a detriment. You wind up arguing. I suppose some people feel that a sense of integrity is more important than the interview, but I think in the long run...

I think the most important thing going into an interview is your knowing so much about it that you wouldn't even need the interview. The interview just carries you over. That's really it.

In court cases, you can read the transcripts. In one way a lot gets printed so you can read it, but also so little sometimes gets printed. So you go to the court papers, you go to the court papers last week, you go to an earlier trial involving some of these same people and read through the court transcripts.

Another interesting thing: so much of the stuff that did get into the court papers the prosecutor doesn't remember or never knew, something handled by an underling. And so by culling that stuff, sometimes you give them the impression you know a lot more than you do know. Even though it's all public record. They forget how much has been printed. "Oh, what else does he know? Who else is he talking to? Is he talking to the prosecutor? Is he going to make the prosecutor look better than me?"

I don't have rules for devising questions, because everybody is so different. I used to do things like write down questions I was going to ask. You know, these things have a way of free forming. And if you stand with your rigid set of questions, you're bending the interview in a way that the person doesn't talk.

You've obviously got to keep in mind where you want the interview to go; you know there are six points you want to know. Well, they're in your head; you don't have to write them down.

Instead of that, when they finish answering, you look at a piece of paper and ask a dull question. It's sort of like daytime TV interviews—the second question is totally out of whack with the first question. So I don't bother with questions in advance.

I get calls all the time. I get letters, lawyers call, "Listen, we've got this guy I think you'd be interested in. He's a great cop, this guy has fought this fight, he's been a terrific cop, he's done this, he's done that, and they shafted him. And boy, does he have a story to tell about corruption! Talk to him!" And sometimes you talk to these guys. You piece together whether it's an article or it's a possible book, or whether it's a movie. These stories lend themselves to different things. And you wind up talking to him.

You waste a lot of time with some of these people. On the other hand, some of these people have wonderful stories and anecdotes—Henry Hill, for instance. A really low-level guy who was introduced to me as a big shot. He was involved in the Lufthansa Airlines robbery, the largest successful cash robbery in American history. He was a major drug dealer; he had done ten years for extortion; he had fixed the Boston College basketball games. They were selling him as a real organized crime guy, even though he wasn't a member.

A major guy, they told me. I talked to him, and I realized he wasn't a major guy. Not on a book level. You

want to write a book about organized crime, talk to John
Gotti. But Henry Hill...

But what it was, I realized, was a book on a low-level,
street-level hustler, and I got the life-style, so it became a
life-style book.

Somebody could have taken that book and instead of
doing it that way, could have believed what Simon &
Schuster, the publishers, believed at the time—that they
had a major organized crime guy, believed it for lots of
good reasons, mostly because the prosecutors were
saying, "Indeed, he's major." That's why they gave him
the Federal Witness [Protection] Program: they were
going to use him in major cases; they were building him
up, in a sense.

From the viewpoint of a book, there wasn't enough
substance there. But as a regular person, there was.
Somebody without the experience and knowledge about
who these guys are and how they fit might have tried to
do a book about him as a bigger person than the book
would have carried, and they're stuck. He really wasn't
the single participant in the Lufthansa job; he wasn't the
mastermind behind it. He wasn't part of the conspiracy.
So you've got this guy who's outside the inner office.
You're trying to write a book about the inner office by
the guy who's outside it. It will never work. So my advice
to people who are getting into these, really be very
careful before they buy the story that's being sold. Even
if the publisher believes it, it's really the responsibility of
the writer, the journalist, for his own sake, to watch his
ass.

Everybody thinks you've got the top guy, and you want
to believe you've got the top guy. The publisher's saying,
"We're going to give you $200,000 up front." Well, for
the average writer, you know, who's running out of
typewriter ribbon, it's a great incentive to get caught up.

You wind up caught up in one of these things. It
doesn't work, and you're going to spend years on the
book. You're going to do four years on something that
maybe isn't worth it.

The preliminary interview with that person is crucial. You've got to make sure this guy can carry your story.

When I started talking to Henry Hill, he talked about murdering this guy. They put his body in a trunk and the guy woke up, came to in the middle of the drive, and started banging on the trunk. Then Henry whacked him with a shovel. He said, "I had to dig him up. We had to dig him up. I had to put him in a brand-new, yellow Bonneville convertible, brand-new. I got it with some policy, and they want the policy back. I could never get rid of the smell. I used to put bottles of perfume..." Wow! This is what I want. He tells me it's a yellow Bonneville convertible, or that he won the car with a bet. That's the way he talked; he talked in that kind of vivid language. He had a memory for color, he had a memory for the moment, he had a memory for weather—"The rain was comin' down." You know, he had that kind of memory and he was a thug and a gangster. Most of them don't talk that way. And once I realized that, I thought, "This guy could be good." And it turns out he was. I knew right away because he told great stories.

You get that with cops, too. You go into the squad room on an arrest day, and they arrested a guy for homicide. Some detective says, "Well, we got him." "What's his name?" "Jack Brown." "How old is he?" "Uh, eighty-two." "Eighty-two! You mean the murderer is eighty-two?" "Yeah." "How could an eighty-two-year-old...who did he murder?" "Uh, Edmond Green." "How old is he?" "Uh, one-hundred-eleven." "What! Where did he murder him?" "Uh, Caravelle [an expensive restaurant in New York City]." They've got an unbelievable story but they don't know how to give it to you. They just have no idea what they've got.

But another guy: "Boy, wait until you hear this one! An eighty-two-year-old guy and a one-hundred-eleven-year-old guy, they got into a fight over their wives. Can you believe those guys? In the middle of Caravelle and somebody's bringing in a baked Alaska, and he hit him

with the baked Alaska and the other guy stabs him in
the neck."

That's the difference. You can't depend on those guys.
If you get one, you're home. But if you get one of those
guys who quotes every fact, they just can't tell a story.
This guy, at his daughter's wedding, will try to stand up
and tell a funny anecdote and everybody will go to
sleep. I mean, he can't tell a story—no sense of language
or drama. They could be wonderful people, but they
just can't tell a story.

I've done interviews where the guy says, "Listen, I've
been burned by the press before, so I'm tape recording."
I don't use a tape recorder. So I say, "Be my guest." So
they make a tape, I do the piece, and I get a transcript
of the tape. The guy calls me up. "You've changed what
I said." I say, "Look at this. I underlined it. All the
quotes were..." "That's what I said but that's not what I
meant. What I meant was..."

Meanwhile, he had hung himself with his own words;
he didn't intend to, but that was exactly what he did. So
I don't know, accuracy is such a difficult thing. You can
be absolutely accurate, but that's not the way they
perceive it.

Sometimes you just get on the wrong wave length with
a person in an interview and you just can't get it. You go
back and the person is sort of off it, or off you, and they
don't like you, or they don't feel comfortable with you.
That happens. Sometimes you do work and you go in
there, but you're not as prepared as you ought to be but
you don't know it. Then you think later on, "Oh,
God..." The errors are just the basic sloppiness and
general incompetence that, I think, is the human
condition.

Then sometimes a guy will say, "That's bullshit! That's
crazy. We'd never do it that way; we do it this way." And
I'll take down what he says. I'm not going to try to argue
with him. If he says something that I've already gotten a
response to and I think he's being inaccurate, I'll say,
"Listen, I've heard something else: what do you say to

this response from so and so?" Then he will say that everybody has a different response.

You know the Dutch Cleanser ad—that girl on the Dutch Cleanser box? You see the girl reflected in the mirror, reflected in the mirror, reflected in the mirror. I always had this idea that if I got to be very, very rich and I had nothing to do, I would just go and interview somebody, a hot shot; and then I would interview an opposite guy, ask him all the same questions and he would destroy the first guy. Then I would take all his answers and go back to the original guy and say, "Now this is how he answers these questions. What do you say?" "That's ridiculous," and he would correct all the responses I got from him to the original questions. Then go back again to the second guy. And you just go back and forth, back and forth, and never resolve anything. You'd go back to infinity.

In all my years of interviewing, I've never seen the interviewer get somebody hammered to the wall. Maybe it's happened to other reporters, but I've never seen it. "The interviewer gets him, just like in the movies!" Never! These guys always know more than you do about a subject.

I mean, you go to interview a politician, and you're a reporter. He's a goddam politician; he's been doing it his whole life. He has a million escape hatches, doors, backrooms, through which he can escape any question you give him. And I find that's what they're able to do. You can get to a point where he might be embarrassed, or look embarrassed, but in the end you're never going to get, "Well, I confess; I'm guilty."

I write fast. I've been a reporter since 1956. So I leave out articles when I'm taking notes during an interview. I don't take everything down. When you're interviewing, you can start taking down stuff that you don't need. I don't care what they're telling me about; I just stay with the paragraph that I know is the key paragraph, because it's the one that has the colorful language, the one that has the insightful thing about it.

Talking to this guy about loan-sharking, for example. There's nothing about loan-sharking that I don't already know. I've got all the clips, I've got all the stuff. And I'm taking brief notes, and then all of a sudden he tells me about this one "lump job" they had. "Lump job"—that's a phrase I want. It's a language that I hadn't heard before. So then those are the lines.

As soon as the interview is over, all the stuff that I really want I highlight. And then I remember things.

I guess I trained myself. I hear it. I hear his inflection, what words he emphasized.

I've used tape recorders, of course. The problem with a tape recorder is that it exhausts you. I mean, it's stronger than you are. It throws all that stuff back at you in exactly the same way. And if you try to fast forward it, you feel you've missed something. Before you know it, you're going bananas and you're spending all your time with the tape recorder. I never had the luxury of having a tape recorder somewhere in the room and having it transcribed.

In preparing for an interview, you have to know pretty much what story you want to work on—for example, if you're working on a story about a major organized crime figure. In all these crime cases, there's all this stuff going on—you've got five commission trials going on downtown, you've got the man on trial, all this stuff. So you can't go into a room and not know what the hell you're talking about. You've got to know almost as much as the person.

Get everything that's public you can possibly come up with; even talk to other people who have talked with him. Have his story down cold. And then go on and try to move it ahead. You've got to spare him the tedium so that he won't go into automatic pilot. Because if that happens, you look at your watch and it will be forty-five minutes and your interview is over, and all you've got is the same crap you could have gotten by clipping the papers, and reading them, and putting together a good file on the story.

I'm astounded at press conferences where you'll go in and there'll be a reporter who will ask a question that was in the paper that morning. Or if not in the paper that morning, if he had done a full clip review on the subject, it would have been there.

What do you have time for in an hour? Ten questions? Eleven questions? If four of them are going to be dead questions that he's already been through, you've lost four questions. On top of it, the dead question, the question that has been answered repeatedly, puts the interviewee in a frame of mind of boredom. He's been through this before. So he doesn't talk; he goes into automatic pilot.

Get him back into reality, into the future. "What's happening this weekend?" And if you can possibly bring off something to these guys they don't know, something that maybe you've picked up among agents, picked up here, picked up there, a little investigation you've heard is going on in the Bronx that he knows about but doesn't think you know about. You're kind of able to ask him about it in a way indicating that you know more than he thought you did.

I think you should just stay with your instincts, doing it in an intuitive way. You do your homework, you do your research, you have every piece of knowledge before going into an interview, and you're going to have extra key questions you want to ask. They're going to fill your head so you'll never be at a loss for a question.

III

Interviewing Celebrities

CELEBRITY INTERVIEWS, sometimes called personality interviews, might be perceived by the public as fun—gossip producing—as opposed to dead serious. Barbara Walters told me, "I'm proud of the serious interviews I've done," distinguishing between the news interviewing she does on ABC's *20/20* (serious) and her "Specials." If she had her druthers, she would do fewer specials, but they are very lucrative for her bosses at ABC.

The five interviewers in this section seem to have very different feelings about doing celebrity interviews. We talked to three women—Barbara Walters, Marie Brenner, and Diane Sawyer—and two men—Thomas B. Morgan and Dick Cavett. Barbara Walters, judging from the sentiments noted above, seems ambivalent about celebrity interviewing. Brenner considers what she does "just marvelous." Sawyer did not comment directly on this particular kind of interview, but appears to be at ease with all kinds of interviewing.

The two men we talked to differ markedly from each other (and from the women) in their attitudes toward the celebrity interview. Morgan found celebrity interviewing harrowing. Cavett, though admittedly star struck from an early age, seems to have wished he were somewhere else doing something else.

Despite the fact that these are five very different personalities, we cannot help wondering if gender has something to do with working happily at this type of interviewing.

What are they after? Diane Sawyer perhaps put it in a nutshell: "Tell me something you've never told anyone else." She says, "Give me another layer of you." When Sawyer spoke of her interview with President Aquino of the Philippines, the revelation she chose to mention was Mrs. Aquino's earlier conjugal visits to her imprisoned husband. That sort of thing makes an interview more memorable to more people than one which reveals Mrs. Aquino's political plans for her country. Walters wants to elicit "what the audience is going to be interested in" (she does not impose her judgment of what the audience *should* be interested in).

A common interview approach is the use of recognized social skills—"incredibly social," said Marie Brenner. It's like flirting a bit; "the whole process is one of seduction," she felt. As youngsters, all three women had social problems (too shy, too aggressive, a loner), but they were all taught how "ladies" are supposed to act.

Morgan, the most disgruntled of the five, summarized his feeling about celebrity interviewing this way: "You never get the truth. At best, a good interview is a kind of defeat." The women here would probably not agree with him.

Barbara Walters

Co-Host and Interviewer, ABC's 20/20, and "Specials"

"Sometimes journalists have a tendency to do the interview that's going to impress other journalists...or that's going to get some attention in the *New York Times*. And we forget that what we should be doing is the interview that the audience is going to be the most interested in."

GETTING AN INTERVIEW with Barbara Walters, the celebrity interviewer, was a lesson in how to get interviews with celebrities.

If you think an introduction from Mike Wallace, a letter from Bill Moyers praising me and urging her to see me, a promised call from Phil Donahue, promised notes from Arlene Francis, Sherrye Henry, Judy Licht, and Marie Brenner would do it, you would be mistaken.

At the suggestion of Mike Wallace, I called Barbara Walters at home, was told to call her office and did, was told to call back in a couple of months to set up an appointment and did, was told Walters recalled having turned me down, and that in any case she had not granted an interview in a year and half because she was too busy.

At this point, I was discouraged and said, "To hell with it," and began a profile on her. I got the idea from Gay Talese, who did a memorable piece on Frank Sinatra, "Mr. Sinatra Has a Cold," after Sinatra refused to keep a promise of an interview. I would tell what had happened in my pursuit of her and discuss her interviewing on the basis of endless press releases about her. Then I changed my mind.

117

Two things made me go ahead. One was Phil Donahue's urging me to see her, "You've got to see Barbara—she's history," and offering to call her for me. The other was reading Walters' account of how she gets people to sit for interviews. Her message is this: (1) give the person a good reason why he or she should see you (for example, one of her ploys in getting to see reclusive, unpopular but famous people, like Haiti's Mme. Duvalier, is to offer them a forum to answer their critics), and (2) pursue, pursue, pursue. She says she stops if she gets a clear refusal.

I wrote her another letter (I had written others). I pulled out all the stops, starting with "When I saw Phil Donahue the other day" and following with reminders of whom I had seen—shameless name-dropping—and ending with a Barbara Walters technique: I wrote that young people who aspired to interviewing careers would want to know how she does what she does (I believe this, so writing this came easy to me).

I was on again. An appointment was made, broken, another made, broken, and finally her secretary called and asked me to hold. Then the famous voice and diction, "This is Barbara Walters. You must think I'm nuts." She apologized for breaking dates, reviewed her horrendous schedule for me, the people she had to interview, a weekend in California, a trip to Paris, and then apologized for boring me with her schedule— she said she wanted to let me know the exact things that made her cancel. At 11:00 AM a few days later, I walked into her office, and she got up from her desk chair, came from behind the desk, extended her hand, again apologized for holding me off for months (eleven, to be exact), and offered me a seat next to her at a table with chairs for four people—she is known to want to be physically close to people in interviews.

A few pleasantries, an explanation of what I was doing in the book, and I asked my first question. I could then really look at her and listen. I was not prepared for what I saw and heard, despite my homework and feeling that I knew "more about her than she could remember about herself" (a frequent statement made by well-prepared interviewers and clearly a conceit).

She is much more handsome than she appears on television and in photographs (it could be said, as my mother used to say, "She doesn't take good pictures," and she hates being told she is more handsome off screen). She has a petite, trim body; elegant, small hands with the trace of pale pink polish (she often shows them when she is photographed). She wears much more elegant and conservative "designer" clothes than I remembered from television. She is an out-and-out knockout.

A slight shyness, to which she admitted, was clear to me. The often cited lisp was not as apparent as it is on television.

But the most surprising thing—something I had never noted especially—was her playfulness and her humor. My being on the receiving end in person may have made them more apparent than they are when I watch her as part of a television audience.

About two-thirds through my requested forty-five minutes, she answered a question, ending with, "And I guess I've always been interested in what makes people tick; maybe that's the whole key. You have to care yourself." I said, "Me, too," meaning this is the way I feel. For a moment, I was startled when she said, "So now you have it all. Thank you." When I caught the playfulness, I retorted, "No, I *don't* have it all. You have fifteen minutes more to go," and we both laughed.

I suspect the quality of playfulness is very important to her interviewing. Later, in reviewing the transcripts of five interviews she selected for me (Katharine Hepburn, Mr. T, the parents of John Hinckley, and two with Richard Pryor—obviously interviews she likes), I saw for the first time how often she uses banter, playfulness, humor. Here is part of her second interview with Richard Pryor:

WALTERS: When we interviewed you a year ago, we asked how you wanted people to think of you.
PRYOR: You know what people say to me about that interview?
WALTERS: What?
PRYOR: They always say, "Boy, did you show her."
WALTERS: Do you know what they say to me?
PRYOR: What?
WALTERS: "Boy, did you show him."

With Katharine Hepburn:

HEPBURN: ... I mean we're much in a similar position. Do

you believe the junk that's written about you? I met you and I thought I don't think she's so tough. I think naturally she's sly and she's going to ask me about Spencer, and I'm going to angle out of that.

Now watch what Walters does with this. She ignores the question asked of her and goes right where she wants to go (or where she thinks the audience wants her to go), and she uses humor to get there.

> WALTERS: Never entered my mind. Spencer Tracy? Why would anybody...
> HEPBURN: But he's an adorable man.
> WALTERS: ...be interested in you and Spencer Tracy? No one ever writes about it. No one ever talks...I wish you would stop trying to bring Spencer Tracy up. Because, well, I had wanted to talk to you about other things. No matter what I do you keep bringing him up...

Katharine Hepburn apparently had been led to believe that Barbara Walters is tough and sly, never playful, and I suspect that most people would have the same impression.

The questions I had always had about Barbara Walters were, Why do people who spend their careers in front of audiences, who have been interviewed countless times, whose professional lives are devoted to watching what they say and how they say it, open up on matters they apparently have no intention of discussing? Why aren't they prepared for some slyness? The answers to these questions can only come from the people she has interviewed.

For *TV Guide*, Roderick Townley interviewed some celebrity interviewees to get their reactions to her methods.

Patrick Duffy, star of TV's *Dallas*, for one, let Walters know ahead of time that he could not discuss the murder of his parents (which had occurred four months before the interview) because the trial was still in progress, but "then in the course of the interview, I was the one who brought it up," he said. There is no explanation for why this happened other than his saying that the interview "was the most honest I've ever been treated. *Ever* been treated."

Angela Lansbury found herself talking about family matters she had specifically said she would not discuss, "choking back tears, unable to continue, while the cameras ground on mercilessly." Townley wrote of Lansbury's response:

> She blames herself for falling, as she says, into Walters' "little trap." "She has this air of being a very close friend...and she asks you, rather sensitively, in a personal way, about all *sorts* of things." The idea is that "you're going to have a chat. You're not going to have a question-and-answer session"...
> "No," concludes Lansbury, "I don't think she went for my throat. But once she *had* it, oh boy!"

Betty White and her late husband, Allen Ludden, were friends of Walters. Of her interview with Walters, White said:

> Barbara kept probing a little further and a little further [about Ludden] without my realizing it. And I started to choke up. She stopped immediately—pulled back and went in another direction. And, bless her heart, she didn't air that part.
> ...If I were terribly sensitive...and thought she was invading my privacy about Allen, I could have been resentful. But knowing her feeling for him made it like two gals talking about somebody they loved a great deal...You're dealing with somebody who's going to cut right to the heart [she said of Walters]...

It never occurred to her, White declared, to refuse to answer Walters' questions, much less lie to her.

Why did Patrick Duffy talk about things that could have altered the murder trial related to his parents? Why did Angela Lansbury see the interview as a "chat" with "a very close friend" (which Walters was not), when she knew perfectly well that she was being watched by millions of people? Why did Betty White not realize she was being probed "a little further and a little further" on a very sensitive topic?

The answers to these questions lie, of course, in what Barbara Walters does. We have suggested in answering similar questions about Mike Wallace that he is like a snake charmer. This is not the term for Barbara Walters; she is something else.

When I had time later to think about our interview, I felt I had seen what interviewees see, not what viewers see; and perhaps this is part of the explanation of her effect on people in interviews. Her physical appearance in person—the good looks, the clothes, the hands—must be an asset. The subtle show of shyness and the slight lisp give her a vulnerability which offsets her "slyness." The playfulness gives one the feeling of intimacy, and that can win over almost anyone (Mike Wallace gives the same feeling in a different way). She is polite (like John Chancellor), and that can usually get you anywhere. She made an effort to relate directly to me as a person rather than merely as another interviewer ("You're a nice man")—much as Mike Wallace and Gay Talese had done in analyzing me as an interviewer. I was charmed, and I suspect that the people she interviews for television are generally charmed—and say much more than they expect to say.

As Phil Donahue said, "She's history," a landmark in the story of television. Barbara Walters is credited with giving women a foot in the door of the high visibility, mega-salaried, power jobs on television. She is a symbol of the degree of fame and money a woman can achieve as a television interviewer. However, any young person aspiring to a career like hers who thinks that these things come easily would be mistaken. Barbara Walters paid her dues for her money and fame.

In 1976, newspaper headlines announced her signing of a five-year contract with ABC for a reported $1 million a year plus perks (at the time she was the highest paid newscaster in the history of the medium). She was the first female anchor on a network evening news show. However, by her own account, the job was a "disaster." Her relationship with her co-anchor, Harry Reasoner, was rocky, and her presence did not increase ratings. In a year, she was out of a job (but not out of her salary). As often seems to happen to her, even the "disaster" was front-page news. With all the money and fame, it was a bad time for her. Many years later, while receiving an honorary degree from Ohio State University, she told the graduating class that she once was "a flop, failing and drowning...but I'm here today, and it wasn't all luck."

I asked her what she thought influenced her in her career as interviewer. She hesitated.

■ I'm not sure; I'm really not sure. If I had to... I
don't... I don't really think anything. If I had to pick
certain things... I grew up in a world in which I was
surrounded by show business. My father in his time was
what would be called today an entrepreneur, producer.
He owned wonderful nightclubs at the time and he did
the shows. He didn't have a business sense; he was the
showman. So I met stars when I was very young, and I
found they were just people. Therefore, I wasn't tongue-
tied or in such awe that I couldn't deal with them. I
knew they also had problems and clay feet and that you
could talk to them like people. So that helped.

Then I went to an all girls' college called Sarah
Lawrence, which was considered a very progressive
school. I don't think I learned a great deal academically,
but we were encouraged to speak out, so that you
weren't ashamed to raise your hand and ask a question.
Maybe that helped.

She was born in 1931, the daughter of Lou Walters, the
widely known owner of New York's Latin Quarter and other
nightclubs. She was raised in Boston, in Miami Beach, where
she attended public high school, and in New York, where she
went to private schools.

Barbara Walters at one time wanted to be an actress, but she
told me, "I didn't have the courage to be an actress; if someone
turned me down I would take it personally." She worked for a
master's degree in education, planning to teach. "I thought I
would work with children.... I didn't know what I wanted to
do."

She was a secretary for a bit but soon found her way into
television, first in publicity, then fairly soon in producing and
writing, where she gained experience in researching, writing,
filming, and editing, all skills she made use of later as an
interviewer, skills she uses to this day.

■ I got into television as a writer on a local station. Most
of the interviewers in those days did not know how to
interview. I would do their research, write their
questions, get the props, arrange the pictures, hand

them the script. You know, in a local station you do
everything.

I was at that point a "female writer"—there was always
one female writer. Then a new show would come on and
they'd hire a whole new staff. They had to have one
female writer—I was the female writer. So it went way
back—my writing interviews.

Hired to join the staff of the CBS morning news show, she
wrote for star interviewers Dick Van Dyke, Will Rogers, Jr.,
Jack Paar, and Anita Colby. Stymied, she left and went to work
for a theatrical public relations firm, a period she calls her
"dark ages years." Eventually she was hired by the *Today* show,
where she wrote for Dave Garroway, John Chancellor, and
Hugh Downs. She waited while thirty-three relatively well-
known women, mostly actresses, were tried out for the
program.

■ I would write for all the women, all their questions, so I
learned to write in other people's styles, and I learned to
write precisely. "These are the four questions you must
get to in the five minutes you have. If time allows, ask
this and this and this." And you learn to organize, and
as I said, you learn to write in different people's styles.
And I certainly knew when I scribbled notes for myself
what my own style was, though I didn't think about it
then.

Watching on the sidelines while woman after woman was
tried out, she said to herself, "Hey, fellas, look at me, I'm right
here, how about me?"

Finally, in 1964, she was put on the air on a trial basis, and
she was off and running. She quickly impressed people with
her professionalism, her producing and writing know-how, and
her persistence in getting interviewees who interested the
public.

Twelve years later, in 1976, she made her publicized lucrative
but "disastrous" move to ABC, where she has remained,
surviving the initial problems.

Over the years she has won prizes, praise—and criticism. She has been thought of by some critics as too cream puff and by others as too tough, too show business, not enough newswoman. She has said of herself. "Yeah, I'm called too strident or too fawning...I can't win for losing. Part of the problem is that the entertainment Specials get more attention than the news interviews on *20/20*. If I had my druthers, I probably wouldn't do the Specials at all. But they do so well for ABC; how do you give up a golden egg? Now *nobody* says I'm too fawning or too nice on *20/20*. I'm proud of the serious interviews I've done." Despite the criticisms sometimes leveled at her, she was considered essential for this book by more of her peers than any other interviewer.

Barbara Walters continues to be highly paid to do both political and celebrity interviews. She writes this about herself:

My Lord, I'm lucky and I know it. But perhaps my daughter summed it up best. I happened to walk into her room early one evening while she was talking to a friend, and I heard her say, "My Mummy can't drive a car, you know. My Mummy can't fix a fuse. My Mummy burns the meat loaf. Come to think of it, my Mummy really can't do anything but talk."

And here is how she makes her living talking:

■ I think you have to start out saying, "What do I really want to know? What does the public really want to know?"

I interviewed Bette Midler and she was very funny about how she asked everybody's opinion. She said, "The janitor will walk by and I'll say, 'Do you really think this is a good career move for me?'"

Well, I will walk around and say, "If you were going to interview the President today, or if you were going to interview Barbra Streisand, what do you really want to know?" and I try to start with that. What do I really want to know most?

Sometimes journalists have a tendency to do the interview that's going to impress other journalists or

that's going to get some attention in the *New York Times*.
And we forget that what we should be doing is the
interview that the audience is going to be the most
interested in. So I think you have to start yourself with,
What do I most want to know? What's the essence of this
person? Almost a theme in your mind.

And of course, there's a difference between doing a
personality interview and doing one for information. Or
an interview that's going to be fifteen or twenty minutes
on the air or something else that's going to be two-and-
a-half minutes on the news that night.

I have a very A-B-C kind of mind: What's the point of
this? Let's go to the heart of this. I like interviews to
have a beginning, a middle, and an end. And I think if
you have a very good beginning and a very good end,
the rest of it in the middle can be a little mushier.

Then if you have a short interview, the way you do on
the *Today* show, or *Good Morning, America*, or if you're
doing a live interview on the evening news programs, it
is all the more important to have what I call an A-B-C
kind of mind. What am I trying to get out of this? You
want to get the hard news, but you also want to get, if
you can, what I call the juice. If I have time, one more
question, another thirty seconds, I want to get something about the person that will make you understand
why he or she did what they did. It may not be the one
that's going to make the headlines, but it's the juice so
that the interview isn't a dry piece of toast. You wouldn't
put toast with juice, but you know what I'm saying.

I think we all would probably say the same thing
about what goes into a good interview: curiosity,
listening, and, I would add, homework where possible.

You can do the fast interview, and many people have
to, especially at the White House, you know, the kind of
run-and-grab, here-they-come-there-they-go kind of
interview; but if you're really going to do an in-depth
interview, then I think you have to know an awful lot
about the person, certainly enough to know when he or
she isn't telling you the truth, isn't telling you the whole
story. But beyond that, so that you can ask the questions

that reveal the essence of the person, it really does help to do your homework.

There are certain interviews, certain people, where you do your homework and then you just sit and listen. An example is a Special we did with Debra Winger some years ago. Very hard interview to do, because none of the questions that you use with anybody else work for her. You really just have to go with it. When I was done with the interview, I wish I had been able to start from the beginning, because I understood it. But once I let it go, it just kept opening up and I just had to sit there and have a conversation. But if I hadn't read some stuff about her, it wouldn't have been the same.

I try not to pre-interview. Most interview programs, the entertainment interview programs, even the morning news programs, do a pre-interview. A staff writer walks up, talks to the subject, asks the questions, gets the answers, and gives the questions and the answers to the person doing the interview. This is the way it works on *Good Morning, America* and on Johnny Carson. You can use the questions and the answers, or you can throw them away.

But with a pre-interview, there's no surprise. Well, sometimes there is, but not often. And my tendency is not to want to use the questions at all. So that means that when I meet the person, I have to get myself started as much as I have to get him started, because we're strangers to each other when we sit down. And fifteen minutes later, we're going to be having a rather personal conversation. And I will *know* in that interview where it suddenly takes off—or doesn't.

No one we interviewed seems to have studied the craft of devising questions to the extent that Barbara Walters has. Unquestionably, her long background as question-writer for many celebrity interviewers focused her attention early on this skill. Watching Barbara Walters on television, we are reminded of the shy people we know who have found a way of getting through social encounters without too much pain—they make up questions to ask others so they themselves will not be uncomfortable by having to express their own views or suffer through lapses in a conversation. The rule seems to be, If you cannot converse, interview. Walters has, in fact, written in *How to Talk to Practically Anybody About Practically Anything* about how her career aided her in overcoming the torture of shyness.

Walters puts extraordinary effort into making up questions for an interview:

■ I really do a lot of preparation. I write all of my questions out on three-by-five cards. I write each question individually. I have lots of them; I can do two hundred of them.

Then I put them in order. And nobody can really do that for me. Sometimes when I'm busy, I've said to my assistant, "Do it. Do the way you think." It doesn't work, because I sort of know what's going to lead to something else. After I have done hundreds of these, I narrow them down, and then finally they're put onto larger cards, which are what I actually work with.

As often as I have done it, I will worry about whether one question comes before another—it's ludicrous—because by the time I sit down, I never use the questions, or rarely, but I've had them, and I've written them and I've gone through them so that they're in my head.

There are people who can have their questions written for them. One of the things that made Mike Wallace so hot during the Westmoreland trial was that it turned out that three-quarters of his questions were written for him. I know this because I did an interview in which I asked him. He simply didn't have the time to do it, and in many cases the producer will write your questions, just as the producer will do the editing. I'm very uncomfortable with that. Even on the *Today* show where we had writers, I used to rewrite almost all of the questions.

And I do choreograph interviews. Depending upon who the person is, I will very often start with the childhood. It's safer, it opens the person up; everyone will talk about his childhood. And if he or she doesn't, there's a reason why and that in itself is fascinating. I

will save the tougher questions, obviously, for the end.
What if the person gets up and walks out? What if the
person cries? What if...? You almost have to know
instinctively when you've gone too far, or when you're
going to push this person. In the interview I did with
Bud [Robert C.] MacFarlane [Ronald Reagan's national
security adviser], the first television interview he did
after coming out of the hospital following his suicide
attempt, I remember asking him two or three questions
about suicide. The last one was, "Why did you take
Valium?" And he said, "It was all I had." And he
laughed and said, "I guess it was the one thing I hadn't
researched," and his lower lip began to tremble. And I
thought, "One more question and he's going to break
down," and I didn't want that. So you have to have an
innate sense of when you stop.

Political interviewing is something different. I think
what I say most often in a political interview is, "You
didn't answer the question." Then you ask yourself,
"How long do I pursue this? When do I realize that
there's nothing else to pursue and go on to the next
question?"

Now, when you don't do an interview live, you really
do have control over it, and it's wonderful. The
interviewer always comes out looking good, because he
or she can edit it. They can put questions in and take
questions out, do a voice-over introduction.

We opted to do the Nixon interview live; we wanted it
that way. And it was an enormous challenge, because I
remember thinking, "I'm damned if I do and damned if
I don't." If the questions are too soft, they'll say I'm so
soft on Nixon, and if the questions are too tough, they'll
say, "You took this man and you really killed him." And
I went crazy; I wrote more questions and asked
everybody under the sun, and I narrowed the questions
down. It was the extreme of what I do.

It was the first network interview that he had done
after Watergate. He had done the big interview with
David Frost, but that had been a syndicated interview
over which he had control; he had done hours and

hours and hours. We were going to have less than an hour with him. He had originally thought about going to *60 Minutes* or us. It was sort of a toss-up, and *60 Minutes* refused to interview him live.

I remember being so concerned about the questions and whether they were the right ones or not the right ones that in the middle of it all, about an hour before I was supposed to go on the air, I called Johnny Carson to see if he would do an interview with me for a Special. It was my way of kind of giving myself some relief. And I remember Carson saying, "Ask him why he didn't burn the tapes," which was what we were going to ask. I don't know why I remember so well, except that I do remember that I needed some kind of…and I knew that I was going to do it all the time. I was only allowed so many questions; I had to be very careful that each one was important.

I also did not want Nixon to fillibuster, which is why *60 Minutes* had not done it. They said, "Oh, he'll go on and on and on." So what I did was to put the obvious answer in the question, so that he had to then go on to the—I don't have the questions; I should have kept them—but "President Nixon, you have said that dealing with the Russians, one must be very strong, that you've got to have the carrot and the stick. Now, knowing that, would you…? In other words, so that he couldn't give me the same clichés, I put them in the question.

I also took the question about "Why didn't you burn the tapes?" and I told the crew to give me a fifteen-second cue at the end of the program. And with the fifteen seconds to go, I could ask him that. So that, again, he had to give me a short answer and he couldn't divert.

I learned at a very early time on television how to edit. When I was very young, I was working at NBC in a program called *Ask the Camera*, which was a nice cheap program to do (it was local). What happened is that viewers would write questions and we would find the footage that would answer that question. "How big is a pelican?" "Well, here is a pelican," and we would get footage of a pelican somewhere. Or if they didn't ask, "How big is a pelican?" and we had a pelican, we would make sure that somebody wrote a letter about the pelican even if I had to call my mother and say, "Mom, are you interested in how big a pelican is?" In those days it was film, not tape. And it would be up to me to sit and edit this piece on the pelican, do the research on the pelican, and write the voice-over for the person on the program to do.

I think it's important to be able to do your own editing. And not to just turn it over to somebody else. I can't remember an interview of mine that I haven't been involved with from beginning to end. And we have superb producers. But I can't let it go.

And I'm also compulsive, so I will not only agonize over questions; I will agonize over editing.

To get interviews, I usually make the calls myself. I'm not as courageous as most people think, so I very often will write a letter rather than make a call. And in the letter I try to think why this person who doesn't do interviews should do an interview.

What comes to my mind as I talk is an interview with Bob [H.R.] Haldeman [Nixon's chief of staff], remember him? He would give *no* interviews at all. When he was in the White House with Nixon—this was before Watergate—he was beginning to get the reputation of being very hard-line, sort of Prussian. Haldeman and Ehrlichman—the two Germans. People would speak about them with humor, but underlying the humor was that these were two very tough guys, and I remember writing to Haldeman and saying that I thought not only was this a bad image for him to have but a bad image for the President, and that perhaps if we did this interview, we could clear up a great deal of misconception. People could see him as a human being. We could do it in his office, light a fire. And, by God, he agreed. So my point is that first you have to think, "Why should this person want to do this interview?" Obviously, if they're plugging a book or a movie, you know.

While I very often will write first, I will also, if I can, call, and call again, and call again. A lot of interviewers don't have to; they have a producer who does it. They have an assistant. I will do it myself. And sometimes it takes years. I don't mean that I call every day, but everybody thinks, "Oh, it just happens." I will say to someone, "Look, if you ever do that book, will you do your first interview with me?" Or if I'm turned down for an interview, which happens all the time, I say, "If there's ever a time that you feel you want to talk, will you let me know?" Something can happen a year and a half later.

Sometimes I meet people personally, but I don't usually. In the case, for example, of the parents of John Hinckley, who tried to assassinate President Reagan, they had agreed to do *60 Minutes*. But they asked if they could meet me, and by the time we finished talking, they decided they would do it [the interview] with me. I think they felt I understood.

So getting an interview is a combination of things: their feeling something about you, their plugging something, their wanting to defend themselves publicly. And it can work negatively. There are people who don't want to do interviews with me for all kinds of reasons.

Another thing, by the way, is I do keep my word. And people know that. And I think I don't trick people. "This is what it is, this is what we're going to do."

I won't allow anyone in the room who is not actively involved in the interview. I don't want somebody sitting in the background, because you'll see the interviewee's eyes darting away.

I have to sit very close in interviews, and I begin to bend forward. I want to forget there are lights and cameras. I sit very close; I want the person just to look at me. And I only look at them. If I look at them, they have to look at me.

And I guess I just sit there very intensely, scrooch up my face, you know. I try not to now, because I used to have that terribly intense look. But I know I try to make it just the two of us.

Marie Brenner

Special Correspondent, Vanity Fair, and Book Journalist

"I credit San Antonio and Texas and growing up as I did with whatever confidence I'm able to go into an interview with. There is something about growing up in that hyper social atmosphere of Texas where a woman, in a sense, is trained always to please, always to ask questions, to pull the other person out—all those refined tenets of upbringing."

MARIE BRENNER, special correspondent for *Vanity Fair*, interviewer of celebrities, and author of celebrity books, was raised on the right side of the tracks in San Antonio, Texas. More than right side, really; rather, the old-money, WASP section of town. Raised with money (her father owned a very successful discount store, and there was money way back, too), she had wealth going for her. Born of a Jewish father and Catholic mother, however, she had a few strikes against her. Minorities in San Antonio are a mixed bag of tricks to the landed gentry (Jews are in the minority; Catholics aren't, but of course are not WASPs). Prejudice was shown in numerous ways. For instance, no Jews were allowed to be members of the San Antonio Country Club.

An admiring high school teacher characterizes Brenner in those days as abrasive and domineering: "She couldn't stand not to be the best." In college, a classmate recalls, "She was just full of herself. She was an expert on everything....She had absolute nerves of steel. She had no fear of going up to anybody and talking to them about anything." The fight Marie Brenner had to wage to assert herself may have been one of the best things that ever happened to an ambitious young woman. Look at the product.

One writer characterizes Brenner in her early days in journalism as "the Tiger Lady going for the jugular." People she writes about are frequently unhappy about what they read. Henry Kissinger, for example, screamed at her for an hour over the telephone when he read the profile she did of him in *New York* magazine. An old friend and current colleague still says of her, "People shouldn't speak to Marie—and they always do....She's the most seductive interviewer." Today, she still feels that if her subject approves of what she writes, she has not gone far enough in her interview.

Like Mike Wallace, she seems to have mellowed over the years. The writer who characterized her as the Tiger Lady now calls her Tiger Lily and sees her as "open, engaging, smart, and warm." The high school teacher who called her abrasive says the aggressiveness is gone—"She knows how to make people feel comfortable, she's much more polished, has an ease of manner, knows how to put herself in another person's place."

This seductive interviewer has practiced her wiles on well-known folks such as the most glamorous of the British royals, Lena Horne, Clare Booth Luce, Norman Mailer, Ronald Reagan, Elizabeth Taylor, and on and on. Her interview of Mme. Duvalier, the wife of the deposed despot of Haiti, won the *Front Page* award for the most distinguished magazine story of 1986. Her "Marie Brenner's Red Sox Diary" (she was the first female baseball columnist to cover the American League) was nominated for a Pulitzer Prize. Her book on a well-known newspaper publishing dynasty, *House of Dreams: The Bingham Family of Louisville*, was a best-seller. Throughout her career, she has free-lanced, and some of her interview profiles have appeared in book collections.

She has earned her stripes. After getting a master's degree in film, she worked as story editor for Paramount Pictures, then began her career as magazine and book writer. She did a stint as foreign correspondent in London, was a columnist for the *Boston Herald-American*, spent years as contributing editor for *New York* magazine, and assumed the same job for *Vanity Fair* when it opened up shop.

I was introduced to Marie Brenner by Diane Sawyer, who said, "I've been told that the genius among women interviewers is Marie Brenner, and indeed she did that stunning thing with Jeane Kirkpatrick—really stunning. She's really talented in what she extracts."

I wrote to Brenner and was invited to her New York Upper East Side town house ("built in 1891," her publicist's handout reports). She met me at the door, hung up my coat for me (like her fellow Southerner, Roger Mudd), and guided me to the kitchen where she was making coffee for us. I made the mistake of telling her that I, too, was raised in San Antonio. She began a "Do you know...?" "You must know..." query (my responses were consistently "No"), until I finally laughed and said, "I don't know many of those folks. You were one of those rich kids from the other side of town; I was raised on the wrong side of the tracks." I felt we were not off to a good start, but she is the social pro that everyone says she is—and just plain nice, and we got along well.

The Tiger Lady, now called Tiger Lily, the seductive interviewer, had this to say about how she practices her wiles.

■ I feel good about an interview when the person is really honest with me, when I've gotten the person to break down in some fundamental way. Usually people who are used to being interviewed have a manner they adopt, and when you can get them in some way to reveal themselves, that makes a great interview.

How do I do that? Just sheer luck, tenacity, hanging in. It is the most difficult thing to do because people are scared of actually revealing themselves. It's very, very hard to do. I have my own way; everyone has her own way.

My way is to be incredibly sociable, as a good Texas girl, and try to create a social situation where you get them so relaxed that then you can ask them anything as if they're an old friend. In other words, not to prepare too much. Before I go into an interview, I write out about fifty possible questions, and then I don't think about it. I just put the questions in the spiral notebook that I take with me. If I get stuck, I flip open the notebook and refer to some questions.

When I get to the interview, I just do this thing about, "Oh, what a lovely house, this is so great," just as if I were at a San Antonio party. That works for me most of the time, because then the person feels relaxed, and they're able to forget that they're with a reporter. This isn't everybody's method, but it's the only method I find that really works.

There are certain people who believe in asking very blunt and direct questions, but I don't. For example, the last two weeks that Jeane Kirkpatrick was at the United Nations, I was traveling with her. Now, this woman is one of the most difficult women to interview, because she is so much the diplomat, so doctrinaire, and so used to giving statements about world policy. But once we started traveling together, I found her also very motherly. Once she realized that she wasn't being interviewed about world affairs, she relaxed and told me extraordinary things—her marriage was bad, she didn't get along with her daughter-in-law—a whole different side of Jeane Kirkpatrick. The same thing with Geraldine Ferraro. When you're there with them, they finally do let down their guard and stop making the kind of cranked-out statement they're used to giving the daily reporters.

Being a woman interviewer makes a huge difference. Huge. Because I think people trust a woman, don't you? Sometimes it works against you, because they don't take you seriously, they think you're an airhead, or a troublemaker, or a news hen, or something like that. But in general, it's helpful, I think. Since my approach is to be very sociable, it works better to do that as a woman. To do that as a man, they'd think you were silly.

I get to people by calling them up and saying I want to write about them. And they will say yes or no. Generally you don't take no for an answer; you must keep at them. "Well, may I call you next week? Can we just talk about it? I'd just like to meet you." In the face of this, there are very few people who are all that resistant. Of course, there are certain classic examples, like Mrs. Onassis, who never will give an interview. And certain people who are having legal problems, but you can often get around that by saying that you will meet with them with their lawyer present. There are usually ways you can circumvent things.

A thing like the Duvaliers posed unique problems. I had many facts about them, so it was just getting in to see them that would give my piece the final authenticity. The interview was less important because the deposed tyrant is not going to rend his skirts and cry and scream, "If only we hadn't been sacked by our country." They're going to say the usual things, "We did nothing wrong. It was the system. It was the vile American press. My husband was great." You just want to get in, see what they're wearing, the cut of their face, the slant of their eye, and put it all together with all the other facts. [I asked if she saw the Barbara Walters interview with the Duvaliers.] Yes. That caused so many problems, because after the interview the Duvaliers said they would never give another one. It really took us four months to wear them down.

The difference between a single interview and living with a person? That's a good question.

In a one-shot deal you have to be very prepared because you know this is it. You've got two hours, an hour sometimes, to get in and get out. Sometimes you just beg for thirty minutes, which is tough if you're doing a magazine piece of seven-thousand or eight-thousand words. So you go in, and you have ten questions in mind, and you hope for the best.

But normally, when you're in a one-shot interview, you extend it. If the person likes you during the interview, at the end you can say, "I didn't get what I need. Can we see each other again?" It's very rare that someone will say, "No, go away."

Because, you see, the whole process is one of seduction. They want you, as interviewer, to like them and to be impressed by them, just as much as you want to get interesting things out of them. So if they feel you're responding to them in a good way, often they'll give you more and more time.

Yes, it's a seduction, absolutely. Normally, you want the person you're interviewing to respond to you, because if they respond to you, then you can loosen them up. And if you loosen them up, they'll really let their hair down and talk to you.

I was on the David Susskind show with a writer who said he goes out drinking for five days with the person he's writing about before he turns on the tape recorder. I don't think this is right somehow, because it seems unprofessional. Maybe I'm from the old school—you go in, turn your tape recorder on, and hope for the best and that you can keep the person talking.

It isn't always seduction on my part. It depends on whom I'm interviewing. At times, it's like trial by fire, total agony. For example, with someone you find politically reprehensible, like the Duvaliers, it's a performance. You keep up a breezy façade and not turn on them in a Fallaci-esque manner and have the whole thing come crashing down on your head and get yourself thrown out of the interview. So, in that case, it can be a real trial.

Interviewing is a social talent. You have to be a good listener. You have to not be afraid to speak up and ask very direct questions in a way that doesn't alienate someone. If you'd gone to a lot of parties as a child, you would probably do this pretty well, because of the seduction and the performance and the flirtation and the confidence and esprit that you have to go in with. You have to be the kind of person who, when you get into a taxi, wants to know everything about the driver. If you don't have that as part of your personality, then you should probably forget it, because you're not going to be very good at it. You have to be willing to efface your ego and your personality, want to know about the other person, not put yourself forward.

Often interviewers seem very warm spirited, but they don't really want to talk about themselves too much.

They're brilliant at pulling out the other person but not comfortable babbling on about themselves.

Maria Shriver is a perfect example of this. This girl is a pretty good interviewer, especially on television, which is very demanding and different from what I do. Maria Shriver is so camouflaged as a human being that she's in the perfect profession for her. She can exude all this warmth, this Kennedy charm, and no one can ever ask her a question, never can pin her down about what it's like to be a Shriver, a Kennedy daughter, because she's too busy bombarding them with questions. I interviewed her once for *Vanity Fair* and when I broached this to her—I said, "This is your personality"—she completely cracked, like a walnut, and said, "Yes, that's it. No one can ask me any questions. I don't want to be asked questions. My childhood was so terrifying and this is a kind of elaborate defense I created. It works perfectly."

I think it's an error to come in too hard on your subject, or in the wrong way. An example of doing the opposite is what I did with Elizabeth Taylor. You know, this woman has been interviewed more than any woman in the world, and, inevitably, about the husbands, the jewels, Mike Todd, and so on, but she takes herself very seriously, ironically enough, as a political thinker. And so for the first ten minutes of the interview we talked only about Israel, because she had been in Israel six months earlier. Once she had gotten her point across about her views of Zionism and what she had told Sharon at some cabinet meeting, then she was totally relaxed and became that other kind of person. But she would never have dished about herself as a movie star without the introduction, because when you're doing one of those luxuriant star interviews, you really want all the great hyperboles. But if I hadn't given her ten or fifteen minutes to talk about Israel, it wouldn't have worked; she would have been too up tight.

I'm sure many interviewers are in this situation, too. You're just much more comfortable in the questioning role, not in the answering role. Many times reporters give very bad interviews because they get so uptight about it. They're used to asking the questions.

I credit San Antonio and Texas and growing up as I did with whatever confidence I'm able to go into an interview with. There is something about growing up in that hyper social atmosphere of Texas where a woman, in a sense, is trained always to please, always to ask questions, to pull the other person out—all those refined tenets of upbringing. I really think that helped me a great deal. I don't go on the attack. In a way, sometimes that works against me, because often I won't go in for the one-two punch at the end. I really think that gentle South Texas training had something to do with it.

Interviewing is just marvelous. One of the great things about doing this is that you get to meet some of the most interesting people in the world and ask them anything you want. I mean, it's amazing. It's like open season. You know, to walk with Henry Kissinger through the Boston Common and hear about his father and his childhood in Germany is not exactly hardship duty. It's not a bad way to spend a life, plus you get paid for it.

Thomas B. Morgan

Writer and Broadcast Executive

Interviewing is "a delicate game, a very savage battle—complicated and savage."

Despite his dire statements about the savagery of interviewing, Tom Morgan, now president of New York City's WNYC Communication Group, seemed to savor every minute of his two hours talking with me about interviewing. Morgan has interviewed and written profiles for *Esquire, Look, Harper's,* and other national magazines, sometimes producing fifteen to twenty pieces a year. Some of these interviews ended up in a book, *Self-Creations: Thirteen Impersonalities.*

Prospective interviewers of celebrities might heed the warning about interviewing famous people implicit in Morgan's idea of an Impersonality: "Over time, deliberately, they create a public self for the likes of me to interview, observe, and double-check. This self is a tested consumer item of proven value, a sophisticated invention refined, polished, distilled, and certified okay in scores, perhaps hundreds, of engagements with journalists, audiences, friends, family, and lovers. It is not really them, but curiously it is not *not* them either." Among the Impersonalities he interviewed were John Wayne, Sammy Davis, Jr., and Gary Cooper.

Getting to celebrities is difficult for almost everyone without names like Ted Koppel, Mike Wallace, Oriana Fallaci. Tom admits that his name is "unknown to millions." How, then, did he get his foot in the door of a host of celebrities?

The answer is that most people see me, talk to me, and let me live with them if necessary, because I represent a

141

national magazine. Whether I like it or not, I come bearing the gift of potential publicity. They want to be even better known. They want to be beautiful—I might be out of work if they didn't.

Vanity is the most deadly sin. Since we all possess it, it is a matter of degree. Everyone wants to be better known, or at least, everyone I have met. We want to be loved publicly, perhaps to compensate for hating ourselves privately. The difference is only that some people strive to be better known than others.

Getting to famous people is one thing; wanting to interview them once you have them is another, according to Morgan. *Holiday* magazine asked Tom to interview Ayn Rand, the cult author, but in preparation for seeing her, he read *Atlas Shrugged,* her best-selling novel, and hated it, so he turned down the job. Jean-Paul Sartre, who had turned down the Nobel Prize, wanted to be paid, and Tom refused. Frank Sinatra wanted the right to censor the final piece, and Tom refused. Prince Rainier, J. Robert Oppenheimer, and a few others wanted to check what Morgan wrote, and he acquiesced, but reserved the right to reject their suggestions. Morgan rejected Rainier's suggestions, but the magazine acquiesced, and Morgan stopped writing for it.

Morgan, unlike any other interviewer we talked to, finds his career as interviewer and profile writer harrowing. Interviewing for him is "a delicate game—a very savage battle, complicated and savage."

■ The interviewee finally says, "I can trust this guy even though he's out to get me," and the interviewer says, "I can trust this guy even though I know he's lying." What you get is a kind of long battle. The result is, as I've lamented, he gets his name in print, which is really what he wants, and you never get the truth. At best, a good interview is a kind of defeat.

Morgan was, from childhood, an "information freak," like other interviewers we saw.

■   The best way to prepare for an interview is to be a born
information freak. I absorbed over time, over the years,
an unbelievable amount of information. That doesn't
mean I know everything about everything, but I know
something about damn near everything. I know about
particle physics, and open heart surgery, and
Shakespeare, and nuclear warheads, and politics. That's
the nature of the beast. When I was a little boy, I said,
"How am I going to get out of this mess called
Springfield, Illinois? Get plenty of information and
you'll get out."

Tom Morgan was born in 1926, one of three children of a
"handsome, devoted, Puritan" mother and a "lovable, inefficient merchant" who died broke, leaving the family poor.

Tom decided that he "had been born an artist," the silver
lining his mother had always spoken of. He was influenced by a
high school teacher to write fiction and by his Carlton College
English professor to write novels. He never got over this latter
influence—his dream all of his life has been to write novels.
But after college, he got sidetracked and shuttled for nine
years between the editorial departments of *Esquire* and *Look*.
Still determined to write novels, he quit the magazine business
and wrote two, neither of which was published. Hungry, he
began free-lancing and discovered that he could employ his
predilection for fiction in writing profiles—nonfiction pieces
which he discovered were virtually short stories. Still, as was
evident in our interview, interviewing and profile writing were
never totally congenial to him.

He stopped interviewing as full-time work and went on to
other journalistic jobs, including editor of *The Village Voice* in
Manhattan, and press secretary to New York Mayor John
Lindsay. Eventually Morgan came to what he had always
wanted to have the time and money to do: write novels. His
first was *This Blessed Shore*. *Snyder's Walk* was published in 1987,
the same year his piece about himself, "Turning Sixty," appeared in *Esquire* magazine.

Morgan is six-feet-four, and weighs in the two-hundred-plus
range—facts he regards as his "survival equipment" in dealing

with the famous people he has had to interview. He admits to a
"disarming Corn Belt dialect"; his language is salty. Pleasant,
warm, without a trace of pretense, he is easy to like, and it was
not difficult imagining his interviewing the high and mighty.
After our interview was over, he helped more than any other
single individual in this book with endless introductions; he
seems to know everyone under the sun.

Here is what he had to say about the "savage battle" of
interviewing:

■ You have to understand that writers who use interviewing don't think like you do. You think about it as
if it was something. To us, interviewing is part of the
preparation for writing articles. So the purpose of my
questions is basically part of the process of getting ready
to write. What constitutes a good interview depends on
what the purpose of the interview is. If your goal is to
write something significant about somebody or some
issue, and the interview enlightens you, then it's a good
interview. But if the interview is just a collection of stuff
and you could have asked the guy fifteen other questions on fifteen other subjects rather than what you did,
what does it mean?

The purpose of my questions was to get information
so I could write about this person—his character, his
life, the meaning of his life. I never read *Playboy*
interviews where the interviewer asks a question and the
person answers. That's just dictation. It hasn't been
processed by a mind.

I guess the definition of a good interview is, when you
get back home and you sit down at the typewriter and
you're going to have to write something, somewhere in
that pile of nothing is something to write about. I don't
think you ever know that, really, until you sit down and
say, "Oh, my God, I've got to read all this stuff. That's
boring. What does it mean?" You realize that those three
questions you asked at the end of the interview—that's
what it means. That doesn't mean that I didn't have to
sit there for three weeks until my ankles swelled up and

my hearing didn't work, and finally something would happen and I'd have it.

The interview process has a lot of osmosis to it. When you go to see someone, you don't know what is going to happen. That's one of the joys of it. You don't know where it's going. Some guys know where it's going, but I don't.

You always feel that you've made a million mistakes, because when you sit down to write, you realize that you asked all the wrong questions and you don't know what the hell you were thinking of. But what usually happens is that when you sit down to write, you realize that there were fifty questions you should have asked but you didn't ask and you can't go back. He's gone to Europe, your deadline is staring you in the face, and you're in trouble. I think the biggest mistake I have made is the failure maybe to be well enough prepared to know in advance what questions this person must answer. I must say kind of defensively that, of course, it's endless. If you ask a guy five-hundred questions, and you realize that you should have asked him five-hundred-fifty questions, then if you'd asked him those extra fifty, you think of another fifty you could have asked.

I never did much preparation. That doesn't mean I wasn't prepared for the interview. As I said, I'm an information freak. If I was going to interview someone like David Susskind, for instance, I already knew an enormous amount about him. We'd never met, but I knew he was the producer of this and that and he had this and that show; his name was in the paper. I write him a letter and ask him, "Would you talk to me?" I don't do any preparation until he writes back and says he'll see me. I don't have any time to prepare for some guy who writes back and says he won't see me.

With a subject that is highly technical, it behooves the interviewer to get some background. For example, I did two pieces for *Look* magazine on J. Robert Oppenheimer. The first time I went out to see him in Princeton, he asked, "What do you know about nuclear physics?" I said, "Well, I don't know too much, but I know a little. I know about the bomb, and all kinds of stuff." Then he said, "What do you know about my work?" And I said, "I have to admit that I not only don't know anything about your work but I wouldn't even know how to find out." He said, "If we're going to do this, Morgan, the first thing you've got to do is read this," and he had prepared for me a stack at least four feet high of his monographs, going back to the beginning of his life, an unbelievable thing! And I said, "Holy shit! What am I supposed to do with that?" And he said, "I will only give you an interview if you read this. If you don't read it, I'm not interested in having another conversation with you." I said, "Okay." So I filled up the backseat of the car with this material.

It took me about two weeks to plow through it. I was very serious; all you needed to do was to give me a challenge. And not only that; I went out and bought the essays of J. Robert Oppenheimer. So I went back and he said, "I can't believe it!" "Test me," I said. He said, "I believe you." I said, "No, ask me questions." So he said something like, "Well, what about such-and-such debate between Niels Bohr and Faraway on heavy water or something?"—(something which he wrote about). I said, "Oh, I remember that." Jesus Christ, I happened to read that. "I remember that. That was really something. You guys out there in Chicago having this debate and you wrote this paper, blah, blah, blah," and he was all convinced.

Oppenheimer was one of the few guys who would not have the interview if he could not read the manuscript. And I always said I wouldn't do that. Except in his case, I said, "I'll do it, but the only control you have is if I've made a factual mistake. You can clearly make any factual change, but my opinion is my opinion." So he said, "That's a deal."

The article came out, and you wouldn't believe it—we made a mistake! After all that effort trying to get it right. You see, he'd been ostracized by that time [Oppenheimer was suspected during the McCarthy era of being soft on communism], and one reason he would talk to me is that nobody else wanted to talk to him. He'd been a hero of mine, anyhow. We were both very concerned that whatever he said, and whatever I wrote about what he said, at least the material would be accurate. He checked it; I checked it; *Look* magazine checked it. And we left a zero off a number, which made it ridiculous. I think we said that one kind of explosion was equivalent to one-hundred-thousand tons of TNT, and it should have been a million. "Oh, my God!" he said. He said that he knew he'd said it. And it was in my notes. It was like a mental block, and we still went with it. Of course, we got eighteen-thousand letters from people saying, "What are you talking about? No wonder they kicked him out; he doesn't know the difference between...etc., etc."

I did make mistakes for whatever psychological reasons; sometimes I got blocked, I guess. I failed to ask questions that you really ought to ask. For instance, I don't think I ever asked Roy Cohn if he was homosexual, but it was a big issue at the time. In a way, I was afraid; in those days it was kind of insulting. Now people ask those questions. In those days, you didn't bring that up. Yet there was something about Cohn that comes through in the article that I think that I thought he was homosexual. That's what I think I thought.

I don't write about anyone's sex life, except with Susskind, because he demanded that I do it. "You want to know why I go out with all those bimbos?" says he. But in general I left that out; I don't think that was a mistake. I could have asked Cohn if McCarthy was homosexual, but I didn't. Was I afraid? I don't know. Was I blocked? Did I think it was inappropriate or did I think it was wrong? In my heart, I believe that everybody should do whatever he wants to do, sexually, I mean. So it's kind of hard to turn around and say, "See, those guys were queer." You can't play it both ways.

While Morgan tries to stay away from what he calls a person's *private* private life," he felt he could not explain Susskind's "passions" without exposing Mrs. Susskind, and Susskind gave him every opportunity to see her.

■ Here's what happened with Susskind. I walked into his office for the first interview, and he came out and got me in the lobby and he says, "I want you to see everything, hear everything, participate in everything I do, or whatever." (I can't give you the exact quote now.) "I want you to know me as well as I know myself." He was absolutely bananas. So then he drags me by the arm into his office and the phone has just rung. He said, "Get on the other phone," so he has me eavesdropping on a phone call with a guy in Hollywood. And I take out my notebook, and I say, "Can I write this down?" And he says, "Yeah, write it down; I want you to get this." So I'm writing this unbelievable conversation between these two maniacs. That never happened to me in my whole life. I'm sure it never happened to anyone.

So that's what went on for weeks with this guy. He took me to his house: "You want to know what I live with? I want you to see what my wife is *really* like." So we go to his house in Westport and he walks in and she throws a dish at him. It was insane.

So by the time I sat down to write the article, to tell the truth was to leave this guy like a bloody wreck on a Normandy beach somewhere. I was his personal land mine. When the article came out, he went crazy. "You've done me in, Morgan. You've destroyed my career; you've ruined my marriage; you've destroyed my life. I didn't know all that stuff was on the record." I said, "Wait a minute, wait a minute. You said you wanted me to hear everything." They put that on the cover of the book. Everyone was overwhelmed by it. But I wrote this article without malice. I've never written with malice. Never.

The biggest mistake I ever made was with Teddy Kennedy. I asked him, "Why did you leave Harvard? I've heard you left Harvard because you were forced to leave. I heard you flunked out." He said, "No, I didn't flunk out; I thought it was time to do my service." I

must have talked to fifteen people after he said that to
me. I even talked to a reporter for the *Boston Globe,* not
the guy who was the family patsy, another guy, who said,
"Everybody knows something happened and it's been
totally covered up, suppressed. Nobody knows what it is.
Try the registrar at Harvard." And he said, "If you can
get this, your life is made." So I called the registrar on
the phone. I said I was from *Esquire* and I was writing
this story on Mr. Kennedy—I think he was running for
the Senate—and I'd like to know what were the
circumstances of his leaving Harvard. They said it was
sealed. "We can't tell you." "Listen, this guy is running
for public office. We've got a right to know." "Well, he
left Harvard." "I'll ask you another question; he says he
left because it was time to go into the army. Is that why
he left? Or did Harvard force him to leave?" They can't
answer that: "His file is closed."

I gave up. I'd been working for three weeks on this
thing; I had a deadline. It was cold. I had a pain in the
neck; I'd been hurt when a horse fell on me; my foot
was blowing up with blood blisters. So fuck it, I went
home and wrote the article.

I should have called Kennedy back and said to him,
"Mr. Kennedy, I've talked to fifteen people who say that
your answer is not true and I want to know. Will you call
the registrar at the university and release this
information?"

And here's what's so funny. Kennedy thought I had it.
That's why they told the world about it a couple of days
before my article came out. They leaked it to their
favorite ass-kisser on the *Boston Globe* just before *Esquire*
was to come out with my profile on Kennedy. "Kennedy
Admits So-and-So." [It is reported that Kennedy paid a
friend to take an exam for him.] They wrote a kind of
tender story; he was just a young person and he was all
upset, and blah-blah-blah. That's like on Monday, and
I'm out on Wednesday and I say he left school on
account of the Korean War. I published a guy's
statement that he said was the truth. I'll never forgive

him for that. I don't trust him and I never will trust
him. Partly my own mistake. I should have given it one
more shot. That was a big mistake. Big, big mistake.

But check it out.

Teddy Kennedy for years thereafter thought he could
get away with anything. Up until the famous Roger
Mudd interview. [See our interview with Roger Mudd
for his version of the Kennedy interview.] He got his
comeuppance that day.

Sometimes people love tough questions. A lot of
people love that combat. Those are the best people;
they're the ones who always win in the interview. Like
John Wayne. He knew damned well I was a liberal. I
don't know how he knew, but he knew. He just loved it.
We went at it for ten days and he himself thought it was
the best profile ever written about him. He didn't care
that I said he was this Fascist bastard; he loved that, he
loved everything. The last time I interviewed him, I
asked him all these political questions; he was just ready
for them. He kept hitting them right out of the ball
park.

I must have quoted thousands of people in what I've
written and I've never had a single person, with one
exception, say, "I didn't say that." Even David Susskind
didn't say that. All he says was, "You schmuck, I didn't
think you'd print that!" The only guy who ever said, "I
didn't say that" was Nelson [Rockefeller] and of course,
he did say it; he absolutely said it. [In a profile of
Rockefeller in Morgan's book, *Impersonalities*, Rockefeller
was quoted as saying of a politician anxious for a
judgeship, "Never met a more sensitive man. He bled to
make you understand him, then when the blood is all
over the floor and you're slipping in it, he gets through
talking and you still don't know what he wants."]

I used a tape recorder for the first time a year ago. I
never used a tape recorder. I felt, and do feel, that it is
very inhibiting to the interviewee [Morgan did not seem
a bit inhibited by my tape recorder]; it's like being on
TV. The interviewee is inhibited by the fact that he's on

record in a way that, for some reason, he doesn't feel when you're sitting there scribbling away. Part of that, of course, is understandable because he can always say, "You got it down wrong. I didn't say, 'I lusted in my heart after that woman,' you know." "But you did, you did, Mr. Carter. I have it here in my handwritten notes. Maybe your kid spilled his milk on it and it says, 'I rusted after that woman.'" But if you've got it on tape, it's much harder to fix.

There are no really great short interviews. You have to have enough time. There are some people who have been interviewed so often that they can do it fast. John Lindsay, whom I worked for, could give an interview in five minutes; he could give eighty-seven-thousand quotes in five minutes, but there are no good short interviews.

Certainly you can't get anywhere in less than half an hour, and probably not in less than a week. Somewhere between a half-hour and a week is necessary to really get somewhere with anybody, because one of the problems of the interview is that you've got to sit and listen to this garbage for hours, sometimes before you can do anything about it. How can you stop him if he wants to talk for two hours? I'll say, "Wait a minute." Then he says, "I'm not through, kid. You asked to interview me," and goes on and on. That's very hard sometimes. At some point you've got to interrupt and go all the way back to maybe his second sentence—"That first lie you told me; let's go back to that. What do you mean by so and so?"

You have a practical situation: you have to make a living. You can't spend more than a couple of weeks when you're in my situation. Joe Mitchell had a contract with *The New Yorker;* he got paid whether he produced anything or not. I had to produce the goddamned article every three weeks or they'd take my house away from me. So that means you had a week or ten days to write an article. And what I'd do was start another interview while I was writing the article. Or start the research on another piece.

To follow a line of thought that you want to follow
sometimes takes an enormous amount of patience and
an enormous amount of skill to bring the guy back to
what you want to find out about, rather than just sitting
and listening to him go on and on. Joe Mitchell, the
father of the modern interview and the modern profile,
would take five years to do a profile, but you're talking
about a guy who was really spectacular. He would spend
months with a person, never asking a question.

You've got to be patient and still have your own focus,
because the guy will run away with you and you've got to
come back at some point and ask the questions that will
suddenly give it shape. I used to just lay there and wait
and let the guy go on, just keep asking questions that
developed the story and help him go through it, build
up his trust. Sometimes after a week, hours and hours,
and endless notes, all of a sudden he says, "I've got to
end this. I've got to go to Hollywood. We've been having
great fun. Isn't there anything you'd like to ask me?" I
say, "Can you have dinner tonight?" We have dinner; I
have two more hours and I'm never going to see this
person again. And then that's when I ask him, "How
come you lusted after your mother when you were...etc.,
etc.?" And you ask him all these terrible questions.
Sometimes you just see it on people's faces, "Oh, my
God, I've been had."

It's hard, very strenuous. You can't just sit there doing
a job. You have a desire to top everything you've ever
done every time, it seems to me. A guy the other day
was talking about the difference between success and
being good, really good at what you do. It's easy to be
successful, but to be really good almost sets a limit to
how successful you can be and how long you're going to
be successful.

One reason you finally collapse in this business of
free-lance writing for big-time magazines is that it's so
hard. I don't think there's any doubt that I became
physically ill after twelve, thirteen years of this. And my
friend, Dick Gehamen, who did it for twenty years,

finally dropped dead. It's a hard, hard life. So that's why they carry you out after fourteen or fifteen years. There aren't too many people who do it forever. I just burned out, like a bad dream. An impossible way to make a living.

Diane Sawyer

Co-Anchor, ABC's
Prime Time Live

"Interviewing is, after all, a matter of peeling back the layers of your own interest. You get to the thing that you really want to know. We know that you can dance around it forever and not have the nerve to ask what you really want to ask. And that's the kind of practice you need; practice can perfect that."

DIANE SAWYER flew the coop. For five years she was safe in her nest as one of the correspondents of CBS's *60 Minutes*. Then Roone Arledge of ABC stole her away with money and broadcasting scope, and gave her star status as co-anchor (with Sam Donaldson) of *Prime Time Live*. She may never again enjoy the safety she had at CBS.

She was not used to being vulnerable when she was under producer Don Hewitt's wing in the coop of *60 Minutes*. She was used to being written up as Miss Perfect, the Ice Princess.

Like Meryl Streep, Diane Sawyer was one of those Perfect People in whom some would like to find a flaw. The following is typical of the write-ups she would get: "By the testimony of professional colleagues and media critics, Sawyer is brilliant, magnetic, witty, gracious, charming, and loyal—and those are only half the encomiums at hand....Confronted with such apparent perfection, an interviewer itches to unearth even the tiniest of flaws."

Then she entered The Really Big Time—became the star of her own show—and things changed. *Time* did a cover story on her with the title, "Is She Worth It?" Reviews of her new show were mixed, but in general not highly enthusiastic. The headline of a *New York Times* article about the program was "A Ripple of Interest for 'Prime Time Live'." Can Sawyer withstand this new scrutiny accorded the Star, the mixed reviews, the perception of Miss Imperfect? Chances are she can. Her background and current support systems may see her through.

Diane Sawyer has been pursuing excellence (perfection?) since childhood. Born in Louisville, Kentucky, of a lawyer-county judge father and a schoolteacher mother, she admits to a "generic pressure from them to do well... excellence for its own sake....My parents were both full-tilt people....Mother took us to every lesson imaginable." Her lessons ranged from ballet, tap, piano, and voice to horseback riding and fencing. Besides all of this, she was in the shadow of her older sister, whom she saw as "lean and elegant and lovely." In public school in Louisville, she put the pressure on herself: "I was terribly extracurricular. I lived for overextension.... I edited the yearbook, did a little basketball, was a junior varsity cheerleader, joined every club, all of which I took inordinately seriously."

With all of this, she was something of a loner. As a Wellesley College scholarship student, she kept a high grade-point average, acted in college theater, sang with a college group, and was an officer of the student body. But, again, "I wasn't what you'd call popular." All of this prepared her for the schedule she chose for herself as an adult: "To maintain her trim figure and keep her energy level high, she exercises on the rowing machine in her apartment...swims and jogs at a neighborhood health club, and plays tennis on weekends." She would undoubtedly be seen by most people as "lean and elegant and lovely." She told an interviewer that she admires Henry James for his depiction of women who "are never careless about their lives."

She did not waste much time getting to the seat of power. After college she landed a job on television in her hometown, but after three years she complained of being "sort of non-specifically undernourished." There was more to it than that, however. As she later said, "I knew that I wanted to be close to the power. That meant only one place: the White House." She got a job with Richard Nixon, who was in the White House. She moved quickly from writing press releases and drafting some of Nixon's official statements to staff assistant to the man himself. For two years during the Watergate conspiracy scandal, she monitored its media coverage and picked up some wrath from journalists, whom she occasionally tried to persuade to hold back coverage damaging to her boss.

When Nixon resigned, he asked Sawyer to go with him to California. She not only went, but stayed four years. Of Nixon, the man a lot of people love to hate, she said, "Here was a man whose dreams were shattered. If I didn't come through for him at a time when he needed me, I couldn't have lived with myself." She worked with him for three years on his autobiography and then returned to Washington, where her television career began in earnest.

In 1978 she was hired by CBS as a general assignment reporter, which was objected to by some journalists, one of whom was Dan Rather. He insisted that she lacked credibility because of her political work with Nixon. Despite criticism, she was promoted to correspondent in 1980. In a little over a year, she gained real visibility when she was assigned to a morning news and entertainment program with Charles Kuralt, sharing the host position. The show began to make a dent in CBS's perennial poor morning ratings, but the increase did not last, and Sawyer was put in another job. A *CBS Morning News* old-timer said she lacked the "calm reassurance" and "nonthreatening quality" required in early-morning programs—she was "just too rational, too brilliant." However, *60 Minutes* producer Don Hewitt did not see it that way; he wanted a "strong woman reporter" and hired her for the most popular news program in television history.

In 1986, she was courted by the other two networks but she was said to be riding for the gold ring—an evening news anchor or co-anchor position. Neither Rather, Jennings, nor Brokaw would budge. She stayed where she was, among the *60 Minutes* "old tigers," as she called them.

"Life is going to pass her by if she's not careful," a CBS colleague is reported to have said in 1983. Her response at the time was, "I can't imagine anything interfering with my getting married." In April 1988, at age forty-two, she married the fifty-six-year-old, thrice-married, rich, famous, and decorated stage and film director Mike Nichols. Less than a year later, the *New York Times* announced that ABC had hired Diane Sawyer as co-anchor with Sam Donaldson of a new "live" news program with an audience, *Prime Time Live*. It was the time for gold rings to come her way.

I had interviewed many people for this book before I experienced that awful feeling of being a bit intimidated by the person I was going to talk to. I had, of course, done research on Sawyer, and somehow her apparent brightness impressed me so much that I was not my usual respectful but dispassionate self. Oddly, without my confessing to her my state of intimidation, she told me of her ruining a television interview with John Updike because she was in awe of him. Could she have sensed my intimidation? She told Updike she felt she had ruined that interview. In turn, he confessed to her that he had been intimidated by her glowing introduction of him. I reported this story to Updike's previous editor at *The New Yorker*, and he said that he had never known Updike to be intimidated by anyone. Was Updike making Diane Sawyer more at ease, as I suspected Diane Sawyer was doing with me?

Sawyer is not an easy person to read. She gives the impression of vulnerability, despite her reputation for coolness and perfection. I suspect that her apparent vulnerability, if sensed by an interviewee, can make an interview more intimate than it might otherwise be.

She came out to the waiting room at ABC to greet me, and perhaps to get some feel for me. I would guess it was her way of leading into an interview, even though this time she was the interviewee.

She has a kind of peaches-and-cream good looks. She could be the belle of your high school, the most likely to succeed, the girl who does everything well. In high school she was, in fact, just that—she won the national Junior Miss contest through her looks, her "poise in the final interview," and "her thoughtful essay comparing the music of the North and South during the Civil War."

My being a bit intimidated did not in any way hurt the interview, so far as I could tell. Perhaps she would not let it. She took a chair facing the one she offered me on the outside of her desk. We were not completely alone, though the door was closed; one wall of her office was all glass, facing her secretary and anyone else who happened by. She is easy to talk to, as all of the television people we spoke to were.

When we were finished, an incident occurred that suggested how controlled and focused she is. She tried unsuccessfully to get her door open; we were locked in. Attempting a bit of levity and hoping to elicit more warmth than I had felt, I said, "What an opportunity. Now I can discuss Trollope and some of the other Victorian writers with you. We're stuck here together." She smiled faintly, but did not laugh. She wanted out, it seemed to me, and now. She had things to do, and this interview had finished. There is no question that she is focused; perhaps that is why she accomplishes as much as she does, and why, too, she had the reputation of being the "ice princess" when she was with *60 Minutes*.

She had this to say about how she interviews:

■ I think each of us does it a little differently; you'd get a completely different portrait of a person if someone else did the interview.

We all know there's something different about different-sex interviews. It's not necessarily important, but it affects things in a slight way. I'm sure that would have been true with Admiral Rickover, for instance. I think being female had everything to do with it. I think that he was engaged in a wonderful flirt and it brought out the lively curmudgeon, whereas his conversations with men were much raspier and less illuminating. His first words to me, in the piece we used on the air, were, "It's not that I'm so smart as that everyone else is dumb, including you." That was his opening line. And I laughed, and we went on from there. So on my part it was not so much of a flirt as just a nice repartee. I don't know that you flirt back exactly with Rickover. I think it was different for him. He said to me at one point something about men in the nuclear navy getting married and that he never thought girls were very important, and then he looked over very quickly to see if he got my back up, so at that level it was a flirt.

My interview with Mrs. Aquino [the President of the

Philippines] may have been another example of a
difference made by the sex of the interviewer, because
she was talking to me as a woman, I felt. She was talking
to me as someone who could understand when she said,
"My husband just wanted to be number one." And I
think she might have hesitated a little bit to say that
frankly to a man.

We knew it wasn't going to be easy with Mrs. Aquino,
because she is very complicated. On one level she's
guileless, with wonderful simplicity, and on another level
she's very prickly about the way she's treated. Frankly,
she is notorious for not being a good interview. It was a
calculated risk for us to go out and do this. But I was
convinced that if people could hear her talk about
herself, analyze herself a little bit, it would be different.
So we decided that we had to see her before the
interview, and fortunately we got to spend some time
during the day before, which I think is critical with a
personality like that. It makes all the difference in the
world when you walk in the room for it not to be the
first hello. Before the interview, she and I sat down in
another room, so it really picked up in the middle of our
private conversation. We just walked in and sat down
and kept talking at the same pace, and they turned the
cameras on, so that a lot of the personal stuff which
came out on the air really was a direct extension of our
very private conversation, like her soliloquy on her
conjugal visits in the prison.

But again, I've interviewed Margaret Thatcher, and I
could have been male or female; it wouldn't have made
any difference.

I don't think about framing questions too much. At
this stage, I've got to trust my intuition. If I'm sitting
there worrying about reading my question and framing
it, I'm in big trouble. The question is an excavating tool.
When you get so self-conscious about your questions that
you get tangled up, you've forgotten your purpose.
You're worried what your questions say about you and
not about the information that they're going to extract.

In a couple of interviews, I've genuinely tried to

underprepare, and it's very hard for me. I'm sort of a compulsive neurotic about preparation, and I've tried deliberately to just go in and sort of say, "What's happening?" And follow it from there. And it works—sometimes—for example, in personality interviews, where you end up asking off-the-wall questions, like the "What did you dream about last night?" kind of question that you're going to gamble on.

Most good interviews revolve around "You've got to be kidding" or "Tell me what you've never told anybody before" or "Why?" Some of Mike Wallace's interviews are "You must be kidding" interviews. And I guess my Cory Aquino interview was really a "Tell me something you've never told before"—kind of a "Who are you? Give me another layer of you"—interview. And some are "Why? But really, why, really, *really* why?"

With John Updike, I guess I learned that I shouldn't interview authors a lot because they're the only category of person that makes me nervous, and he and I got so nervous in the interview, we could barely talk. I was nervous because I had just read his book in which he parodied a talk show hostess, and that's all I could think about. I think another problem with Updike was that I was overprepared. I was in awe, and I think when you're in awe it's better to underprepare and go simple, because if you overprepare you really get tangled.

Sometimes your mistakes produce interesting results. Sometimes you push harder than you intended to. Somebody blows up and you get something really interesting. They may never speak to you again, and you may burn your bridges forevermore, but you get something really insightful.

You ask about dress. I dress in a way that no one will remember what I wore. Neither too informal or too formal. I have a kind of uniform, which is a white shirt, just a button-down shirt.

Once my nephew and his friends came to visit me—they were about thirteen years old, and I put them through an exercise. I told them that I would introduce them to anybody that I could arrange for them to meet.

We saw the Vice President and all sorts of stars. I said
they had only one obligation to me: if I took them to see
these people, I wasn't going to sit there and make
conversation while they sat dumbly by and listened.
They had to make up a list of questions, based upon the
things they really wanted to know. Why did they really
want to see this person? And if they could ask the
question, no matter how shocking the question might be,
how bold the question might be, they had to go ahead
and ask it. I wouldn't take them in if they didn't ask it.
And I really think that you can do that in a kind of less
formal way yourself with anyone.

Interviewing is, after all, a matter of peeling back the
layers of your own interest. You get to the thing that you
really want to know. We know that you can dance around
it forever and not have the nerve to ask what you really
want to ask. And that's the kind of practice you'd need;
practice can perfect that.

Television interviewing is different, as we know, from
print interviewing. If I were a print interviewer, I would
go for silences hanging so heavy that the room could
barely stand it any longer. On television you don't have
that luxury. Unfortunately, the silences also have the
camera running but there is a measure of that you
employ even on television. In television interviewing,
there is a much greater premium, obviously, on the
rapidity of your reaction, your ability to create rhythms
in the interview.

I guess apart from listening, which is the common
denominator of both interviewing techniques, for
television interviewing the other single talent is an
appreciation of the rhythms of conversation—the extent
to which you push someone, pepper them for short
takes, and then pull back and relax, and then come on a
little stronger again. It's knowing when to. It's almost like
a lens of a camera. It's knowing when to move in
conversationally and when to move back out.

It's like...what's it like? There's a wonderful D. H.
Lawrence phrase about love being two stars in
counterpoise. And a perfect interview is when the

counterpoise is exact at every part. You're pushing, they're pushing back, and you ease up and they ease back. It never has an awkward moment. It really is a dance at its best.

Dick Cavett

Television Interviewer

"If you push me on stage and say, 'You're on, go; we can't even tell you what you're doing; there's an audience and here's the music,' I know I'm all right. Because I know I'm an ad-lib performer and I love that. I love the danger of it. It excites me and starts the flow."

Aｆｔｅｒ ｒｅａｄｉｎｇ Dick Cavett's two books—*Cavett* and *Eye on Cavett*—and numerous articles about him, and then interviewing him, I was mystified. Trying to solve the mystery of Dick Cavett is like trying to solve an Agatha Christie whodunit. The big question is, Who has been sabotaging his career?

Here is an immensely attractive guy who has repeatedly been near the top of the heap in television and is admired by all kinds of people, but as yet has been unable to sustain a television series despite numerous opportunities. What's going on?

Rereading my interview with him for the umpteenth time, I gradually came to a realization. Cavett speaks about interviewing in a different way, almost totally, from any of the others we spoke with for this book. The few things that other interviewers had more or less in common—the emphasis on preparation, listening, following up on answers, and curiosity—were missing.

Then it struck me: interviewing, as it is perceived by almost all the other people in this book, is not what Dick Cavett is all about. He is a stand-up comedian, an actor, a conversationalist. But asking questions and being silent, listening for the answers, are not what really interest Cavett—and never have been.

The whole story seems to be in his two autobiographies. It is difficult to know whether he understands why his career has faltered; he himself seems never to have solved the mystery. As we shall see, he is open about things he wishes were different about himself, but somehow he does not seem to relate these to his career. Nor does Christopher Porterfield, his friend and co-author of both books. His life story is that of someone who never quite fit in, who is bedazzled by fame—his own and that of others—and who has never quite settled on what he wants to do with his life.

Born in Lincoln, Nebraska, in 1936, Cavett attended public schools. In high school, he might have seen the shape of things to come.

> I was president of the student council, the perennial lead in the school play, the witty emcee at football banquets, and quite a sizable frog in the pond in which I dwelt.
> The paradox was that I still was not in the inner circle, not a member of that debonair group of "neat people" who dated and danced and who maybe, in those pre-liberated days, had some s-e-x. I could, even in those days, ad-lib from a nightclub stage like a seasoned pro, yet I felt socially awkward.

Unlike the others we interviewed, Cavett did not mention a curiosity about people, an addiction to asking questions or his being an information freak. Somewhere early on, however, he had a premonition that he would be famous, that he would "make it."

> I did have this sense of inevitability, that somehow, somewhere in the future, people would be taking my picture, recognizing me, asking for my autograph, and writing me fan mail. It was weird, because the rest of the picture was blank. I had no idea what I would be well-known for, just that I would.

Cavett felt that he was just a bit off-center "in terms of what was wanted" and that he "fit no known category." Throughout his life there were always comedy, acting, and talking (he does not mention "listening"), but he did not seem to be able to make up his mind exactly what he wanted to do in these fields.

From early on, he identified with stand-up comedians. Reflecting on Cavett's college days, Porterfield recalled that "Above all, comedy was the thing." Cavett pored over Steve Allen's study of a dozen classic comedians, *The Funny Man*.

On graduating from Yale, where he got a degree in theater, he did summer stock and then went to New York to seek acting jobs. To make ends meet, he finally took a job—copyboy for *Time* magazine—which he cleverly used to open doors for him.

He was always fascinated with show business people. At one point his college buddy (and later co-author) asked him, "What do you want to get out of meeting those people?..."What is it you're after?" Cavett replied, "I can't say exactly. I just know I want to get close to those people. Sometimes I have sort of a premonition that I'm going to meet one of them and that I'm going to be able to make him interested in me. It's sort of a tingling sense that *something is going to happen*."

His premonition was correct. Something did happen, and his career was under way.

As copyboy for *Time*, Cavett one day was able to slip a folder of his jokes into the hands of Jack Paar, the host of *The Tonight Show*, and in a very short time, Cavett was hired by NBC, where over a few years he wrote jokes for Jack Paar, Johnny Carson (who succeeded Paar), and interim hosts of the show (including such luminaries as Groucho Marx).

Urged by his friend Woody Allen, he took the leap into nightclubs as a stand-up comedian, but insists that he hated them. His growing reputation led him to guest stints on notable television programs, and finally, in 1968, he packaged his own talk show and sold it to ABC. The show won an Emmy for outstanding daytime programming, but it was canceled in less than a year, considered by some people as too highbrow.

Nevertheless, in a few months, it was returned to a summer prime-time slot, and in the fall of 1969, he was moved to Joey Bishop's late-night position, where he was in tough competition with Johnny Carson and Merv Griffin. He had an audience of 20 million viewers, and for a while his ratings were competitive with the two veteran talk show hosts. But the ratings did not stay there. Cavett's show was canceled in 1974.

He moved to CBS for an unsuccessful eighteen months and then, two years later, again had his own show, this time on public television. After four years, this too was canceled, and he returned to his first network, ABC, for a short-lived show. Since 1989 he has been hosting *The Dick Cavett Show* on CNBC, the consumer news and business channel.

His up-and-down career as talk show host was matched by his own up-and-down feelings about the job.

> It is remarkable that in all the time I worked on talk shows, and long after I began to appear on them, I never pictured myself hosting one. Talk shows were merely a means to something else. I remember once when I was writing for Carson I said to him, rather tactlessly, I now realize, "What do you go on to from this?"...I realized I had embarrassed him with the question. I guess most people would settle for the hosting of a network show, but for me it remained a stepping stone to some filmy beyond.

At the peak of his career as a talk show host, while writing his autobiography with Chris Porterfield, his co-author asked him, "Now, as a highly paid, well-known, and influential TV performer who gets propositions in the mail every week, would you say that you have the whole package?" Cavett replied,

> If I do, I haven't opened it. I suppose I have some of each [power, fame, wealth], but I am not, as a result, remarkably happier now than I was at any other time of my life. Since I've never found the roots of my ambition, I can't identify my goals with any exactness.

That was 1974. To date, the "filmy beyond" does not seem ever to have been quite clear. At one point he said, "I loved the radio acting and would have been quite happy doing it as a profession." Then: "I would really love to have been a second banana on a variety show like Carl Reiner or Howie Morris with Sid Caesar, or Harvey Korman with Carol Burnett. Constantly improvising and surprising myself and others in a variety of nationalities, ages, and characters would have been great fun. I think I am made for that kind of thing, or was."

Acting was so attractive to him that when he finished a brief Broadway appearance replacing star Tom Courtenay in *Other-*

wise Engaged in 1977, he could still say four years later that his weeks on Broadway were "among the happiest weeks of my life," and two years after that, "I wish I could find something like it again." One trouble was that in this big Broadway role, he obtained reviews that would neither get him another big role nor discourage him from trying again. Later he did a summer stint in the title role of *Charley's Aunt* and said to himself, "No, no this is what I do. The other thing [talk show host] is the act."

Perhaps Cavett himself put his finger on what stood in the way of his having a successful acting career: "I would sometimes sight-read a difficult role in a way that moved those around me, and even me. It would be enough to get me the part, but then I could never quite get it back in rehearsal or performance. Or if I could, it would only be once or twice; I could never keep it."

However, in 1988, Cavett again went to Broadway briefly as a replacement in the role of the Narrator in Stephen Sondheim's *Into the Woods.*

In contrast to someone like Roger Mudd, who is said always to be in the "interviewing mode" no matter where he is, Dick Cavett from childhood apparently always has loved conversation, "chatting," talking *with* people, not just asking questions. About his early days in school, he remembers that he was frequently braced down for "inability to control talking" or "visiting with others." Jack Paar once said, "In my opinion, Cavett is the wittiest conversationalist on the air doing the old *Tonight* format."

In 1983, problems concerning where exactly his talents lay became apparent. Fred Silverman, at the time a CBS program executive, brought Cavett to the network with an eighteen-month contract and then defected to ABC, leaving Cavett high and dry. Silverman had tried to "redefine" Cavett as a television personality, and Cavett quipped later, "It's disconcerting to be told that you could really amount to something once people figure out who you are," adding, "I must admit, though, that who and what I am, as a TV performer, are questions that have long perplexed some of the keener minds in the medium. (At last count there were six.)" During his

eighteen months at CBS, he did everything under the sun—
interviews, specials, announcements, "everything but the
weather report," he wrote.

Cavett cites a wandering mind, a lack of discipline, and an
inability to plan as characteristics which may have affected his
career. He once wrote that he was "incapable" of planning, that
his mind wanders so badly that "it can take me a month to read
a book." (He often interviewed authors.) In our interview he
spoke again and again to both of these difficulties and to his
lack of discipline.

I was given an introduction to Cavett by a previous boss of
his, WNET's Jay Iselin, and after quite a few calls to his staff,
an appointment was set up. I got there a bit early, and at the
appointed time Cavett rushed in, looking distracted. He had
on a red cotton turtleneck sweater, worn jeans, and running
shoes. He is short and thinly muscular; he looked tired. When
we began to talk, I was struck by his looking beyond me, not
directly at me. After a while, he made eye contact; I do not
think he really wanted to be interviewed but did it as a favor to
Iselin. When the interview was over, he seemed relieved and
said, "It was painless." I felt I had imposed on someone who
really was not comfortable talking about interviewing.

These were Cavett's words to me:

■ What makes a really good interview? Hmm. Wow. I
don't know. I can tell you when it's happening though,
because both of us are enjoying it in some way, the way
when a party's going well, you can tell. They both
happen with equal rarity, I think. But, mmm...there's
nothing that makes a good interview. You can be
prepared or unprepared; you can have a good guest and
it turns out to be on a bad day. I don't think anything
guarantees it.

Mmm...then it depends upon what you mean by
interview—if you're trying to get information out of
some lying politician or something, or getting
information in general. In my terms, a good interview
can be if it's funny, on the one hand, or if you can hear
a pin drop, on the other. So I don't know anything that
guarantees it.

It's good if the person can talk; that seem obvious, but you've got to be real careful of somebody you've seen or read, a performer or writer. Writers are the biggest surprise, because some of them can't speak at all. Of course, if the same muse guides their tongue as guides their pen that's different, like Truman Capote, Gore Vidal, Norman Mailer, Jacqueline Susann: of course, that's beginning to date us, isn't it?

What's the next question?

Is there a talent for interviewing? Hmm. Yeah, I think. Though...sure, there must be, but I think you could develop into a better interviewer, whereas I don't think you could go very far in the arts without being born with a great gift. I've seen newspeople who I thought were awfully bad at it after a long time. I've been interviewed by magazine people who I began to think must be using some kind of technique on me because they don't have any notion of where to go or what they want to write about. I suppose sometimes it's a technique...just where you're going to meander.

Talking about an interview for television, for my purposes, if it turns out to be entertaining in any sense of the word, I'm happy, even if it doesn't take the direction I thought it was going to.

I must have developed a technique to look like I was listening when I wasn't, because I know that often you simply can't, at first. You're too preoccupied, you're too new to the medium, and too many things compete for your attention. The timing, the stage manager's signal, "Who during this interview am I supposed to mention?" "Do I have time for three things or just two, or...?"

And you look up and the other person's lips have stopped moving and it's your turn to talk, and you haven't any idea what they were talking about...nothing. So you learn the hard way that at times all you can do is listen with one-fourth of an ear.

I never use an earpiece. The newsmen always have it in case somebody cuts in: "We're cutting away quick, because there's been an accident..." Or there are some directors, producers, who give instructions through these. How anybody can stand for this, I don't know. That glazed look that you sometimes see a newsman get. It's how I've seen myself look when I've lost track of what this person is saying. At times, I've tried to guess what he said, "I'm sorry, but I wasn't listening" will, of course, get a laugh.

I have been anguished because I thought, "When this person finishes this sentence, I've got something so much better I want to talk about. This is really going to be good. I hope I don't lose track of what he's saying." Tune back in and forget what the thing was. And I see myself sitting there and going, "Uh, uh, do you...uh...uh." I really want to keep the show going, but I get so mad that I can't think what that wonderful thing was. Pretty soon it's going to be over and they're going to be on a plane going to Paris and I can picture the laugh it would get or the comment it would get. Where did it go? This has happened to everybody I've talked to.

Ask yourself three or four times before you go on, "Do I know this person's name?" That awful thing happens when you have three people, and you say, "I'd like to thank Bob Hope, and Emily somebody, and my other guest."

I've tried to cover when I forget. Sometimes I cover successfully. Once I said, "I don't know any of these people's names." They were all well-known. I was just tired. Somebody as unmistakable as Carol Channing, or Groucho Marx, and you sit there and say to yourself, "Who are these people? How did they get here?" That will happen at the end of the second of two ninety-minute shows. I realize I have sat there and said to myself, "Odd that I've never started a question with the person's name. I haven't any idea what it is and shortly I have to thank them." Sounds obvious, but be sure you know their names.

I've saved some of those moments with the old memory technique of how to remember names, or how to remember anything—by making ludicrous associations.

Sometimes I put some stuff off-camera so that if I can't remember, I can glance over. Usually in foreign languages, or code, like a one- or two-word thing that I want to get in, so that guests can't read it. Sometimes I put up a sentence, but the guests would go over and say, "You're going to ask me about my years at the Cotton Club, I see." I hate to have guests see these and read them.

Ideally, if I were doing the show the way I would love to, I would go out with three or four things I know I want to get to and let the rest happen. I think when it works well, that's what I do.

Examples of my style? I suppose leading Bette Davis into saying how she felt comfortable with me when she didn't do many shows like this because the press is very nosy. "I'm not going to ask you anything that would embarrass you." And she said, "That's right, you're a gentleman, aren't you?" And I said, "How did you lose your virginity?" Well, the laugh went on for about…and she answered, "I'll tell you."

[Ms. Davis reports in her autobiography her recollection of the event. "With my eyes popping out of my head, and counting to ten, I said, 'When I married my first husband.' Then after a long silence, I said, 'And it was *hell* waiting.'"]

That was a somewhat notorious, famous, funny moment. Occasionally I take a chance like that. It is funny, of course, if you place it right.

I once said to Timothy Leary, "I really think you're full of crap." And I thought that was a nice moment, because he was, and the fact that the network left it in was interesting. Of course, in those days, if I'd said that about Spiro Agnew, they would have cut it out. What's going to be left in reflects the temper of the times.

The danger in the kind of thing I do is watch out that I don't play to the studio audience too much. Sometimes someone on my staff says, "Gee, I'm surprised how good the show looked. I watched it in the control room and I thought it was kind of weird. I didn't much like it, but I got home and I realized it was totally different." What

they don't realize is the atmosphere, all the psychic
energies, the distractions and the tensions at the studio.
I learned that you don't go by anybody's opinion of what
the show looked like who was there. People who watch
in the green room on TV think they would have an
idea, but they're wrong, too.

You just see it in a whole different aesthetic at home.
When I watch I think it's been reshot, because you're
less demanding, you're more relaxed, you're watching
the show in a different setting. Things that seem terribly
dull or terribly good while you were doing them are
never as bad or as good as they seemed.

Why the show looks so different at home is that you're
watching the face on the screen only. When you're in the
studio or in the green room, somebody's agent is here,
and there's tension, and people are saying, "It shouldn't
be in here." "This is going on too long." You're watching
it through sixteen distracting layers of gauze, and
interviewers I've seen at some point do what I do: go for
a laugh. But they're sorry they did, and it comes from
thinking, "Well, this audience is sitting here and they
haven't laughed for a while and it's my job to keep them
entertained." Especially if you've been a stand-up comic
as most of us have been, or some kind of performer, and
you forget that the person at home in slippers with his
feet up doesn't give a damn about the audience; he isn't
aware of them. But I'm facing them while I'm taping,
and I see somebody yawn! People at home don't see the
yawn.

I wouldn't have a clue how to teach anybody how to
do what I do, because when it works well for me, I'm
never sure why, really. It doesn't have to do with my
preparation, or at least I don't use what I prepare.
Maybe going through the preparation is helpful, even if
you abandon it. But I've had things work so well it's a
total surprise, and I had no idea why.

In some cases, it's the presence of an audience that
sparks two people. Or in other cases, the lack of an
audience makes somebody comfortable enough to talk in
a slightly different way. It would be interesting to take

somebody I had done an interview with and then give him or her amnesia and do the same show without an audience and see what the difference would be. That's a big factor: interviewing in front of an audience as opposed to when we have lunch and then get comfortable and talk. I have found that most people are better with an audience, though they think they're not going to be. Anybody, layman or performer, hears that first laugh and you see him straighten up a little. Richard Burton was one of the best series [of interviews] I've ever done. He was at first afraid to have an audience, thought it would inhibit him or something, and I kind of coerced him. The minute he heard the audience, he relaxed.

Katharine Hepburn had definitely said she didn't want one. I knew she'd be sorry, or that she'd be happy with a full audience. People began to drift in, including the band. By the time it got going, it sounded like an audience show.

I still think I prepare badly. I have no methods that I've ever come up with, partly because of that feeling of being a little spooked by preparation, and also finding that the best shows have very little to do with my preparation.

My ways of preparing are so various. The earliest mistake I made was to be overprepared, and then panicked because I had so much stuff I wasn't going to get to. Suddenly I couldn't focus on anything, like going all over the menu and you can't find anything you want. I don't think overpreparing was bad, but my way of treating it was: "My god, this is half over and I haven't even gotten over the first five of the forty-three things that seem essential!"

My wife suggested to me that I be more on top of a show by knowing precisely what I want to say at the beginning. She's right. I tend to go out and sort of feel around a bit, and I don't really have that luxury.

Maybe I should have rules for framing questions. When I watch somebody who's concise, like Ted Koppel, who doesn't waste any time and sticks to the point at all costs, I always admire that. It would be silly for me to do that, although it probably wouldn't hurt to do it more.

I think "*All* this looks interesting," so I'll decide to use all these ten things and I'll get out there and maybe three might be better than seven, and, "Oh, shit, why didn't I make the decision before?" At that point I should, if I had them [the notes] before me on the desk, I should just crumble them up and...If you push me on stage and say, "You're on, go; we can't even tell you what you're doing; there's the audience and here's the music," I know I'm all right. Because I know I'm an ad-lib performer and I love that. I love the danger of it. It excites me and starts the flow. It's like if you're pushed into the water, you swim even though you don't feel like swimming that day. The only time I know I would never be in trouble is when I'm put on stage with no preparation, and then I know I'm fine.

Apparently it *isn't* that simple for Cavett, because at the very end of the interview, he added, "So to this day I'm caught between preparation, and inspiration and no preparation. Yeah. I'm always doing a compromise."

IV

Exploring an Issue

GENERALLY, JOURNALISTS present events, issues, and people. They tell us about the removal of the Berlin Wall, they show us the facets of the abortion issue, and they give us a profile of Deng Xiaoping. How well they do what they set out to do depends to a large degree on the amount of time they have.

Time, time, time. People who present news events in newspapers and magazines, or on radio or television, are extremely limited in the amount of time they have to study their subject—and even more limited in the amount of time they have to present it. The same may be said of presenting issues and people. The individuals who interview celebrities are generally given very limited amounts of time by their subjects, and equally limited time on the air or space in a publication.

The people included in the next two sections of the book have chosen a particular kind of journalism that requires more time than almost any other kind. They devote all or part of their professional lives to in-depth explorations, and they arrange their lives so they have the time necessary. (It usually takes money to have free time, so it helps to write one bestseller after another, as Gay Talese and Studs Terkel do.)

Why is time so important? First of all, the more time an interviewer can have with a subject, the more likely it is that he or she will attain the depth sought. Equally important, time gives the interviewer the room to digest what a subject has said, think up new questions, fill in the gaps left from the previous interview. Some of the people in this book have to digest everything in a few minutes, while others have some time between interviews with the same person. Some journalists spend weeks or years with the same person. Depth is dependent upon time.

In exploring an issue in depth, an interviewer is interested in people only insofar as they give him information about the issue (in exploring minds, the person is the focus.) The problem is to get the interviewee to sit long enough to elicit the information the interviewer is after. How do these interviewers manage this?

They tell us here that confrontation is not the answer, and again Mike Wallace is the anti-model, at least to two of them. Harrison Salisbury says that for his work he is not interested in theater or courtroom drama like Wallace. Talese's approach is "not that Rambo, Mike Wallace, crack-them-in-the-jaw, *60 Minutes* approach."

These people seem to agree that the gentle approach usually works; few interviewees will sit very long (other than in a courtroom, in which they are forced to sit) to be confronted, badgered, exposed, prosecuted. Talese tries to show his "genuine interest" and his lack of intention to exploit. Terkel "works like a Chinese doctor" (he pays them for their time according to their needs). It probably does not hurt to exude the warmth that Terkel is said to show (certainly he did to us).

They are not seeking headlines. Ken Auletta believes that newspeople confront in order to create headlines—"I find that really depressing." The people who seek to understand an issue in depth are after "knowledge in areas where there has been darkness or misunderstanding," as Talese puts it.

Phil Donahue is the special case here. He pursues issues in some depth but is much more limited in time than the other people interviewed for this section. His success and the admiration he inspires from critics and his colleagues seem to be a function of talent and his having stumbled upon an answer to the time problem. To do a decent job of looking into an issue with tight time constrictions, one must quickly digest what the interviewee has said and think up new questions to fill in the gaps. What Donahue discovered was that he had in the palm of his hand an aid never before thought of: he could share his interviewing responsibilities with his studio audience.

The format he developed is, of course, widely used now on both television and radio—with various degrees of success. Oprah Winfrey, copying the format, has been very successful; Diane Sawyer and Sam Donaldson on *Prime Time Live* have had trouble with it; and Morton Downey, Jr.'s version fell by the wayside.

Donahue would be the first to admit that he discovered long ago that, given his goals to explore and the limitations of time, he did not have to do the job alone. On the other hand, the other people presented in this section have to do it alone.

Ken Auletta

Newspaper, Magazine, and Book Journalist

"Humility is the key word. One of the problems with journalists becoming stars today is that they are supposedly in the business of asking questions but wind up being asked questions.... You become comfortable with the idea that you know the answers.... Why in hell should I go interview a thirty-five-year-old who's only been in a few campaigns while I've been in fifteen or twenty?... You become a know-it-all, and I think that's the death of a journalist."

"WHAT I DO as a profession is ask questions," Ken Auletta summarizes. He once said that he likes to think he has the best of both worlds—magazine and newspaper journalism. He might have said he has had the best of four journalistic worlds—magazine, newspaper, television, and books. Auletta writes for *The New Yorker* and the *Daily News*, has co-hosted a weekly television interview program for New York's WNET, has authored five books, and in his spare time does articles for the *New York Times, Esquire,* and other publications.

"Most of my work is concerned with political and economic and governmental matters, though I do stray off and write of the media frequently and, more recently, of multinational corporations." His books are *The Streets Were Paved With Gold* (1979), about the New York City fiscal crisis; *Hard Feelings: Reporting on the Pols, the Press, the People, and the City,* a collection of essays (1981); *The Underclass* (1982), about the hard-core unemployed; *The Art of Corporate Success* (1984), about the Schlumberger multinational company; and *Greed and Glory on*

179

Wall Street: The Fall of the House of Lehman (1986), about the stockbrokerage. He made numerous references in our interview to this last book.

Throughout our talk he spoke passionately about interviewing, sometimes using sexual analogies to describe what he does. "The analogy to sex is not a bad one," he says. For example, there is "less foreplay" in deadline interviewing (as in newspaper work) than in interviews for longer pieces (for magazines or books); "It's really the difference between a one-night stand and a long-term affair."

Ken Auletta was born in Coney Island in 1942. While his mother was Jewish, he was brought up as a Roman Catholic, following his father's religion. In school he was athletic, not a student; his high school average was sixty-four. Despite this, he got a B.S. from the State University of New York, Oswego, and an M.A. from Syracuse University.

I had an introduction to him from Tom Morgan and was invited to Auletta's Upper East Side apartment in Manhattan for the interview. He is dapper, like Gay Talese, and just as Italian looking. What came through to me was warmth, empathy, passion. Speaking about himself for a book of interviews, *Growing Up Italian,* he referred to his emphasis on touch and warmth, saying, "Feeling close to people helps me as a reporter—it helps to make others feel relaxed and comfortable so they can talk to you. Whatever ability that is, I learned through osmosis." A reviewer of Auletta's *Underclass* says of his relations to the hard-core unemployed, "He sees these people as human beings, real and whole, and his empathy for even the most incorrigible of them is contagious."

With his unusually broad background, Auletta seems to be one of the lucky journalists who, having experienced it all, has found his niche. This seemed clear in the way he talked about what he does.

■ What's maddening about day-to-day newspaper coverage, for someone like me who doesn't do it, is the kind of mindless quality of the questions asked. There's a kind of pack of people shouting questions basically to create confrontation, to create news or headlines. This is one of the reasons why there's such tension between the press

and candidates for office. In the coverage of a
presidential campaign, for example, the candidate gets
bored with the same questions, but also sees that these
guys are really out to trap. It's not really an interview;
it's prosecuting and badgering. I find that really
depressing.

I was part of the pack for a short period of time
during one of the campaigns, and I found myself doing
just what everyone else does. John Glenn was there, and
I found myself appalled by the questions that were being
thrown at him. Then Glenn was suddenly standing next
to me, and what do I ask him? "When are you planning
to announce, Senator?" I didn't break out of the pack
mold; I couldn't think of anything else to ask. I was so
embarrassed that I had done that. But that's what
happens.

So guys like me have the luxury of not having to write
daily and not having to be part of all that. And when we
become part of it, we act exactly the same as the people
we're appalled by. Though I must say I could never
shout questions the way some of them do.

I'll tell you when I feel good about an interview. Mood
has something to do with it—my mood and the source's
mood. There can be days when you wake up and your
energy is not up, or your patience or tolerance is lower,
or you've got something else on your mind. Or you don't
feel good. Or you're hot. Or whatever. Things like that
could affect your performance in an interview.

I find that having time with the person is critical. Not
having ringing phones, where they're interrupting, is
critical. Probably no one else being present is critical,
though I've done interviews that were fine with someone
else present. But alone, you're more comfortable, and
the other person is more comfortable and free.

Your questions, or some of them at least, should in
some way challenge the person you're interviewing.
Particularly if you're dealing with business people who
are not used to interviews. You somehow have to
provoke them out of their shell.

The shell that the politician is in is the automatic pilot

shell. They've answered this question before, maybe fifty times before—it's a kind of reflexive response.

The shell of the business person is really a shell of fear. "I don't know you. I'm not used to this. I'm on guard. I'm not going to make a mistake. I don't have to talk to you. I'm a private businessman; I'm not one of those politicians."

So you've got to break both of those shells to have a good interview.

I find generally that successful interviews begin softly. I don't confront people. I try to make them relax, try to win their confidence, try to show them that I'm not just interested in the headline or sensationalism. I'm interested in understanding. And I don't have to be on the air tonight or file a column tomorrow; I've got time.

I'm not in the headline business, so my criteria for a good interview are different from those of the daily reporter. I'm looking for more understanding, either of the person I'm doing the profile on or the issue I'm exploring. And so the more time I have and the more I can get the person to break that shell, the better off I am.

The more experience I've gotten, the more I'm convinced that you need a little foreplay. You can't just rush into an interview and expect someone to open up to you, basically to disrobe. You really need... seduction is the wrong word, because that's more manipulative than I mean. It's really honestly seeking out information. You're trying to get the person to be honest, to talk about things in a fresh way, partly to be introspective, which is something most people are rightly concerned about doing, particularly with journalists they don't know.

There are some exceptions to that. There are times when you burrow right in with that prosecutorial question. That's more when you're on deadline pressure, because maybe they don't give you access. You can only do it at press conferences, where you have only one opportunity. So you ask your one big question, because

you're not going to get any other reflective question. But
in general I've learned to be more patient.

In any case, I find that the questions that force the
person to reflect, and maybe surprise them in the sense
that they're not used to getting asked that question, help
make a good interview.

For instance, former Mayor Koch had made a visit to
the *Daily News*. We had heard he'd been to the *Times* and
the *New York Post* for briefing on his budget, and after
he left us he was going to *Newsday*. So he had done at
least four, counting probably some other media, and he
had been asked a series of questions. I was bored with
his boredom, so I asked, "Mr. Mayor, if you didn't have a
worry about dollars, and you had one thing you could
do to enhance city service, what would that one thing
be?" What I liked about that—I don't mean to pat
myself on the back—was suddenly the mayor paused for
about four seconds to think, which you never do if
you're on automatic pilot. Clearly he kind of enjoyed
thinking about that. It was a very revealing answer he
gave: we should do more about dropouts. It was
illuminating because it told about what Koch's priorities
were, and if you followed him over the years, they
changed. He was challenged to go into uncharted
terrain. And for someone who did everything by rote
increasingly and who enjoyed, as he did, feeling free, he
probably enjoyed that question more then he did most.

This reminds me of something about Nelson
Rockefeller that's relevant. Rockefeller, then Vice
President, had granted an interview to Bob Scheer [a
journalist and correspondent for the *Los Angeles Times*]
who was doing a piece for *Esquire* or *Playboy;* I can't
remember which. Scheer was then a committed left-wing
liberal—probably identified himself as a socialist. He
was very open about his politics. And I asked Hugh
Morrow, who was Rockefeller's longtime press secretary,
why Nelson Rockefeller would grant an interview to
someone who was a committed enemy to everything he
had been associated with. Morrow says, "You know, I

went to the VP and I talked about it, and I was surprised by his answer. He said to me, 'Hugh, the Vice President's job is not exactly heavy lifting anyway, but basically in politics you get bored with the same questions all the time: "Are you going to run for President? Do you support him on that?" How many challenges do I have in my life? The challenge of being able to see whether I could take on Bob Scheer, that I could seduce him, that I could charm him, whether somehow I could shift that piece he's writing—it's a challenge like climbing a mountain.' " People look for challenges.

I feel good about an interview if I feel I've penetrated the shell, if I feel the person has opened up in some way and has been reflective, revealing.

Here's an example. Pete Peterson [a leading character in Auletta's *Greed and Glory on Wall Street* and chairman of Lehman Brothers, succeeded by Lewis Glucksman] was a very manipulative man. He wanted very much to manipulate the story [of Lehman Brothers] and my view of it. He would tend to give me long speeches and not let me get to my first questions for the first couple of hours (we would do three- to five-hour interviews each Sunday morning). And so for the first hour and a half or two I would listen to points he wanted to make, after he had repeated them three or four times, even though I had prepared questions. It was very valuable to me (*a*) for getting the information he was imparting and (*b*) for giving a sense of how he operated. I remember I waited until our twelfth, thirteenth, fourteenth session, and then asked him, "Well, Pete, what about your relation with Generoso Pope?" "Oh, you know, we went to school together; he's a good friend." And I said something like, "Did you ever do any business with him?" "What do you mean, do any business with him?" I said, "Were you ever retained by *The National Enquirer* (which Pope owns) to represent them?" He said, "I never did any work for *The National Enquirer*."

And clearly, he's now alive and fearful; I've got him on my hook and he can't shake it off. He can't dismiss me and my questions and not do another interview with me. You know, he's in too deep. And you're just letting out string and pulling it in slowly.

And finally, you know, I got him to acknowledge that yes, he had received $75,000 a year from Pope. He had said he didn't do any work for *The National Enquirer*.

I then started in the next session with, "Well... " and he would come back and say, "You know, about this question of *The National Enquirer,* you understand why I work with Pope. We were college chums and he had a retarded child and I had a retarded child, and he asked me to work closely with him because of that, and you know..." So I asked, "Did you have anything to do with whom he hired as his lawyer?" "Well, yes..." And I said, "Did you ever attend any business meetings representing *The National Enquirer?*" You see, he didn't know whether I knew of specific situations, and he was really trapped.

But, in truth, that creates some excitement for him, because his brain is now working overtime to figure out "How the heck do I get out of this?" or "How do I put the best face on?"

It's not a happy predicament for the person on the other side, but at least it's one that arouses his energy and interest. So I think in that sense it's a change from what they think of as their seduction to something entirely different, to a kind of hunt. And that, too, gets adrenalin flowing.

I've learned the importance of doing more than one interview. The Lehman book was instructive in this regard. I just thought of this: I've learned sometimes to leave my notepad, don't open it initially, don't put on your tape recorder. Just talk to people a little bit. Create a sense that you're not going to exploit them. You're not in for just a quick sexual act. The analogy to sex is not a bad one.

I'll give you a couple of concrete examples.

When I was working on *The Underclass*—which is about a group of people who are hard-core poor, ex-addicts, ex-convicts, long-term welfare recipients, street people—

I was attending a training school for seven months
with twenty-nine people. These were people, unlike
politicians and businessmen, who never met a reporter. I
was white and many of them were black or Hispanic.

At first I didn't take out my pad. I just sat and
listened and didn't talk. When you listen, it conveys a
couple of things—one, you're interested, and two, you're
not a know-it-all. It's true: you don't know it all. You're
listening because you want to learn. You're not
interrupting; you're letting them go on.

By not having my pad out initially, that created some
level of confidence. And they got to know me as Ken
rather than as Reporter. In fact, then they wanted to
talk to me more than most people I talk to. These are
anonymous people who wanted to shout their lives to the
world, so they were quite thrilled. The poor people love
to talk to the press. You could walk down the middle of
the ghetto street with a pad or a tape recorder and be
safer than if you had a tank.

The one danger that you have to overcome is that they
feel exploited oftentimes by the welfare system, by the
bureaucracy, by schools, etcetera, and by the press. They
sometimes feel stereotyped. And so, once you're there
and they see you coming back day after day, you're
clearly in for the long haul. Clearly, you're not out to
exploit them.

Time is really important in terms of not only
interviewing but whether you get the story. Take the
Lehman case. If I were writing that for *Business Week* or
Fortune or *Forbes* or any magazine on a weekly deadline,
they might have given me two to four weeks to do that
story. I would have reported a very different story than
the one I actually did, because one of the two chief
protagonists, [Lewis] Glucksman, took me five months to
crack. I would have written the story without having
talked to him, and it might have ended up more as an
authorized story as told by Pete Peterson.

If you want to do in-depth stories about things that
are hard to get to, like business, if you want to crack
that, penetrate the wall, you're going to need time.

You've got to free reporters, but there are economic
consequences to that. I mean, can you afford to have
some of your best reporters diverted for six months on
one piece? Do you want that one piece to really pierce
the wall and find out what really happened to Coca-Cola
when they made the decision to change the formula?
You can't just do it in one interview. You really gotta live
there. So time becomes critical.

I was going to profile Roy Cohn for *Esquire*. I went to
see him first. I always call people I'm going to write
about so they don't get suspicious and paranoid. I think
that's another important thing if you want someone's
cooperation. Rather than start reporting without letting
people know you're reporting. If you call their friends
without their knowing, the friends will call, "Hey, who's
this reporter who called me?"

Roy said he would cooperate. I go out and start the
story and I call and he won't return my calls. You could
do a story without the person's cooperation, but it
becomes a one-dimensional account—like Sy Hersh's
Kissinger book, a brilliant prosecutorial brief, but I
don't have a broad sense of what Henry Kissinger was
like and how interesting he is.

Anyway, Roy didn't call me back, so I called his
partner, Stanley Friedman. I said, "Stanley, for some
reason Roy Cohn is not calling me back, and would you
give him the following message: I'm going to start
writing the piece in about a half hour. Whether he talks
to me or not, I've got these unbelievable charges made
about him and I can't believe he won't want to respond
to them." Two minutes later, Roy Cohn called me and I
ended up spending a week with him.

And that's what I did with Peter Soloman [head of
investment banking at Lehman]. It's plea bargaining.
You're wearing a different hat from the nice guy. I
called Peter Soloman's secretary and I just said, "Look,
people have made these unbelievable statements about
Peter Soloman and I'd like him to have the opportunity
to respond to them and I'd also like to get his side of it."
He called back within a few minutes.

But it's true, I wasn't kidding. Look, the truth at that point was I knew letters and phone calls weren't going to do any good, talking to other partners to try to get them to talk to him wouldn't go any good.

I really had to use my atom bomb, you know. And it works. Rarely doesn't it work. Because once you're in deep, they know that you've talked to most everyone. By the time I got to Peter Soloman, I had talked to every member of the board except him. I said that to his secretary. At that point he couldn't afford to be alone; he's out on a limb alone; he's not protecting his interests. So if you've got time, you can play that out.

I remember sitting with Bob Rubin [the president of Lehman Brothers], and instead of asking about the most unpleasant things, which will arouse his suspicions and make him defensive, my first questions had to do with him: where he grew up, where he went to school, how he came to Lehman Brothers. And what you find out is that an hour and half later they're at age ten. It's deliberate in the sense that you want to relax them and it's useful to you in what you're doing. If you're writing a long thing, you really want to understand who Bob Rubin is, what makes him tick, and as you delve deeper and deeper into the story, to be able to make connections, to be able to understand. By understanding Bob Rubin's background I could understand why he and Glucksman were so close—growing up Jewish in Massachusetts, growing up Jewish in Manhattan. So it was illuminating to me, filling in the pieces of a puzzle. And there's another thing I got out of that first interview with Rubin: I also got his agreement that he would talk to Glucksman about seeing me, and that's how I cracked Glucksman. Every time you interview someone, you're trying to get him as your ally to get someone else to talk.

Some of interviewing is a matter of talent. Like preparing questions, figuring out what it is you want to ask, and somehow, as I've said, breaking the mold of the standard questions that people have been asked. You don't want to bore them, and it takes talent not to bore them. There's no reason to ask them biographical questions if the person is in *Who's Who*. It's important to think of questions in a way that is not standard, varying them when you ask them, and interspersing more gentle ones with harder ones. And the ability to listen.

Humility is the key word. One of the problems with journalists becoming stars today is that they are supposedly in the business of asking questions but wind up being asked questions. The process often happens slowly, imperceptibly, and you become comfortable with the idea that you know the answers. If I know the answers, then everyone is asking me questions, and I'm written up in gossip columns, and I hang out at Elaine's [a literary restaurant on Manhattan's Upper East Side] and people come by for my autograph; I go on book tours and appear on the Donahue show. Why in hell should I go interview a thirty-five-year-old who's only been in a few campaigns while I've been in fifteen or twenty? You lose that humility to ask questions, or to ask yourself, I wonder what the answer to that is? You become a know-it-all, and I think that's the death of a journalist. One of the reasons that journalists move on is that they lose their humility. Or they get tired, tired of asking the same questions. That's what we mean in journalism when we say, your legs go. You don't have strong legs anymore to race around.

I have the typical reporter's bias toward television. That is to say, I tend to think of television as more superficial than print. In part that stems from being exposed to a lot of television reporters who always ask those dumb questions. All those poseurs are really seeking a headline, not information.

But I did weekly interviews on WNET [the public television station in New York]—and saw something else. An interview with Louis Lefkowitz [former New York attorney general] was probably the first time I realized television could do things I couldn't do in print. Therefore, I admire that part of television. What I learned was that in television the facial expressions of the person you're interviewing in response to your questions are much more revealing than anything I could ever write.

In television you can allow someone's silences to work in a way that communicates something. For instance, when I asked Louis Lefkowitz a question and he paused and thought, I just played it out and let the camera stay on him. Let that moment pass before the screen. You're revealing something very fundamental. Here was a man who had been an assemblyman when Alfred Smith was governor; he had really served throughout this century in state government before he retired. And when he would talk about politics, his eyes would get a little misty, or he'd get a little twinkle in his eye. And you can capture that on television where you can't in print. So I learned about that power of television as a medium.

For print I use a tape recorder sometimes and notes other times. When I use a tape recorder, I'm always convinced it's not going to work. For my piece on [Laurence] Tisch of CBS, I used a tape recorder a lot. In the Lehman book, I didn't use a tape recorder at all. Peterson right from the beginning said, "I'll talk to you; no tape recorder." I took ten notebooks full of notes, and I wrote very small on both sides as fast as I could. It worried the hell out of me, but I would stop them if necessary. I was more careful in that book because I basically had a kind of mystery about what really happened. I had to interview everyone and then go back over my notes and then present them to someone else, other witnesses in the room at the time of an incident.

So I was constantly checking things. What I would do is go over my notes after each interview and figure out what I wasn't sure of and then go back to them on that. Or a word, or the meaning was unclear because I was writing so fast. I felt very good about it but it's very laborious. You probably can do no more then three interviews a day and then set time after the interviews to really review your notes and to write questions on separate sheets of paper. There is a tremendous amount of clerical work in doing it that way, but it works.

I'm a compulsive note-taker; my wife calls me a
pedant. I'm writing things down all the time. So I have
lots of questions. I go through each one in an interview,
but basically I try to go with the flow of the interview—
I've learned to relax about that a little more. If I ask a
question and he goes off on a tangent, but an interesting
tangent, I stay with that, and later ask the question I'd
planned.

Generally, I plan out an interview so certain types of
questions are grouped together. That way I'm
controlling the rhythm of the interview.

I generally try not to confront the person right at the
start, and I don't put too many negative questions in one
area—I try to space that. Let's say if I have prosecuted a
point and asked a series of questions that will make the
source uncomfortable, I'll say, "Let's talk about
something else." And they relax again. I mean, you just
can't throw fastballs all the time without the person
getting his defenses up. They clam up, and you're not
going to get them to be expansive and honest with you.
So I find it's really important to vary your pitches as an
interviewer. I think more about that now than I did five
years ago.

I've learned that people do things for very human
reasons, including making very big decisions for very
human reasons that are not 100 percent rational. As it's
crystallized in my mind, I realize that many decisions
that are made in government or business or in life are
not the result of rational planning, not necessarily the
result of scheming and conspiracy, but in fact they come
from people who act out of panic, or who wake up on
the wrong side or right side of bed that day. I think life
has some of that in it. I don't know what weight to give
it—50 percent or 10 percent—but it's there, it's a factor.
I've got to take that into account in what I do as a
profession, which is to ask questions.

I talked to Henry Kissinger. I wasn't just dealing, as
Sy Hersh would have you believe, with a manipulative,
brilliant, evil genius, but someone whose decisions were

sometimes taken out of panic or ego or fear or guesswork. If I don't take this into account, I'm robbing him of his humanity.

If I follow the consequences of that truth, I then say that it's really important that I look at the human side of the equation or I'm not going to give as good an interview. What does that mean? Look people in the eye, not appearing to be sneaky, not throwing prosecutorial questions first, coming back for more than one interview so they don't think that you're just interested in exploiting them, giving them an opportunity to respond to criticism, listen—all those "techniques" become important.

What you want to do, particularly if you've got time to do it for a book or a long magazine piece, is try and understand the whole person if you can. Understand that other people are reacting on a piece of that person. For instance, Peterson's partners, who basically disliked him, in general, were acting on that part of Pete Peterson who was very cold and furious. But obviously there was another part of Pete Peterson, father or good husband or generous man of charity, public-spirited citizen. He's all those things. You have to somehow convey all that and yet realize the limitations of what you're doing.

It seems to me you have to keep two truths in mind: that you're writing about a person, so you want to get the complexity that's there, and at the same time you're telling a story which has to narrow its focus at some point. If you're writing about Kissinger and Cambodia, for example, more of the manipulative side of Kissinger would come out, rightly, and less of the humanity. But you want to convey that the person has some of these other qualities so the portrait's not one-dimensional.

No one is a snapshot. We're all complicated people. I think it was Christopher Morley who said that truth is a liquid, not a solid; and that's about right.

Harrison Salisbury

Political and Historical Writer

"If the person I'm talking with tells me something which I
know is very sensitive to him...I let him go on and talk about
other things. If there is more to be said about that, I take it
very easy. I don't want to lose him. It's like playing a trout,
you know. There are different ways of bringing him in.... You
can't jerk too hard or your trout is going to get away from
you and you will never get the rest of the story."

AT THE SUGGESTION of John Oakes of the *New York Times*, I
wrote to Harrison Salisbury, the Pulitzer Prize–winning writer,
characterized by a *Times* critic as "the exuberantly contentious
journalist who has brought his stubbornly independent witness
to many of the major events of our times." His work has given
him access to three of the areas of the world most troubling to
Americans—the USSR, Vietnam, and China. He has taken full
advantage of his opportunities.

Salisbury's newspaper reporting and his books have brought
him mixed blessings: prizes and the withdrawal of prizes,
extravagant praise and severe criticism, denial of access to
public files, expulsion from the Soviet Union, and libel suits.

Following my letter, Mr. Salisbury called and asked me to
come for our interview to his small Upper East Side Manhattan
pied-à-terre (he has a home in the Berkshire foothills).

He offered me a seat very near him in the small living room,
and I began my questions without much explanation, feeling
he had understood from my letter the nature of our book.
From the beginning I could see Mrs. Salisbury nearby in the
open kitchen, where she seemed to be washing dishes or
preparing a meal. While I was listening intently to her husband

talking about interviewing, I became aware of her passing back
and forth from kitchen to bedroom, a few feet from us. I was
surprised to find I was self-conscious, wondering what she
thought of my questions (Was I passing muster?); I also
wondered if she was looking out for him, protecting him from
I had no idea what. (Was she going to give him a signal to get
rid of me? Did she think I was an impostor about to rob the
apartment?) I finally pulled myself together and ignored the
distraction.

Salisbury is over eighty years old, tall, thin, patrician looking, with an impressive head of white hair and a white
mustache. As I sat listening to him, I pictured him sitting in
New York's prestigious Century Club (of which he is a member)
having a scotch with another journalist, or on the porch of an
old-money, gray-shingled house on Squam Lake, New
Hampshire, like Henry Fonda in the film, *On Golden Pond.* Also
like the film character, he is saltier in his language than I
expected. For example, when I asked whom I should interview,
he suggested I call the *New York Times's* Seymour Hersh at his
Washington office where he is "every goddamn day."

He admits to being skeptical and "contrarian"; qualities that
may be compensated for by his politeness and general good-
will. In one unexpected incident in our interview, I saw all these
qualities. Near the end of our time together, I had the feeling
that despite my written explanations, Salisbury still did not
quite get the idea of our book, and I asked if he understood
what our purpose was. His reply startled me, particularly after
he had given me a rich description of his use of interviewing:
"I haven't the faintest idea; I can't imagine why anybody would
want to write a book about interviewing techniques." I again
attempted to describe the book, and for the first time during
the interview, he seemed uncomfortable, as if he realized that
he might have offended me. He promptly complimented me,
falteringly, about how "interesting," "fascinating," the idea
was.

In describing what he does, he extols the gentle approach to
interviewing and then, seemingly off guard, he admits to more
aggressive tactics. I suspect that the combination of aggressiveness and his obvious decency and good manners produces very
frank interviews.

Harrison Salisbury was born in Minneapolis, in 1908, into a family whose ancestors emigrated from England in the mid-seventeenth century. He was shy and solitary, somewhat younger than his classmates in public elementary school. He wrote from an early age, generally poetry and essays; one historical essay earned him a prize from the Minneapolis Historical Society. He started in journalism early. He edited his high school and college newspapers; during college he also worked as a reporter for the Minneapolis *Journal*.

On graduation from college in 1930, he was hired by United Press and stayed with the organization for eighteen years, working in London and Moscow. In 1949, he moved to the *New York Times*, where he remained till retirement. There he reported from the Soviet Union, other Iron Curtain countries, New York City, and North Vietnam.

Placed in the *New York Times* Moscow bureau (he *was* the bureau) during the Cold War, Salisbury got only a fraction of his pieces through the Soviet censors, and those that were allowed out were so doctored-up that he was accused by some Americans of "glorifying" the Soviets. He got heat from both sides, however; later he wrote of his experiences and the Soviets expelled him for five years. His fourteen-part series in the *Times*, "Russia Re-Viewed," later brought him the Pulitzer Prize.

The first American reporter to be allowed into North Vietnam during the war (through his untiring efforts), Salisbury wrote pieces on American destructiveness there. For this reporting, he almost received a second Pulitzer, but an unexpected thing happened. He received a Pulitzer committee vote of four to one in favor of his winning, but the advisory board refused him the prize. It denied that he was rejected for "ideological reasons," although many suspected that this was the case. In the background was the fury of the Johnson administration, which tried to discredit Salisbury; some people even questioned his patriotism. He was called a traitor. (In his 1989 memoirs, he wrote, "for a blinding moment I had become the focal point of the great agony of Vietnam.") Surprised at the hostility against him, he explained in his book, *Behind the Lines*, that he simply reported on what he had seen and heard. His response to losing the Pulitzer Prize was, "I have a little distrust for a newspaperman who gets too many bouquets. He must be missing part of the story."

As noted above, Salisbury has seen a peck of trouble in his days in journalism. Besides the ire of the Johnson administration, accusations of lack of patriotism, expulsions, and the "unwinning" of the Pulitzer, he wrote pieces on Birmingham's racial tensions which brought on a $10-million libel suit against himself and the *Times*. (He later won the case, however.)

After his retirement from the *Times*, he did some television work for PBS, and wrote a history of the *New York Times*; a book about China, *The Long March: The Untold Story*; and his memoirs, *A Time of Change: A Reporter's Tale of Our Time*. During his career, he has published more than thirty books.

"A good interview should have the character of a good novel," he told me. This is how he manages to achieve this:

■   I think the principal thing that makes a good interview is a well-prepared interviewer. The interviewer does his homework before he sits down with the person he's talking with. He knows enough about the background and the personality of this individual to be able to move the conversation along easily with a minimum of interruptions (I think interruptions are things which spoil an interview more often than not). Then the interviewee will tell his story. If the person has any gift for storytelling (people love to tell about themselves, once you get them going in the right direction), they go on and on, and you occasionally nudge them, and you come out with a first-class piece of work.

You have to be able to recognize the areas where the subject either has had a very exciting, dramatic experience, or is bound to have something very revealing to say. Very often the interviewee is scared away by an interviewer pouncing on something which is said in an easy manner because he hasn't realized perhaps how significant it was, and that really ends the interview as far as content is concerned.

I happen to believe in the easy, friendly interview. I don't much care for the Mike Wallace type of interview; I don't think it produces very much.

In my own practice, if the person I'm talking with
tells me something which I know is very sensitive to him,
but has told it perfectly openly, I don't really go back to
that. I let him go on and talk about other things. If
there is more to be said about that, I take it very easy. I
don't want to lose him. It's like playing a trout, you
know. There are different ways of hooking this fish, and
after the fish is hooked, there are different ways of
bringing him in. You have to sense the personality of
the individual and usually, I think, you can't jerk too
hard or your trout is going to get away from you and
you never will get the rest of the story.

I don't have any very brilliant opening lines. I usually
like, almost whatever the subject is, to start a long way
back: get someone talking about his childhood or his
early years and then lead him gently up to the area of
interest. You begin to build up a fabric of personality,
which is a little bit the novelistic technique. It should
reveal in depth what this person is about, and what kind
of emotions move him, and what experiences he had in
life which brought him to this particular stage.

I think in that kind of an interview, the private life
and the public personality become blended, as they
should be, because the public façade may conceal a great
deal which we really ought to know about his actual
personality.

If you want to understand the making of a very
successful general, like MacArthur, for example, you
must know what he was like before he was MacArthur.
You have to encourage him to talk about nonmilitary
matters and personal matters and what he was like when
he was growing up. Try to get away from the stereotypes
that he's apt to feed you, because he's used to dealing in
stereotypes. Getting him to do that is a very difficult
task.

To some extent, the same is true with important
diplomats or important politicians. They will tend not
necessarily to fabricate a boyhood and a personal life,
but will present you with a picture of the barefoot boy
who went through all these struggles and so forth, and

you have to know enough about the reality to match it up against the real economic and social status of the person. But you want his image of himself, you want to know if it differs from what is the real image. It's hard to get that out of the person in the course of talking, and yet it may come out.

Most people feel much more comfortable talking about their life and their personal affairs than they do about matters of great public policy. For obvious reasons, they're not going to be crucified for having had a problem in childhood, but if they make the wrong remark about the budget, maybe it will be picked up.

Nonetheless, if they're talking very freely and easily, then they may perfectly well get into areas that are wonderful and discuss them at great length without any sense of embarrassment or any sense that they're impinging on things that shouldn't be said. I want them to feel that way because that may well be the most interesting part (generally it isn't any material that has any security value). It may be politically embarrassing, but that's their business, not mine; they're adults, they're big boys, and they can take care of themselves. I don't feel any compunction to say, "Ah-ah, you said something there that maybe you shouldn't have said."

I've often noticed in watching *Meet the Press* and the President's press conferences—these big, staged things— that the reporters have a tendency to dive right in when something is said, and the first thing you know, they've driven the person way off from the declaration he's made into ground that is innocuous and banal, instead of letting the story tell itself. I would never do that myself. Some of these people, like Nixon, are quite paranoid, and for good reason. That's why I favor the easygoing approach, not pressing the subject in any way, but showing a genuine interest.

If you don't show a genuine interest in the person you're interviewing, you're not going to get the kind of empathy that you want for a good interview. I have always been able to feel empathy for whomever I might be talking to, even though I might basically not have very much in common with him or not like him at all. I try deliberately to find some bridge there that will enable the subject to feel comfortable and to talk in a fairly easy fashion.

It's impossible, however, if you're interviewing somebody like, say, Kim Il Sung, the man who runs North Korea. You cannot establish empathy with a man like that, so that the interview is bound to be flat. You can put in touches that you want, but they will be touches of observation; they won't come out of the subject. Unless, of course, he condemns himself in his own words, which he sometimes would do, not understanding what the hell he's saying. But there's not much you can do with a character like that. You can't push him into feeling comfortable with you, because he's not comfortable with you. He suffers you for some reason of his own, and he's just going to go as far as he wants to go and no further. It's a waste of time to try any type of bridge technique with him.

Most people you interview do not have that kind of built-in resistance. They may be standoffish vis-à-vis newspapermen in general; that's true of lots of people. It's true of politicians. Even though they want the attention of newspapermen, they are also very wary of them. In that case, it is possible to reduce the tensions and make it go more easily if you show a sensible and intelligent interest in the man and his policies and his life and his experiences.

The only contribution I would say I make to the interviews is in creating an atmosphere in which the subject feels comfortable and doesn't feel that he has to have his dukes up all the time because this guy's going to come at him. If he's got his dukes up, I won't get anything out of him.

I do different kinds of interviews. If I'm working on a spot story for a newspaper, I'm usually looking for specific comments or positions on ongoing affairs of some kind. In that case, it's a very factual sort of interview. I want to know their response to something that's just happened or what's going to happen in the future. These are rather dry interviews of an information nature, not too exciting.

Sometimes, for a newspaper piece or a book, I'm on a hunt for lost facts or lost information. In a complicated situation, nobody seems to know the answer to an important question, for example, of chronology, and so it is sort of a hide-and-seek game. The individual is cooperating in the interview, but his memory is not as good as it might be. So it turns into a sort of joint endeavor to reconstruct some event in the past and see if we can put it together. I can help out perhaps by feeding in lines and information which are drawn from my own research.

When I was interviewing people for my book on the *New York Times,* for example, I was putting together the complex circumstances about the publication of the Pentagon Papers. People were so busy at the time they didn't remember exactly the sequence of things. I would interview maybe half a dozen people about exactly the same thing. I let them tell the story as they remembered it. Then when I had interviewed five or six other people, my tactic was to come back and ask whether they remembered what so-and-so did. Sometimes they would and sometimes they wouldn't. And then I'd match that up with what so-and-so had told me. In that way, sometimes very interesting things would come out.

Many, many times you will find an absolute direct conflict of testimony, which is what you get in a courtroom trial. These people are perfectly sincere, but their memory is just totally opposite. You have a helluva time then.

When I was in China interviewing for *The Long March,* I talked to these old men about events which had happened fifty years ago. Again and again and again, I got diametrically opposed accounts of the same battle or the same happening. That posed a very real problem for me: which guy was right? I'd have to try to find somebody else to interview, and if the second man that I talked to was giving me a version that was totally different from the first, then I would simply test him by leading him on to other things that were well known. We knew what the actual circumstances were to test the reliability of his memory. Many people, when their memory becomes vague, will spin a story for you. They're just as apt as not to say, if you suggest something, "Oh, yes, I remember that." And you can't trust it. You simply have to do the best you can and then fly by the seat of your pants.

I know some reporters who will deliberately lay a trap for the interviewee, knowing perfectly well that he hasn't told the truth, and then wham him with that. I suppose I have, upon occasion, used that technique, but usually the subject doesn't admit anything. He gets sore and you're only demonstrating your own superior knowledge.

You get this a good deal on television, in what used to be the old Dan Rather-type interview: lead the person on and then say, "But, look here, I have this document and..." then read it back to the witness. That is show biz, not really what I call interviewing for writing purposes.

I'm interested in getting at facts and information and I don't think that those are the tactics that give them to you. I've had a couple of television shows on PBS which involved a lot of interviewing, and I use the same tactic on the air as I do in what I regard as more serious interviews—interviews for writing. That is the only kind I know, the only one I feel comfortable with, and the only one I regard as being wholly fair and productive. The others have a very strong element of courtroom procedure which is, as you know, imbued with show-biz tactics. That's why we have so many courtroom plays and courtroom scenes on television. It is theater. I'm not interested in theater.

I think good interviewing takes a lot of time and patience. You have to go at it very slowly and easily. If you're doing something major, it may take you several hours to create the atmosphere in which you have free flow back and forth to make it really work.

I would say that some of my best interviewing has

been done with politicians on campaigns when there is enough time in between the appearances in the day just to sit around talking in a very leisurely manner. Very often in those informal settings, you may get quite marvelous vignettes about people.

That was true of two very unlike people. One was Adlai Stevenson and the other was Richard Nixon, and each of them in his own way, in this kind of relaxed moment, was able to paint, quite without intention, a marvelous picture of himself and his personality. I was just lucky enough to be there.

I was thinking about Khrushchev. He was a newspaperman's delight because he was always open to interviews. He talked incessantly, and his talk was interesting. He was a mugger, he liked to be in the spotlight; he liked to talk about himself and his experiences. You just had to keep him going. All you needed was a moment when he was not otherwise occupied and when you had him at your mercy, as it were, and he would just talk and talk and talk. We would get great stories out of him just by being there, getting him going, and then steering him in directions which we thought were most interesting. He was quite easy to steer because one thing would remind him of another, and you would just push a little button, and off he'd be going onto another anecdote. Endless, endless good stories.

In terms of specific questions, I don't have any formula. My questions are always designed to guide the person into areas that I am interested in, in which I know he has interesting views, has had interesting experiences. If it's a very important interview and a complicated one (I'm thinking of the newspaper forum), I will have done my homework so far as the type of questions I want to ask. I may have written out or committed to memory a general line of how I want to proceed from points A to B to C to D. I know that occasionally you can slip in a question out of context and maybe get a really good answer just because it has come out of context. I never dismiss that possibility; but usually I try to make the sequence fairly logical because here again your subject will feel comfortable in moving from points A to B to C to D in a fairly straightforward manner; if you dart around, he may be confused.

I have used the darting-around tactic occasionally, again with Communist reporters and officials and people of that kind. I know these people are very uncomfortable with that tactic. They like to have things in a precise, orderly way, and they very often insist on written questions. If they insist, I'll give them a sheet of written questions which are in logical, serious order, but in the actual conversation I will dart from point to point to point, deliberately violating that, just because I would like to get a little spontaneity in the interview. And it usually comes through. It does make them uncomfortable; they get shifty, they look at the questions and try to get back to them, but it's very hard for them not to answer them if we're in full swing. It is a little needling tactic, but it's probably necessary.

I think that the interviewer is just an ear. He may just guide the interview a little bit. He is not a personality in the conversation. He may create an atmosphere so that the person feels free and easy in talking, but I'm not one of those who puts his own personality into the interview. I don't think it belongs there. Some interviewers say, "Well, I believe such and such," that sort of thing. That's not my style. You get it sometimes in magazines like *New York*, but I think that's a reversal of roles. It may be entertaining but it isn't what I call interviewing.

In the last few minutes of our interview, I asked Salisbury whom I should interview for the book, my usual ending. In the course of answering this question, he gave an analysis of two opposing television styles of interviewing, and then two opposing print styles.

■ I think Ted Koppel does the best interview of anybody on television, without question, and he does it because he is able to interview, even asking the sharp questions, without ever showing any sign that he is pressing, that he is antagonistic to his interviewee. He's able to keep a marvelous neutral tone in the interview, which results in magnificent results.

Whereas, you take Mike Wallace—not now, I think Mike is a great interviewer now—but in his early days he was the prosecutor, and his victims would blow up and march off the stage and all that kind of stuff. It was great drama, but it wasn't interviewing. It was show biz, really.

On the newspaper side, I think of two totally different styles of interviewing.

One is Scotty [James] Reston who's interviewed every important statesman and political figure in the world for the last thirty to forty years and is the master, in my opinion, of establishing an identity of viewpoint between himself and the person he's interviewing, regardless of whether it actually exists. From the very first move and gesture, somehow or other Reston sees the world the same as the foreign minister does, and they become two statesmen discussing a common question. Boy, that's a great trick, you know, if you can do that. And it's mainly because he feels that way, and it gives him that empathy that enables him to get them to speak very frankly in a marvelous way.

The other person is Sy [Seymour] Hersh. Sy is the ultimate prosecuting type of interviewer. Sy does his homework magnificently; he knows exactly what the people he's talking with are guilty of before he talks with them. I say guilty because usually he's talking with guilty people. He just comes at them like gangbusters. Before they know it, they're in such hot water, they've lost the game in the first minute.

It's astonishing, the contrast between these two styles. Reston establishes rapport in the first minute, and Hersh devastates his victim so that he may spill his whole story out before he knows it.

I cannot help pondering whether Salisbury has spent his interviewing life wondering which kind of interviewer he should be—the Reston kind or the Hersh kind. It appears that he has compromised with a bit of "contrarian" and a bit of "soft touch." Perhaps it is best that he never completely made up his mind; he has done very well the way he is.

Studs Terkel

Writer and Radio Interviewer

"I compare myself to a gold prospector. I hear about a certain person...and I head for him like a gold prospector heads for California. The gold prospector starts digging and I start asking questions and up comes all this ore...all these sixty pages transcribed. Now you gotta find the gold dust... so I start editing, cutting.... It's not just gold dust; it becomes a ring, a watch, a necklace, a tiara."

PRACTICING WHAT he calls "guerrilla journalism," Studs Terkel has been traveling across the country for more than twenty years with his tape recorder to get Americans to talk about themselves. These interviews have been the basis for six books: *Division Street: America* (1967), reflecting the divisiveness of America in the 1960s; *Hard Times: An Oral History of the Great Depression* (1970); *Working: People Talk About What They Do All Day and How They Feel About What They Do* (1974); *American Dreams: Lost and Found* (1980); *"The Good War": An Oral History of World War II* (1984), for which he was awarded the Pulitzer Prize in nonfiction in 1985; and *The Great Divide: Second Thoughts on the American Dream* (1988). In addition to all this, he has acted in a movie (*Eight Men Out*), has narrated a PBS documentary (*The Good Fight*), has written an autobiography (*Talking to Myself*), and hosts a nationally syndicated daily hour-long radio program of interviews, commentary, and music on Chicago's fine-arts station, WFMT. Busy man.

We wrote him cold, with no introductions, and he called back. An interview would be fine with him. I had made it clear that I would go to Chicago, but Studs Terkel, the man who travels all over America to interview people, suggested that we do it by phone. He recommended a gadget which sells for under two dollars that connects the tape recorder to the telephone, and we set a day and an hour which would not interfere with his daily radio program. I had wanted to see Terkel in person, but I said fine.

I called the radio station at the appointed time and had to wait a couple of minutes for Terkel to get from his program to the telephone. In that warm, gravelly voice of his, he apologized for keeping me waiting and we began our forty-five-minute interview. I soon caught the "air of wonder" he is said to have; you catch it in his voice. When he became particularly intense, his voice would shift to almost a whisper. He is full of enthusiasm and good feeling—no wonder people open up to him.

■ Most people I've interviewed for the books are the noncelebrities, those we call the "ordinary," which is a phrase that has no meaning, because every individual is different. We have a common denominator—we breathe, we eat, and we live in a certain society with certain values—but aside from that, every individual is different, so I look for certain kinds of people.

A friend of a friend tells me about someone who's articulate and sensitive—but ordinary people, yet in a certain way extraordinary, those are the sorts of people I look for. Not the big shot of the community, although I'd probably see him for another reason. Like in *American Dreams,* I had a chapter called "Boss." Now and then there's a celebrated name, but the name is used for a certain purpose. The name of Joan Crawford is in *American Dreams* because somebody else is there—the autograph seeker, who is the key, and to show that both their lives are based on a kind of illusion and sort of an escape from reality. Otherwise, it's the noncelebrated.

A partial list of people interviewed for Terkel's books includes designer, poet, film director, town mayor, business executive, homosexual former Marine, swimming and tennis champion, schoolteacher, surgeon, stockbroker, certified public accountant, lawyer, actor, producer, playwright, cabdriver, policeman, priest, millworker, journalist, chairman of the board of a bank, president of a baseball club, traveling folk singer, movie star, autograph collector, college professor, building developer, housewife, historian, bellhop, bodybuilder, maintenance man, farmer, grandmother, general store proprietor, prisoner, wrestling promoter, photographer, nurse, radio commentator, president of the Daughters of the American Revolution, professional auto racer, pro football player, lottery winner, senator, ghostwriter, security guard, publisher, soldier, teenager, unmarried mother, Hare Krishna member, logger. Apparently Terkel can talk to anybody, and does.

Terkel's gifts as an interviewer are widely recognized, almost universally admired. Studs Terkel "understands [that] what people need—more than sex, almost as much as food—and what they perhaps will never find, is a sympathetic ear," a *Newsweek* reporter wrote. He has "a formidable gift for evoking and recognizing articulateness in a variety of people." Terkel exhibits "an uncanny flair for engaging people in spontaneous interviews, thanks to his warmth, curiosity, and empathy."

His facility as an interviewer is, he says, partly the result of his background. He was born Louis Terkel in the Bronx in 1912, the third son of working-class parents. When he was eleven, the family moved to Chicago. Subsequently, his father, a skilled tailor, became chronically ill, so his mother helped support the family by running the Wells-Grand Hotel—a hotel for blue-collar workers, skilled mechanics, and craftsmen—on the north side of the Chicago Loop.

■ I lived in this hotel from the age of about fourteen to twenty-four—about ten years. In the lobby there were the guys, a variety of opinions—working guys, not a flophouse—a workingman's hotel back in those days. And so I was open to all kinds of talk and opinions. I imagine that the hotel was a factor in the way I talk to people—all varieties.

He attended junior college, spent two years at the University of Chicago, and three years at the University of Chicago Law School. He found law intolerable, failed his bar examination, and fell into jobs in Omaha and Washington, D.C., unrelated to his future career. After a short period, he returned to Chicago for good. In 1935, he joined the Federal Writers' Project as an actor and portrayed villains on radio soap operas such as *Ma Perkins* and *Road of Life*. It was in this period that he renamed himself "Studs," after the colorful and sagacious Studs Lonigan, the hero of James T. Farrell's novels about Chicago during the Great Depression.

During the 1940s and 1950s, Terkel's jobs were as varied as the people he interviews—radio actor, interviewer, successful stage actor, sportscaster, disc jockey, journalist, lecturer, playwright, and TV talk show host. In his first television show, *Stud's Place*, Terkel played the role of a bartender who chatted with his waitress, his house musician, and invited guests. The show was canceled in 1953—his liberalism and a resulting set-to with the House Un-American Activities Committee made his show a casualty of the witch-hunts of the period. He had been a member of a left-wing theater group and had signed petitions for "Commie" issues like rent control, ending Jim Crow, Social Security. He is apparently unendingly grateful for the blacklist; otherwise, he believes, he would have gone on to big-time television and would never have experienced the life he has made for himself—writing books and interviewing for a "little FM station playing classical music."

The blacklist could not stifle Terkel for long, and he resumed a series of highly successful radio shows, including his current *Studs Terkel Show*.

In 1966, someone at Pantheon Books had the good sense to see the book possibilities in what Terkel did and offered him a commission for his first book based on interviews, and Terkel began his series of studies of American life. His books have been enormously successful.

Interviewing is, of course, largely a matter of getting people to interview. And if anybody knows how to do it, it is Terkel. He gets many of his subjects from friends, or friends of friends—"scouts," as he calls them.

■ In a block, I might find someone whom everybody knows. They call her Florence. She may be a housewife, and yet that person is able to say something others can't, maybe because of a certain way she has of thinking or talking, yet she's part of the community. So what she is doing is articulating what others may feel but can't express or even be aware they feel at the moment.

I read about a guy in North Carolina who had been a leader of the Ku Klux Klan but now is a union leader and he travels with this black woman, you know, on civil rights matters. How did this happen? So I look him up.

Friends have offered me tips and they called others: "I know someone who knows someone who knows exactly the person you're looking for." Help has come in the form of a casual comment or a letter or an address or a phone number scrawled on a scrap of paper.

I compare myself to a gold prospector. I hear about a certain person, maybe this ex-Marine who's teaching biology—this old guy—in a university outside Birmingham, Alabama, and I head for him like a gold prospector heads for California. The gold prospector starts digging, and I start asking questions and up comes all this ore—you know, ore, dirt, everything—all these sixty pages transcribed. Now you gotta find the gold dust—sifting, or whatever the prospector does—so I start editing, cutting—ending up with eight pages out of sixty. Now you've got to find a form. Then it's not just gold dust; it becomes a ring, a watch, a necklace, a tiara.

Besides the interviews set up for him by his "scouts," Terkel seems to take any opportunity to satisfy his insatiable curiosity about people. Apparently almost everywhere he goes an interview presents itself. An encounter which for many people would offer merely a routine interchange or perhaps no communication at all is, for Terkel, an opportunity to listen to the person's story, to hear "the person's natural eloquence flowing out." In *American Dreams*, for example, he writes of different encounters: "We met accidentally at a railway station." "He had volunteered to drive me from Frankfort to eastern Kentucky...on the way back, there is time for reflection." "A casual encounter during a Los Angeles-Chicago flight; an ensuing conversation at O'Hare International Airport while he's between planes." To him, a "casual encounter" is almost a contradiction in terms.

Terkel will go almost anywhere in the country to find his subjects. For example, for one book he traveled hundreds of miles through southern California, through New England, the bluegrass country and the Carolinas, across the expressways and dirt roads from Tougaloo College to a Mississippi farm, and to a Chicago neighborhood.

How does Terkel "elicit so much grief and passion" from people, getting them to confess anything to him? Everyone asks him that. He resisted my attempts to get him to offer specific techniques or rules—"There are no rules, no rules"— and then he gave some rules.

■ Listening is the key. You might not start talking immediately—just a casual conversation—the news of the day or something. Very often you meet somebody on a train or a bus—they'll start talking to you. People want to open up; allow them. But the person has to be sure you are seriously listening. Listen not just to what he's saying. Listen for pauses, silences.

Sometimes a person may laugh at a certain moment— black people, especially. There's a laugh when this black person is recounting a bitter experience—that old idea: "laughing on the outside, crying on the inside," and that laugh is a safety valve. "I went to this tavern and they served everybody but me. 'Sorry,' they said, 'but we have no glasses,' and they laugh." It is a bitter moment. Sometimes there's a pause and the person goes on to something else. But let it go. You don't shove a mike into someone's face and say "And then what happened?" That would be like asking a mother who is carrying her dead baby out of a fire, "How did you feel?"

My advice is openness, being interested in people. I don't have any other prescription. Why did somebody do that? I may interview someone whose thoughts and ideas I find appalling, but I want to understand the person. For example, why did he join the John Birch Society? And as he is talking—he was never accepted, and suddenly he's with these people, these big shots: "I'm in the big time!" "Why don't you join the Klan?" His life has been so miserable and wretched he's got to

blame someone at times, otherwise he'd never make it.
Yeah, that's it! And that's his story. "Look at me—I'm not
nothing." It may be a horrendous outfit he joins, but he
belongs to something, has some sense of self-esteem.
And you have to respect that in anybody.

When you do an interview, it starts in an arbitrary
fashion. There's no one way to start, like "Where were
you born?" Since it doesn't begin in any one way, you
can alter the sequence in any way you want. It's not
something written in stone. It may be, "When I say
'depression' to you, what's the first image that comes to
your mind?" and they'll say, "Rotten bananas" or
something like that.

There are no rules, as I said. But casual, casual; it has
to be casual. It's having a cup of coffee—which I often
do, by the way. A cup of coffee and talk. I prefer the
word "conversation." "Interview" makes it too formal.

At the end of every interview, Terkel asks his subjects to sign
a release form.

■ You have to do that. And a token payment. It could be
$1, it could be $100. I work like a Chinese doctor;
someone poor I might give $100, $200; some I give $1,
just as a token. And they sign a release: "I hereby, in
consideration of $1 (or $50, or whatever) give Studs
Terkel the right to use part of this taped conversation
for his projected book on whatever." That's about it, and
they sign it.

Sometimes I change people's names in my books, but
more often, when they are asked, people tell me, "I wish
you'd use my real name."

Unlike some interviewers in this book who do not like the
tape recorder, Terkel is wedded to it. He believes it captures
not only the words but also the voice, and reflects what a
person is feeling.

■ Today, the tape recorder is everywhere. Once you start
the interview, it's forgotten. I goof up on tape recorders

a lot, but that's a factor in my favor. I don't do it deliberately, but sometimes I goof up on the mike. This way you don't come through as somebody from Mount Olympus; you come through as vulnerable, flawed, human. But the tape recorder—it's marvelous.

There was one woman in a housing project here years ago. She had four kids around, and we had to play the tape back because her kids wanted to hear the mother talk. She says, "I want to hear what I sound like; I've never heard myself on a tape recorder before." And I play it back and she gasps and says, "I never knew I felt that way before!"

Well, that's a remarkable moment. It's a discovery—she said something she never even dreamed she felt, let alone thought. That's a tremendous moment. That tells me something really happened—to her and to me. You get a tingle, you get excited. People are like a fountain, a reservoir.

Gay Talese

Writer

" ... interviewing isn't a con game. It is not even a game. It is a quest, at least as I see it, for the expansion of knowledge in areas where there has been darkness or misunderstanding."

Y OU WOULD NEVER THINK, on first looking at the dapper Gay Talese, that he is shy (as are Barbara Walters and Phil Donahue). His shyness, however, does not prevent him from doing almost anything to get—through interviews and firsthand observation—what he wants for his books. He engages in a kind of total immersion in his work, suggesting anything but shyness. Once obsessed, he lives with his work until it is finished.

Gay Talese's writing, based largely on interviews, has brought him fame and fortune on a grand scale. His first major work, *The Kingdom and the Power,* about the *New York Times* (where he worked for twelve years), was a best-seller for six months. *Honor Thy Father,* about a Mafia figure, sold more than 300,000 copies in the first four months of publication and brought a record (at the time) $451,000 for paperback rights. *Thy Neighbor's Wife,* about the darker sides of sexuality in America, was also a best-seller, and United Artists bid a then record-breaking $2.5 million for screen rights (but has yet to film it).

I was introduced to Gay Talese by Byron Dobell, previously an editor for *Esquire,* for which Talese has written profiles of, among others, Frank Sinatra, Joe DiMaggio, and Floyd Patterson, pieces which are "now considered classics of the genre." Dobell called Talese "one of the great reporters."

Invited to his Upper East Side Manhattan town house for

our interview, I arrived minutes early and waited across the street. At what I thought was exactly the appointed time, I rang his doorbell, then looked at my watch to discover I was one minute early. Talese's voice came over the intercom, saying he was tied up and would be down in minutes. I had no idea that my reply, "Take your time; take your time," would be specially noted by him. I had underestimated his observational powers and attention to detail, both of which help account for his writing success.

Talese is a trim, tan, nattily dressed man with a gentle manner. He ushered me through the first floor to a comfortable chair situated near his. I turned on my tape recorder and began by asking him to warn me of unquotables. He launched into a polite and long tirade about tape recorders, none of which seemed aimed at me. His replies were measured, as if, stuck with this abominable machine, he might as well choose his words as carefully as possible.

Talese was born in 1932, the son of an Italian immigrant. He had a repressed, unhappy childhood and remembers himself as a loner who failed most of the classes at his conservative parochial school. Then, when he was thirteen, he made a discovery. "I became involved with the school newspaper," he told Francis Coppola in an *Esquire Film Quarterly* interview, and realized that "you can be shy, as I was, but you can still approach strangers and ask them questions." He said of his school days:

> I wasn't a student, an athlete. I didn't have a girl. I didn't even goof off. I didn't do anything. I didn't go to the prom. I just concentrated on people. That's all I've ever been interested in. They don't give grades in my subject: curiosity.
>
> I don't know why certain people are more curious than others are. In my little town of Ocean City, New Jersey...I had a sense that the people around me appeared to be one thing and were something else. I had a natural curiosity about finding out what they were. I wanted that more incisive view of people.

At college, Talese majored in journalism at the University of Alabama, wrote for the school newspaper, and was campus correspondent for the local city newspaper. On graduation, he had his heart set on the *New York Herald-Tribune,* which, along with five other New York newspapers, rejected him. To his surprise, the august and prestigious *New York Times* hired him as a copyboy. Two years later, he was made a reporter and later was appointed chief human-interest writer. He stayed at the *Times* for ten years, and then, in 1965, he left to write books, each of which has taken years to research and write. He spent three years working on *The Kingdom and the Power,* five on *Honor Thy Father,* and eight on *Thy Neighbor's Wife.*

For *Thy Neighbor's Wife* Talese did two things which are perhaps unique in the field of interviewing. First, he not only wanted people to talk frankly about their sexual desires and experiences (Alfred Kinsey had already done this years ago), but also felt it was important to use their names. The book took eight years to complete, partially because he was not going to do it without the names. And he got them.

Talese also decided that since he wanted others to open up completely, it was only fair that he do the same. As he reveals in *Thy Neighbor's Wife,* he went whole hog.

> After reading several books on sex laws and censorship, watching many obscenity trials in courtrooms, and interviewing the editors of *Screw* and similar publications, Talese began his personal odyssey in the sex world by venturing into massage parlors and becoming a regular customer. The masseuses massaged him and then masturbated him....He visited dozens of parlors on such a regular basis that he became socially acquainted with not only the masseuses but also with the young managers and owners....They accepted his invitations to dine with him in restaurants, submitted to his interviews, and allowed the use of their names in his possible forthcoming book— and two of them finally permitted him to work in their parlors as a nonsalaried manager.

The word got around about Talese's unusual research, and, naturally, he received a lot of publicity (one article was called "An Evening With Gay Talese Nude"). Interviewers who go into the field of battle for their information risk their lives; Talese risked his marriage. On one occasion when he brought a magazine reporter home to discuss his project, Talese found a note from his wife saying that she had left and it did not say when she would return. He wrote, "That the marriage survived at all was due not only to their love but more to the fact that through the years they each had developed an insight into the labyrinth of one another's ways, a special and not-always-spoken language, a respect for one another's work, a history of shared experiences good and bad, and a recognition that they genuinely liked one another."

Talese's intensity about his work and his frequent use of personal references were dominant themes in our interview.

■ What drives me into other people's lives is always something personal within me. I get most of what I think I've learned in the years I've been alive from talking to people.

Honor Thy Father, for example, which is about a Mafia family, is not really about that to me. It's about the embarrassment felt within my Italian-American home toward the existence of these gangsters with Italian names. It was a sore point in my father's life, and I wanted to explore that somewhat forbidden subject.

Equally forbidden was the subject that followed in *Thy Neighbor's Wife.* Reared in a very rigid Irish Catholic church in a Protestant town, I, as an Italian Catholic, was a minority within a minority within a minority. As an altar boy and later as an older practicing Catholic, I was always subject to the rigidity of Catholic teaching and a form of censorship espoused by the church toward written or visual matter or even thoughts that were considered impure. This kind of censorship provided my curiosity to look into the forbidden. Who are these obscene people?

There is, even if it isn't always visible, a semblance of myself in everything that I've chosen to write about. Now, even more, subjectivity dominates my work.

As a young person, I always had a sense of myself in isolation and I would be looking at people with this inordinate amount of curiosity I think I was born with, and wonder how they see the world. I'd be seeing the world in my distant sense of being an isolated person, and the feeling that I was conveying some of me into that person as I got to know them. It was almost like a Ouija board, something of me understanding them better than they understood themselves. I got them to define or to go deeper into themselves. I became a partner in their own understanding of themselves.

I've always sat across from someone as I'm sitting across from you now, asking them what they're like, what they like and do not like, and what they are inside themselves, and what it is like to be them? It is shifting attention from one's ego and directing it toward someone else, and asking them, "What is it like to be you? Tell me about yourself."

Some individuals will say, "What right is it of yours to know about me?" If that would be the reaction, for someone like myself, I would have to convey respect to that individual and to suggest that there is a lot to be learned from that individual's sharing what it is that makes the person unique, or worthy of such respect that it should be disseminated.

One might say this is a bit of flattery, cajolery, maybe a little bit of conning. Well, maybe it is, initially, in trying to get the person to open up, but interviewing isn't a con game. It is not even a game. It is a quest, at least as I see it, for the expansion of knowledge in areas where there has been darkness or misunderstanding. So my work is usually in areas that are unexplored.

My first book, *New York: A Serendipiter's Journey*, was interviews with obscure people in the shadows of New York, the people that were overlooked, misunderstood, the supposedly unimportant people. In another book, *The Bridge*, I interviewed people who were on the high structures in the wind doing such a piece of art as the Verrazano Narrows Bridge, people that were not usually interviewed. I asked the question, "What is it like to be you?"

Or the person sent to prison for ten years for circulating an obscene picture. "What is it like to be you now? How do you interpret the circumstances in your own life in this free society that put you behind bars for selling a book to someone who wanted to read it? I mean, What is it like to be you?"

And a lot of people have never been asked, in so many words, that question from someone who has patience, who is genuinely interested.

In interviewing, curiosity is step one. I don't think you can teach that. You have it or you don't have it. And the second thing that I think is equally impossible to obtain through education or any other means is patience. You have to sit there, sometimes in an atmosphere of stress, with a reluctant or suspicious individual and be able to communicate your own genuine curiosity and interest in them as a fellow human being without any attempt to harm, inadvertently or deliberately. You have to have the patience to persevere, sometimes in the face of being turned down once or twice, or maybe if not turned down, being in the presence of a person or persons that you know have misgivings about being interviewed.

I listen with a care that, I suggest, is becoming less and less a part of the daily habits of the younger generation of interviewers, be they working for newspapers, magazines, or even people with book contracts. Developing the ear, knowing how to listen, and retaining it, and then, while hearing it, knowing that it isn't quite all that could be said on that subject, knowing that going back with more questions and more questions and more questions will achieve greater depth in that person's understanding of himself or understanding of the subject which he might be an expert in.

I believe I get people to talk to me because they sense genuine interest. I'm genuinely interested in certain people, and I believe that they are attracted and swayed by my interest. And I do not exploit their availability, so that of all the people I've interviewed over a period of more than thirty years and published many, many, many writings or magazine pieces, there is not one person that I could not call up again today and see again. Which does not mean that I've written a series of valentines. It's just that I try to be fair and open to different views and never see the person as one-dimensional. I try to capture conflict, which all of us have.

When I'm going to an interview, I wonder how I'm going to begin. I might have an idea of how to begin, because I did know quite a bit about the person before I met him. Maybe checking the files of the newspapers or the magazines. But then I feel a kind of harmony with that person's presence, and I start transferring myself into that person. This is, I believe, part of what I do. I am able to share that person's position in the room without moving from the chair I'm in. I can almost move over and be on the other side of the table.

I reminded Talese that he has been called the master of the direct question.

■   That's a flattering comment, I imagine, but the "direct question" sounds like it's a singular harpoon aimed into the nose of an animal. That's not it at all. I envelop the area; I move all over with a kind of shroud, I move softly, and I move in time in all areas, so it is more indirect. It is more getting to know a person in a way that will finally bring that person to light, into focus, not in a way that is going to bring embarrassment to the person being denuded. Rather, it's going to show the humanity in that person.

It's not that Rambo, Mike Wallace, crack-them-in-the-jaw, *60 Minutes* approach, is it? It's not that kind of district attorney or crime buster or "Knock down the door, let's get the facts, ma'am." It isn't that at all. It is gentle on the exterior, but in the interior more ambitious, wanting to get into the psyche, into the heart and soul of someone, and wanting to come back to something on paper that is going to last, is going to have some meaning after the magazines and newspapers of this month are thrown out into an eternity of obscurity.

When talking people into sitting for interviews, Talese is also gentle on the exterior, ambitious on the interior.

■   There is a kind of patience, a polite persistence, a *polite* persistence. A rashness, a brashness, or just thoughtlessness, a crude persistence will get you nowhere. I'm not saying that persistence will always meet with fulfillment. Sometimes people do not want to be written about or interviewed.

But I have not found people being aloof or unavailable to me. I have found them to be accepting of me, and I think part of that has to do with my conveying in my own manner acceptance of them before I even start talking to them.

In his book on the Mafia, *Honor Thy Father*, Talese refused to use secondary sources and went for a Mafioso directly, despite the fact that people told him a Mafioso would not talk to him. He stalked his man, Bill Bonnano, the principal figure in the book, from the time he saw Bonnano talking privately to his lawyer outside a courtroom during a recess in a trial. Talese watched him, and Bonnano caught his eye and smiled. Talese approached them and the lawyer said that Bonnano had nothing to say. Talese responded politely that of course this was an inappropriate time for an interview but that someday he would like to do a book about Bonnano. His polite stalking began: he called the lawyer's office repeatedly, wrote Bonnano letters, sent him one of Talese's books. Finally it all paid off. Bonnano agreed to see him in his lawyer's office and to have dinner with him. Next, Talese asked Bonnano and his wife to his home for dinner; then more meetings were arranged between the two men and sometimes between the two families. Talese got what he wanted—countless interviews over years. Such persistence might put even Barbara Walters to shame.

The exercise of "imagination and choreography," which Talese considers essential to his work, is not furthered, in his experience, with the use of a tape recorder, which I was using in my interview with him. Here is his "tirade" on the subject of tape recorders.

■ Well, here's what I think of the tape recorder, if you
don't mind my being candid with you. I myself do not
use a tape recorder. I know that in the profession of
interviewing these days, it is considered almost essential.
Newspapers recommend it to reporters because it
guarantees a kind of verification of verbatim statements.
It is felt that it protects newspapers against libel action,
and lawyers love it.

I do not like the tape recorder because what it elicits
from people is what we in the writing business recognize
as first-draft responses. You're getting from me, and for
the duration of this interview you will get, ˋcorrectly
stated, my words that will be verifiable in a degree that I
think is almost superficial. Because if you were to ask
me to put some paper in my typewriter and write the
first thing that came into my head in response to
something you suggested I try to describe, I would try to
type something clearly. However, on first try, the first
draft, I would not come close to saying what I want to
say, even if I'm knowledgeable about the subject. How a
thing is said, the shadings, the nuances, the subtlety, the
preciseness, does not come, at least with me, when
writing, or even when speaking on first attempt.

I think nonfiction writing in my lifetime has disinte-
grated, and part of the reason, I think, is the tape
recorder, if you don't mind my continuing to attack this
machine that records what I'm saying.

The tape recorder is a way of falsifying interviews.
Interviews in magazines, the question-and-answer type
of interview, whether it's done by the *Paris Review* or
Playboy, these interviews suggest in their question-and-
answer format a verbatim response to the question
posed. It's not true. Those interviews are really the
result of edited transcripts, sometimes even submitted to
the interviewee and rewritten, and the questions later on
are inserted. And yet there's never in these magazines
any explanation to the reader that this is the way the
interview is conducted. One might say, "Well, who cares?
Most readers do not care."

However, in my own style of interviewing, I do not use the direct quotation, except in those instances where I want to be precisely accurate and where the use of the person's words adds to the understanding of him.

I take notes in place of a recorder because I do not really want direct quotations. After I've completed an interview with a person—I might see that person thirty, forty, fifty, sixty times over as many days—I go home each night and type up what I've got. In typing, I have clarified those notes for myself, made them easier to read, and by going over them I have understood a little more thoroughly the extent of what the person has said. I remember it better. I'm also aware that there are things I wish I had asked the person.

On the following day, as I go back for the next interview, I've already reviewed things, a sort of postinterview with myself, and then I'm able to follow up more closely on the previous session because it has been absorbed by me thoroughly. The typing process is what's done it.

Our interview was coming to an end. I had requested an hour, and when my watch indicated that my hour was up, I tried to close the interview. Talese urged me to continue, and I replied, "A contract is a contract." He urged me to go on; I asked one more question, actually out of politeness. I got up to go, and then a surprising thing happened: he began to give an analysis of me as an interviewer. I realized that although he had not asked me any questions, he had been sizing me up throughout the interview and could easily give me a summary of what he had observed.

I had turned off the tape recorder, so I reached down to turn it back on, we both smiled, and he began again so that I could record these last remarks. I quote these closing words because I believe they convey what he thinks is important in interviewing, and because they appear to present a picture of himself.

■ I'll repeat this—my impression of you. You have this youthful enthusiasm, exuberance, that you communicate

over the telephone when you seek an interview. You have
this burst of enthusiasm, this sense of naïveté, this
eagerness—this almost bridegroom eagerness—in
anticipation of the great event that's going to be the
interview. You build it up, you build it up on the phone,
you generate all that kind of enthusiasm so the person
on the receiving end of this call from you is taken, as I
was, by your courtesy, and by your enthusiasm, and how
much this interview seems to mean to you. You
communicated that—that's important.

And then you arrived very promptly, you were even a
minute early, but promptly, promptly. I said, since I was
on the fourth floor, and since I do not have a push-
button system and I had to come all the way down to let
you in, I said I was on the phone but please be patient,
"I'll be down in a minute." You said, "Take your time.
Take your time." You're very courteous and deferential,
and you watch the clock. You're very attentive, you're
well-mannered. These are all important qualities to the
interview.

When the interview begins, you maintain this
enthusiasm about what you're hearing. I have no doubt
you've heard the same thing again and again and again,
but you do not let the interviewee know.

You have an eternally youthful quest for knowledge
and a sense of discovery that you convey. That's what
interviewing must be, it has to be a shared sense of
discovery—the person who's being interviewed is to be
discovered, and it's going to be shared by both people
and will be edifying to both.

Phil Donahue

Talk Show Host

"One of my bromides is 'The sooner you make your point, the more likely it is that other people will have an opportunity to do the same.' The guests and the audience must understand that this is a community event in which the clock is a tyrant."

THE EXTREMELY POPULAR syndicated television talk show *Donahue* had a lot going for it almost from the beginning. Phil Donahue discovered that in addition to having the interviewer and interviewee as the stars of a talk show, he could employ the audience and make stars of them. While widely copied today, the use of the audience as part of the show was unheard of back in 1967 when *The Phil Donahue Show* premiered.

The obvious star of the program is Donahue himself. An *Esquire* description of him when he was forty-four is still true of him today:

...his charm, the thick, silver-gray hair, the Irish good looks, the wit. He is handsome but not a knockout.... The whole is much better than the parts, but he does exude a beauty, an athletic grace...and few people around him are unaware of it. Yet all that would go for zot if every woman in every chair and each one watching at home didn't think that he was somehow vulnerable, that they could talk to this guy and he would talk back....

A *Newsweek* interviewer said of him: "He has the ability to place himself in his audience's head and ask the questions they would ask....Donahue...knows his audience, perhaps because he's basically one of them. This is a guy whose father was a

Cleveland furniture salesman and whose mother...was a shoe clerk in a Cleveland department store (who retired only after Donahue had been a star for twelve years)."

Next to Donahue, the stars of the show are the unusual guests he arranges. "He never shied from any topic or anyone," wrote the *Esquire* profilist. On the show's premiere in 1967, he had a winner—not only a controversial guest, but a controversial issue as well. The guest was Madalyn O'Hair, the atheist whose legal actions produced the United States Supreme Court ban on compulsory prayer in public schools. The calls and letters were overwhelming.

This auspicious beginning was followed over the years by the widely publicized display of an anatomically correct male doll; interviews of such people as the leaders of the American Nazi party and the Ku Klux Klan (together on the same program); and hospitalized AIDS victims. Donahue's topics have included impotence, venereal disease, faith healing, transvestism (Donahue dressed as a woman for the show), women's rights, and male-female relations—and sex, sex, sex.

He has always stressed issues rather than celebrities. Donahue thinks the viewing public is far more prepared to accept sensitive subject matter than is often assumed, and he sees television's problem as blandness, not controversy.

The third star of the show is the audience. Donahue recognized almost from the beginning—*The Phil Donahue Show,* out of Dayton, Ohio—that during the commercial breaks, the audience, largely women, were asking questions which were sometimes better than the ones he was asking. It was then that he jumped out of his chair and went into the audience for a three-way interaction among himself, the audience, and his guests, who were seated on the stage. When that happened, it was "nirvana" for him—he had his signature format, a major television innovation.

The show, which has come to be called simply *Donahue,* has been broadcasting five days a week for more than twenty years, is seen daily by an estimated nine to ten million people, mostly women, and was estimated by *Forbes* magazine in 1987 to bring Donahue a gross annual salary of $8 million. He has won at one time or another most of the awards available to him and is extravagantly praised by the press.

He has not escaped criticism, but the criticism sometimes ends in praise. For example, after faulting him for not going as deeply into subjects as does Ted Koppel (Donahue admits that if he could, he would be doing something more like Koppel's *Nightline*), for not giving some of his serious guests more time, for leaning too heavily on guests, Kathleen Fury in *TV Guide* said simply, "The man is smart. The man is a gift to television."

He has a habit of thinking about what happens to him, as if he were following the oft-quoted statement, "The unexamined life is not worth living." An interviewer for *Woman's Day* wrote, "Get him going and he talks like an earnest Catholic intellectual, a wrestler with questions of conscience and clinger to values that may not be as popular as they once were—unobstructed freedom of the press, for example, and equal rights for women."

The progress of Donahue's career may seem like one success after another. It wasn't.

Before graduating from Notre Dame, Donahue began a decade of working in and around radio and television.

■ I grew up professionally on plane crashes. I covered the West Virginia primary in 1960 between Humphrey and Kennedy, mine disasters, strikes, floods, power failures, murders. You know, when Jimmy Hoffa's coming out of the hotel room door, you don't have time to check your notes. He's walking from here to the limousine—you either get it or you don't. And that's the best way to grow up in this business, in my view. You know, you had to think on your feet. Those are the days in which I grew up, and it sure did serve me well. I didn't realize it at the time.

While he became a celebrity in Dayton with a show called *Conversation Piece*, Donahue became discouraged not only with his professional progress but with the Roman Catholic Church (he had been an altar boy), the American Dream, and his own personal life. "The money was good, the wife was beautiful, the kids were healthy, the job was prestigious, but the man was miserable. And so was his wife," he wrote in his autobiography, *My Own Story*. (He later divorced and, after some time, married actress Marlo Thomas.) He told an interviewer, "I'd like to be known as someone who's recognized his own imperfections, his own feather against the Rock of Gibraltar, and, despite his minuscule contribution, hung in there."

After seeing him perform and then meeting him, I was surprised that, like Barbara Walters, he thinks of himself as shy: "a shy, insecure, vulnerable man-child." If he is shy, a quality that did not come across to me, then he must pay a price for the charm he is widely known for. He told a *Newsday* reporter that he is happy to get home at night where he does not have to be charming.

Part of his charm is undoubtedly his "stroking" of people, a trait sometimes referred to in profiles of him. I felt stroked, too. He was solicitous of me from the beginning to the end of our interview. Right away he said, "I didn't want to go to hell and turn this interview down" (referring to the array of celebrities we had interviewed, and therefore complimenting me on how well we were doing). Later he suggested that I had known about the importance of interviewing long before he had, and ended (without my solicitation) by trying to figure out which people he could introduce me to whose names would enhance interest in this book.

In our interview, he was self-analytical, intellectual, philosophical, interested in broad issues of conscience and morality. In addition, he focused an unusual amount of attention on the people involved in his program—his guests, his audience, and his largely female staff.

■   I spent a lot of time in this business without knowing what I did. They asked me to hand out awards to singers, ventriloquists, for set design, reporting, investigative reporting, on-the-scene reporting. I gave awards to actors on Broadway and on the screen. There was never an award for interviewing, and there still isn't today. So I never really thought about it.

I was into my thirties before I thought about it necessarily as a discipline to study. That's why I'm so impressed with your...you say forty-one years you've been interviewing....obviously you identified this thing long before I did.

I started getting some attention for being an interviewer, and then I started thinking about it. "I'm an interviewer!" Someone may say, "How do you do that? How do you get to be an interviewer?" Well, there's no interviewing school, there's no certificate, there's no award for it. For an hour a day for more than twenty years, I have been serving as a host for what we call a talk show, and the tool that I use while presiding over this program is the interview.

I'm sure there are some obvious things that you've heard as you've made your way through this scholarship. I think first of all you've really got to have a heartfelt curiosity about the issues that you're exploring (if you really care, I think it will show), to have some sense of who the interviewee is, and to have some notion about how important this is to the audience or the general public.

I think you have to be comfortable and secure while lots of people are watching you—especially on live television—in knowing that all the experience that you've brought to this will serve you well without notes when the guests stop talking. I think that if I ask you a question and you respond, it's very important for me to be secure enough not to be concerned about my next question. Once I start looking ahead, I'm going to miss what's being said. The more notes you have on your sleeve, the more your head is going to be on your sleeve. You have to be comfortable with what's just been said, give yourself permission to take a beat and process it, and then respond either by asking for more clarification or allowing the information that's just been shared to provide another question. If you're not comfortable doing that, your temptation will be to worry about the next question while you're in the middle of the answer. I've seen it a thousand times on interviews.

You can see in the interviewer's face whether or not she's dropping out. It's a very disconcerting place for an interviewee to be. On more than one occasion interviewers have asked me questions, and I've started as best I could to cooperate with them. And I can see the curtain drop when I start to speak. It's certainly not with malice, but it's an unintended back-of-the-hand from an interviewer who feels he has launched this vessel and it will carry on its proper course at least for a while, until he can think of another question.

An interview, in order to have a soul, has to have some time to breathe. You can't interview Henry Kissinger in six minutes, and I think it's cruel to put an interviewer in a situation where he has to talk to some world figure on a satellite for six minutes. I can't say the rosary in six minutes.

The interviewer must have an opportunity to chase down answers and demand specificity and cut through a guest who, for example, may be asking a question without taking responsibility for it. There's a lot of that. I find myself in my own show chasing down irresponsible commentary. "What do you mean? Why don't you tell us what you mean?" The person says, "Doesn't the Bible tell us we're supposed to increase and multiply?" I say, "What do you think?" "I think it does and I think homosexuality is a sin." "Thank you; now I get you." It is the interviewer's responsibility to do what he can to give the guest the maximum opportunity to say what he means.

Sometimes I think we have to risk appearing to be impolite in order to insure that the guests don't take you around the world in their answers, and I think this is especially true of public figures who have a responsibility to speak clearly about their own positions on issues that concern their constituents.

I don't think you're born to do this. I think you obviously have to have a certain amount of curiosity and ambition and intellectual energy going into this thing, but I think that ability is something that is slowly nourished over the many assignments where you're on the scene of a bank robbery and talking to the FBI, trying to get it down right because the news is in an hour and you've got film which has to be processed.

That's the beauty of this system. We don't have to have a degree; we don't have to have a certificate. A lot of people think it helps, and I'm not going to argue with them. But the point is there is no law. That's the wisdom of our whole First Amendment approach to information, that you don't want to require anybody to pass a test to do this, because what you want is as many people as possible reporting the news. The more people you have reporting the news, the more likely it is that somewhere in the collective middle of this vast crowd of variously talented people will be found the truth. And will also be found issues and answers which are necessary for the citizen to make an informed contribution to the democracy.

The larger the companies, the less likely they are to cover all the news. We still have some very good work under way. Journalism has not yet lost its soul, but in my view it has lost a large piece of it.

Anti-media juries, increased litigation, and the impossibility for two papers to survive in some of the largest cities in this country, including my own hometown of Cleveland, should make us all wonder what is not being reported. How do you prove what's not covered? Should Gannett own ninety-six papers or whatever? Journalism today, interviewing today, is at risk, because the fewer media companies there are and the larger they are, the more insecure are the jobs of those who work for these media companies—ask somebody who works for CBS. The larger the company, the more likely it is that your journalistic community will engage in a kind of consensus boosterism: find out what the establishment wants. We have politicians doing that—spending major dollars on media advisers who poll the people to find out what they think and then the candidate tells them what they want to hear. And newspapers are doing the same thing.

As we have seen earlier in this book, interviewers can differ markedly in the amount of leeway they allow themselves to openly express their own views. Interviewer opinions can be expressed in everything from "You don't really mean that, do you?" to "You Fascist bastard." Donahue does not express his views as openly as Oriana Fallaci (perhaps no other interviewer does), but no one watching Donahue in, for example, a program about women will doubt that he is pro-women's rights.

■ There's so much that goes into this show, as in every human pursuit. You can't have a successful human enterprise without it being fueled by ego. The problem, of course, is managing it. And I think that the interviewer is in special need of ego management. But I don't think that it's absolutely necessary to work overtime to present yourself as a mechanical man, walking down the center of every street, never revealing how you feel. I would argue that the humanity of the interviewer might be appropriately expressed in interviews.

But we have a press in this country which is desperately interested, and not surprisingly, in presenting a balanced view, and in the process I think we may be using balance to explain the lack of passion.

But we should be careful here. I'm not suggesting that it's necessarily good for all journalists to be advocacy journalists, but I do not think it would hurt if we relaxed a little bit and occasionally allowed our souls to show up on our sleeves. Having said that, I also think it's very important to try not to use the interview to advance our own political views.

Our job is more often to feature unpopular people with unpopular ideas, and yet we are trapped in a business, especially the electronic people, who are rewarded for being liked.

Today you can't have a real, a respectable, party in Washington unless you have a journalist. So that journalists, instead of covering bandwagons, find themselves invited to ride on them. This is especially true in Washington, a city preoccupied with who's in, who's out, who's in trouble, with the rise and fall of the careers of powerful people. Some of the old guys with pencils behind their ears would be surprised to know that you can't be a journalist in Washington now unless you own your own tuxedo.

You can't cover Henry Kissinger and have dinner with him. I can't go to your house, meet your wife, talk to the kids, comment on the apple pie, retire to the parlor for cigars, and then come home and wring the edge of my journalistic talent to critically review your job performance as a public servant. You can't do it.

You know, one of the first perks when I was a reporter, interviewer, was that we got to know a lot of cops. We sat in the newsroom all day long with the police radio. "One X, P, I, 10, 4, Roger." "Two X." And then when we went down to the cop shop, as we called it, we went to lunch with the cops—Burger King and two Cokes, and usually we bought. We could turn that in as an expense. With how much enthusiasm could we record a police scandal? With how much enthusiasm would we chase it? With how much energy would we deal with the tedium of covering it, especially when we knew that these were our friends and maybe there wasn't a story there anyway? That's the first example of, I think, the danger of the press being co-opted. Walter Lippmann, you know, was the friend of Presidents, and I'm sure he had his cigars at the White House, maybe even on the balcony overlooking the rose garden.

I don't think that a journalist has to live in the basement or in a vacuum, but I do think we have a responsibility to wonder if we haven't become part of the beat rather than observers of the beat.

The temptation to talk too much—when you have your name on the program and a mike on your tie and two-hundred-fifty people who have waited thirteen months for tickets in the audience—is occasionally overwhelming. This natural human condition is, I think, humorously manifest at a social gathering. The next time you're at a cocktail party, pass a microphone around and watch what happens, especially after a little white wine. It alters consciousness, and it alters behavior.

I had Woodward and Bernstein [the journalists

credited with exposing the Watergate scandal] on my program, and I was just fascinated with their work. I always wanted to be a White House correspondent for a network news program, and that never happened. I suppose I'm a little jealous of those in that position, like the big shots who write for the big papers, including the *Washington Post*.

In advance of the arrival of Woodward and Bernstein, I hung calendars on the stage showing the sequence of the major events. I was convinced that the public at large didn't really get the sequence of what happened. So, borrowing from their book, I was just going to take a moment and point out what led to the resignation of Nixon before I introduced Woodward and Bernstein. So I started right at the top of the show, this magnificent visual, so everybody could see: "What did he know? When did he know it?" And by the time I got through, you weren't sure whether Watergate happened in the United States of America or even in this century. I was so overwhelmed with this mission of explaining it, and apparently so overdeveloped in my own opinion of my ability, without notes, to express it, and I was so keenly in admiration of the work of my guests, that I squeezed too hard. And I looked pretty foolish out there.

So by the time Woodward and Bernstein got on, the audience was much more confused than if I had just relaxed and tried not to be so wonderful and come right out with the first question for them and given them the ball.

I find that's true of guests as well. Guests who take you around the world are guests who are not too sure where they stand on a position. It's much easier to write long than short. Writers will tell you that. The good folks, the talented people, come right in at you, crisply, with a grace note here and there. I don't think that journalism has to be flat and bland, but I do think it has to not waste the reader's time. And I feel the same way about the answer—and the question—in an interview on television.

Some of the best answers to questions have come from people who have offered them by interrupting me, you know, when it's clear he or she knows where I'm going. I like that kind of simpatico.

The opportunity of falling on your face is ever present, and in my years on the air I've done that. The idea is to try to limit that from happening to a manageable number of times. It should be said that I don't do this alone.

I think a good interviewer is an available sponge who can accept information from those whose job or responsibility is to keep the interviewer alert and informed. And it's good to have somebody watching from afar; they're more likely to have an objective view of what's happening. During a commercial break, they can make you change course or remind you of something that you've forgotten. Or if you come to my show you would see that in the five commercial breaks that we have for the hour-long program, each of which is two minutes in length, they are almost always used by the producer of the program to come out and put ideas in my ear. And I'm grateful for that. They can't do it when I'm on the air because it's a bit of a loss of dignity for me, but they can certainly do it off the air and I encourage them to do so. I'm not comfortable with a teleprompter, never had to use one in my career, thank goodness.

You know, I bring varying degrees of enthusiasm to work; I don't come to work whistling every day. I am less excited about some topics than others, but when the lights go on I throw myself on the sword.

I get to work between 7:00 and 7:30 and I, of course, commit myself to the program that night. If it's more complicated, I work on it the day before. Obviously I'm involved in the planning of the program.

It's hard to imagine after more than four-thousand shows that there's any subject we haven't discussed, and so we have a base, you know. We know a little about a lot of things. I suppose you could say for that reason that we're dangerous. We've built on that experience. I bring the experience of those four-thousand hours with me every time I go in to do the program. The producers write notes for me. I often have thoughts as I read this magnificent research that they have done, that some of what they're writing could be published, truly. They know their job is to try to make me as smart as they can. It enhances the chances of the success of their program: "This is my program"—a possessive feeling.

We have a very real dependence on each other. I can't be as good if their research is only partly done. And if I'm not conscientious and don't review all of the material that they have provided for me, then I can take what should have been a great show and make it only good, because I didn't thoroughly rehearse myself on the material. I do find that there's nothing better for retention and comprehension than to be facing an audience—250 living, breathing people in the studio and another several million at home. That is apt to get my attention.

Thanks to a little anxiety and fear on my part, making sure that I am ready, and a lot of hard work by the creative people in the office here, we've been able to stay for over twenty years.

"Why does it work?" Donahue was asked by a *TV Guide* interviewer. "Well, I've got no desk and no couch and no bandleader. I don't have funny gags and a sidekick to laugh at all my jokes. It's the audience that makes it work. I'm not mock humble. I think I'm the best guy in the business with an audience."

Donahue is not shy or "mock humble" with his studio audience either. Just before he goes on the air, he shouts to them, "Help me out! Make me look good!"

Donahue emphasizes the briefing of his interviewees much more than any other interviewer we spoke with. He does, after all, have two sets of guests—interviewees on stage and the studio audience. The complexity of the show is staggering. A world-class juggling act.

■ One of the important responsibilities, I think, of an interviewer is to do whatever he can to at least reduce the anxiety of the interviewee, the person on stage. We have a responsibility to meet and make a nonpatronizing effort to familiarize the interviewee with who we are. However, I do not think it's in our best interests to sit around and talk for a half hour before we go on. The energy goes out of the balloon if you do that.

I also think it's important to at least shake hands. I think I have an obligation to tell you how glad we are that you're here, to look as sincere as I can when I say, "Welcome." To say positive things like, "You're going to love the show," which is something I mean. "The chances of your being happy about having been on the program are very high. But it is nerve-racking; you're alone, you're up there against 250 people." "When am I going to talk?" "We beg you not to talk too much. I remind you that you do not have to have my permission to speak. This is not a law and order program. I ask you to remember that I have a divided loyalty. I have a responsibility to you, but I also have a responsibility to the audience—they fought the traffic, the weather, the subway; they're here. The better shows are the ones where a community develops between us and them. So I don't have one guest today; I have potentially 251 guests. Please remember that as we make our way onto the stage."

If I don't say this, many guests come here full of passion about their own book or their own subject or whatever might be the reason we ask them to appear in the first place. If you just bring the guests out there, they will orate, not in an egomaniacal way, but as a natural response to their own hard work and feelings on the issue that we happen to be discussing that day.

We have a very demanding and fickle audience, which is accustomed to seeing a man give $10,000 to a woman dressed like a chicken salad sandwich, especially on daytime TV. So since we believe it doesn't do any good to talk when nobody's listening, we do remind the guests that they are part of an exercise in democracy here, and that they're going to be frustrated. They're not going to have as much time to say all the things they'd like to. "I'm telling you that now, so you won't be ambushed out there. The biggest trap door is that the program will be over like that." [He snaps his fingers.] I say that to everybody, and every time I come to them and say the program is over, they say, "What?" I've seen countless interviews where the guest was not conscientiously briefed, and in the middle of his first thought, the interviewer is saying something like, "Thank you, and now back to..." And that's really unfair.

I spend a lot of time with my own audience during the commercial breaks, schmoozing, chatting, touching, joking, teasing, in an attempt to create as natural an environment as I can.

This is a very, very unnatural environment. There are several cameras, all with a kind of invasive look about them, the lights are somewhat like an operating room, and you've got a guy running around with a black instrument in his hand thrusting it in your face. This is not an environment which promotes the expression of heartfelt feelings. In many cases, it promotes posturing, and that's what will kill you. You want to save people, some people, from their own pompous selves. At the same time, you don't want to be the moral arbiter of all things good and wonderful.

There's a certain amount of managerial responsibility that goes with this. One of my bromides is "The sooner you make your point, the more likely it is that other people will have an opportunity to do the same." The guest and the audience must understand that this is a community event in which the clock is a tyrant. This is not the high school gymnasium where you can talk all night about drugs, rock 'n' roll, or sex education.

It's made worse by the frustration of being interrupted five times by commercials, and we also take phone calls. This is a very, very, very busy show. You have to share that with the guest without scaring him:

"I want to make it clear that you do not have to

perform on my show. It's very unfair of me to ask you to perform. It's not your job; you're not a performer." But I'll gently say, "If it's comfortable for you, consistent with your personality, energy doesn't hurt us. If you look like you care, they'll care. But be yourself; don't be who you're not. Please don't talk faster than you normally would; be comfortable in the knowledge that in this platform we can only get to a couple of layers. Let's raise the curtain up; let's get some argument here."

That's where our ego gratification is: knowing that we can start an all-night argument at home.

V

Exploring a Mind

INTERVIEWERS WHO LIKE to spend a long time on one topic or issue, sometimes also spend a long time—often years— interviewing and observing one person. Gay Talese, for example, has spent his free-lance career in investigating—often for years—one topic at a time (as when he focused on sexuality for *Thy Neighbor's Wife*). He then found an interesting Mafioso and interviewed him and anyone he could find who knew him for *Honor Thy Father*—an exploration of one man's mind and life, an effort which took Talese years.

Susan Sheehan of *The New Yorker* spends years with only one person before she writes about him or her. On television, Bill Moyers has spent his career exploring both topics and minds, and has been successful at both.

The minds these interviewers have explored run the gamut from Joseph Campbell (whose television interviews with Bill Moyers on religion have reached almost classic status, in print selling thousands of copies) to a schizophrenic woman, as she goes in and out of a mental hospital. (Sheehan's book, comprised of her *New Yorker* articles, won the Pulitzer Prize.) Sheehan likes to investigate for years "people who haven't been written about.... They will give you more time and have more interest in talking because they've never had a chance to talk before." Moyers typically will choose a person who "*wants* to talk, *wants* to share his ideas."

Like Talese, whose basic question is, "What's it like to be you?" Bill Moyers thinks "the most interesting question in the world ... is 'What makes a life?'"

He likes to interview the individual who has something of value to say "but usually does not have the time on television to say it." Moyers gives the subject time and provides questions, patience, and attention to reveal his mind to the viewing public.

In general, these interviewers seem to possess the curiosity many of the individuals in this book talk about—the difference is, their curiosity about one person is intense. In addition, their patience is extraordinary. These are not people whose attention, curiosity, and patience last for only a few questions. These qualities persist.

Susan Sheehan

Staff Writer, The New Yorker

"I think you've got to find the patience to find a way to get the hard questions asked and answered, or just to be present. There's a lot of interviewing where I'm just there and not asking a thing."

SUSAN SHEEHAN, a woman raised in the upper middle class on the Upper East Side of Manhattan, has spent years listening to the life stories of a mother on welfare, a frequently imprisoned robber, a mental patient, and an aged woman on Medicaid.

Sheehan was hired at the age of twenty-five as a staff writer at *The New Yorker* magazine (about as prestigious an inner-circle a print journalism job as you can get), and she has remained there. She says of herself, "I like to be off by myself and write about people who haven't been written about. They will give you more time and have more interest in talking because they've never had a chance to talk before. They have the kind of information that I'm interested in learning."

Four of her books (all are based on interviews) center on people lost in the cracks of humanity; another is a collection of sketches of Vietnamese people; and still another is a biography of famed publisher Alfred A. Knopf. She has also written long *New Yorker* profiles of Ethel Kennedy and Jacqueline Onassis. Her work is highly praised and she has won numerous journalism awards, including the Pulitzer Prize (for her book on an often-hospitalized schizophrenic woman, *Is There No Place for Me?*).

She was born in Vienna, Austria, in 1937, came to the United States four years later, and was naturalized at age nine. Her life, at least on the surface, seems to have been charmed. She graduated at twenty-one from Wellesley College with a Phi Beta Kappa key and a Durant Scholarship. For the next two years she worked in journalism as an editorial researcher (for *Esquire-Coronet* magazines), did free-lance writing for two years, and then began her work at *The New Yorker*. As if that were not enough to turn aspiring women writers green with envy (the way aspiring actresses respond to Meryl Streep), at twenty-seven, she married Harvard-educated *New York Times* reporter Neil Sheehan (who later also won a Pulitzer Prize).

I did not realize that interviewing Susan Sheehan without an introduction from our common friend, Tom Morgan, would have been impossible. As Ms. Sheehan and I sat down, she said, "If you write to me and say, 'Tom Morgan suggests that I see you,' I have to do it, although I don't give interviews. I don't really care about being interviewed; I like being the one who interviews. I don't like talking about myself."

While her work is sometimes criticized as being cool (a *New York Times* critic said of *A Welfare Mother*, "...laughter, tears, and emotion were missing"), she was open and warm in our interview:

■   In a good interview, I get what I want to know to the best of the person's ability to tell it. That takes a lot of time. You try to go directly to it, and if that doesn't work, you try indirection, and then you try to get back to direction. You just pursue.

The kind of work I do is not daily journalism; it's not monthly journalism; it's every-other-year journalism. So you have to know the most important thing they have to give, and they're not going to volunteer it in the first interview, or in the tenth interview—maybe in the fortieth interview.

I place no value on daily journalism. I'd be too frustrated. In that work you have to say, "The President said today..." and write what he said. You can't say, "The President was lying." In the kind of interviewing I do, you can make people tell the truth. If they're lying, you can say they're not telling the truth. You can find out what the truth is, which is what matters to me in

journalism, not just getting a comment on a current
disaster, a current crisis. I would not be suited to flit
from story to breaking story, working in herds or packs.
I don't really care what the President says in a press
conference. You don't find out the truth about that until
years later.

I just find the person I need. For example, I go to a
prison and I need a certain kind of prisoner who's
representative of something. I go to a prison to write
about the prison. I don't pick a first-time offender, I
don't pick the guy who killed his mother-in-law. I really
look for the career robber who's guilty, because that's not
at issue. I start talking; they never know how long it's
going to take, and I don't myself. But I know I'm going
to be there a long, long time. Gradually, I become
friends with my subjects. There's no hostility because I
spend enough time with them, even if I don't approve of
them. I don't approve of robbery. The robber I've
written about has been back to prison several times since
I've written about him, but he writes letters from all the
prisons. I stay in touch with all my subjects, including
the schizophrenic patient.

So it becomes not anything formal, not like I was
interviewing the president of IBM or Coca-Cola, where
you keep it very stiff and formal. With those people, you
have all the PR staff there fighting you and keeping you
out, because he's not going to tell you anything that's
going to be truthful. There are too many secrets. The
history of corporations has shown that sooner or later
the scandal is going to emerge, but you're not going to
get that from interviewing. But you can get ordinary
people of a certain kind, whose lives to me are more
interesting than executives', to give you the time and to
tell you the truth.

How do I find them? You'd almost have to separate
the books I've done. The welfare mother was the hardest
to find, because how are you going to get her to trust
you? She'll probably be cheating on welfare in one way
or another. It was horrendous. It took me more than
three months to find a subject. At the prison I was quite

lucky; they knew some career robbers who didn't mind
being written about and weren't Mafia connected (and
therefore would never talk), and who weren't hostile.
That was not too hard, and there I just made sure he
was representative and talkative enough.

For the schizophrenic I chose, I had to work through
the bureaucracy. You've got to protect mental patients
from themselves and you've also got to stay alive, so you
can't pick one who's too dangerous, who's too paranoid,
and who could injure you. You really do have to choose
carefully. You need someone who's articulate, not
someone very self-contained. And what happened there
was that I asked the state for a representative mental
institution. I don't use the word "typical," but
Creedmore was representative—not the best, not the
worst. As far as I'm concerned, it probably can't be
much worse than that, but as far as I know, it hadn't
been singled out for being the worst.

And then you try to look for a representative subject.
They said, "Isn't it a shame that so-and-so (the woman I
called Sylvia Frumpkin) is not here. She would have
been perfect. However, we're afraid she'll be back." Well,
in June she came back, quite psychotic, and I was
introduced to her, and she was thrilled to have a book
written about her. I drew up consent forms and I kept
having her sign them as she became less psychotic so
that no one would ever feel that she had been taken
advantage of. And I just really got lucky. You couldn't
have found a better textbook example of schizophrenia.

I was lucky to have her cooperate. But you just listen
and listen and listen for years. I have never done a long
book with fewer than eight hundred or nine hundred
pages of single-spaced transcribed notes. So it's a long
haul.

I don't go over a sheet of questions. At the beginning,
we're just talking. No rules at all. Often you don't have
to ask anything; they just talk. You really play it by ear
until you've written a rough draft—maybe a year later—
and you've got holes in it, and then you have specific
questions. At the beginning, you're just talking. You've

got to do a whole new set of interviews that are more to
the point. What I don't know is, What do I ask? What
should I ask about the meaning of the thing that
happened in the second month or the fifth month, or
whatever? You'll be looking to fill the holes in the
manuscript.

I don't know if there's a talent for this kind of
interviewing. Faulkner once said, "I've heard of talent,
but I've never seen it." I think what makes a certain
kind of writer is curiosity, and I think I'm curious about
knowing about people. I think you've got to find the
patience to find a way to get the hard questions asked
and answered, or the patience just to be present. There's
a lot of interviewing where I'm just there and not asking
a thing. In the Sylvia Frumpkin book, some of the
scenes that the reviewers liked the best, I hadn't asked
anything. There's a scene where I'm at the Frumpkin's
dinner table—I believe it was Passover—and what they
were saying was startling. I wanted to be under the table
when they were really going at each other.

So many things don't have to be asked if you're there.
The idea is to be there, not always to have to ask
questions. In fact, what's seen, or heard, is often as good
as what's asked, although, of course, it's a combination.

I will use a tape recorder if I need it for legal reasons,
if I think *The New Yorker* is really going to want it on
tape. I don't have any money to transcribe tapes, and I
hate the sound of my own voice. And so at Creedmore,
everything was tape-recorded and I listened for five
minutes. I know where the tapes are, but I never use
them. I do speed writing so that my notes are perfectly
good and it's just too inefficient for me to use the tape
recorder. If I had the money, I would love it. If you have
a transcriber, it's great; but if you don't, it's hellish. So I
don't have a choice. I don't worry about a tape recorder;
I find that people forget about it. So it's not a problem
that way; the problem is quite financial.

Being a woman has been a great help in interviewing,
in that you're less of a threat. Somehow, once you
establish the fact that you're not a bleeding-heart liberal,

not trying to help the prisoner escape, or smuggle things in, or break the rules, they're pretty decent about a woman who's doing her job. In the mental institution, since I picked a woman patient, it was probably good that I was a woman. We became friends. That helped.

To do this work, you have to be a reader and not a television watcher, because you really want to be a literate person and not someone who loves the quick fix of television. They are very, very incompatible—what I do and TV. I don't watch any television—maybe three hours a week—lousy shows that I've become addicted to. I don't see the news on TV. I didn't grow up with television. I think if you want to do what I do, you must have read books you cared for and wanted to write them. You'd have to have in your head what great books are. I don't read much, but I reread every year *Tender Is the Night* and *In Cold Blood*. I reread books I care about, the ones that I take as models of one thing or another, whether they're fiction or poetry. But I don't read most modern books; modern books are bad. I don't want to read that style.

You can't prepare to have curiosity. I think that's got to be there. I think what I do is a little different from other people. I have an aversion to writing about people who are similar to most others. I don't get interested in the world of the upper middle class. I really don't care about the lives of the rich and famous. Goodness knows, books about celebrities sell; those about nonentities don't. But I'm not interested in the kind of people I would know professionally.

Sure, I learned from my mistakes. In 1963, my first long *New Yorker* pieces were on the subject of burglary. My error was to take the police side of the account. It never occurred to me—I was pretty young—to go to talk to the burglars. I think that's a young person's error—to believe the police. You should get both sides. But to mistrust the police altogether— that's too simpleminded. Fourteen years later, I get both sides of the story. In the early 1960s, we had different notions of the police as

being good. Today, our notions are more complicated;
police are good and bad, like the rest of us.

You don't take everything people say as the truth. You
check it out and then see what the meaning of the lie
was. Often people don't know, they don't understand the
truth. The prisoner I wrote about really wants to think
he committed the crimes because he had an unhappy
childhood and was poor. He really believed that. I didn't
believe it. I let him talk to me, then I wrote it my way.

I don't have bad luck with interviews because I have
time. I think the thing to have is a lot of time.

To earn a living doing what I'm doing will be harder
and harder as things are going. It's wonderful if you can
work for *The New Yorker*; they pay very well for pieces.
You could not earn a living writing books this way,
because they don't sell enough. You have to be
independently wealthy. Our older daughter wants to be
a journalist; I grit my teeth and hope she will change
her mind or that she'll get into a form of journalism
where she's more likely to earn a living. I used to think
of going into TV; and then you hear about the firings at
ABC or CBS and you find there's not much job security,
and you do worry about young people.

I would tell someone never to enter this work; you
won't be able to make a living at it.

Bill Moyers

Interviewer, PBS

"The interviewer's job is to create an environment, as in a good conversation, in which the person eavesdropping doesn't feel guilty about eavesdropping, but feels delighted because he's invited, and is sharing a moment of true communication, a true encounter. There comes a moment when it's a religious experience to listen to somebody speak who speaks well, and to share that person's experience, mind, ideas, vision, or just confession. I think there's no better production value than a mind thinking in front of you—literally, in front of you."

HOW DO YOU get to be Bill Moyers?

This is a question that countless people must have asked, somewhat jealously. What intellectual would not want to talk tête-à-tête and at length with some of the most erudite people in the fields of philosophy, religion, science? And then, who would not want these interviews to become the basis for best-selling books?

The range of knowledge Moyers exhibits in his interviews is stunning. This range comes from a wide array of experiences.

Back in 1986, someone in the television industry commented to me, "Bill Moyers still doesn't know what he wants to be when he grows up," a comment prompted by Moyers' having had a more varied career than anyone else we interviewed for this book. Moyers himself, somewhat defensively perhaps, told an interviewer more than ten years ago, "I know not many people have drunk from as many cups as I have.... But I'm not just a wine taster. All the jobs I've had, as different as they may appear to be, relate to public affairs. Just as a doctor specializes within the general field of medicine, I've 'specialized' in government, publishing, and broadcasting—all branches of public affairs." Examining his statement carefully, one would be hard put to place his three major occupations under the heading of public affairs. It might be more accurate to say that Moyers has been searching for the ideal funnel for his interests, intelligence, and schooling—and for a job which fits his values.

What are his values? They seem pretty clear from a statement he made to a *Saturday Review* interviewer almost ten years ago:

My mail suggests to me that people of all persuasions watch me on TV....That's power. The stewardship of air time is critical. It's not the ability to change the course of things directly, but you can change a person's view of the world. You can affect the quality of his day. As Thoreau said, "To affect the quality of a day, that is the highest of the arts."

From all indications, Moyers does change people's view of the world and affect their day in his television interviewing, most notably in his series, *A World of Ideas*. Moyers apparently has finally found a role that can take full advantage of his background in interviewing, his study of religion, his wide experience in publishing, writing, government—and still satisfy his values. But as we shall see, he has paid a price for this position.

Billy Don Moyers was born in 1934 in a very small Texas town where his father was a dirt farmer. The family moved to a somewhat larger town in Texas where Billy Don went to school. In high school, he had his first brush with something he loved—the newspaper. Afterward, he kept returning to newspaper work; in 1982, having had great success as a television interviewer, he said, "There will come a time when I quit this life and either teach—at the University of Texas—or go back to a newspaper, which was truly my first love."

Upon graduation from high school, Moyers entered North Texas State College. At this young age, he wrote a letter to then Senator Lyndon Johnson—the first of two he would write to LBJ which would alter the course of Moyers' life. In his letter, he offered to help Johnson with his reelection campaign. Johnson accepted.

Johnson urged Moyers to leave his small-town college and go to the University of Texas for a journalism degree. Moyers agreed. Johnson added a bonus: he introduced Moyers to television by helping him get a job at a station owned by Mrs. Johnson. Moyers received his journalism degree with honors.

Graduating from college, he dropped journalism in favor of another major interest—religion. (He had been preaching on Sundays at small Baptist churches while attending college.) He was awarded the prestigious Rotary International Fellowship to study ecclesiastical history in Scotland for a year, an experience he considers a powerful influence on him. Returning to the United States, he became even more serious about religion: he entered Southwest Baptist Theological Seminary, where in two years he obtained a Bachelor of Divinity (his second degree with honors). During this time, he acted as publicity director for the seminary and preached at three rural churches.

Then Lyndon Johnson entered his life again. Moyers was invited to rejoin Senator Johnson's staff. He accepted, giving up a college lectureship and doctoral studies he intended to pursue. He became the senator's personal assistant, then special assistant, then executive assistant, where he coordinated the senator's vice-presidential campaign (on the Kennedy ticket). But working in the Vice President's office after the successful campaign was not challenging enough for Moyers, and he became associate director of the Peace Corps, which had interested him from its inception. In less than two years, he was deputy director.

Then an odd twist of fate—nudged on by Moyers' assertiveness—placed him back with Lyndon Johnson.

While Moyers was lunching in Austin, he heard the news of President Kennedy's assassination, immediately chartered a plane to Dallas, wrote a note to Johnson, and got it to him through a Secret Service agent just before LBJ, standing in Air Force One about to take off, was to receive the oath as President of the United States. The note read, "I'm here if you need me," and Moyers was, in a matter of seconds, on the presidential plane headed for Washington, not to leave Johnson's side for the next four years. (The President asked him to leave the Peace Corps and Moyers did.) Within a year Moyers was White House chief of staff, then became press secretary. Some journalists dubbed him "the best White House press secretary in memory."

By 1966, the Vietnam War was splitting the nation and things soured for Moyers. To him, the government had become a "war government," not a "reform government," and Moyers saw no "creative role" there. He left the White House to become publisher of *Newsday*, the most popular suburban newspaper in America. Within three years, the paper won fifty-three journalism awards and two Pulitzer prizes. Then the paper was sold and Moyers resigned.

Footloose, he decided to see firsthand "what the country is about and who the people are," and he traveled by bus all over the United States interviewing people, producing the much-praised *Listening to America: A Traveler Rediscovers His Country*.

Moyers' real television career began in 1971, the year his book was published, but the path was not smooth. For ten years he moved back and forth between CBS and public television, where he hosted the acclaimed *Bill Moyers' Journal*. He ended up as a news analyst for CBS, where he was paid well but the working conditions were not to his liking.

The television industry was experiencing what *Time* magazine called "the decline of the furrowed brow," referring to the sober quality of news analysts. Moyer and others, like John Chancellor at NBC, were allowed less and less time to comment on the news. Up until 1984, Moyers averaged twenty-three hours of television a year; in 1985, he did one hour, in 1986, four hours. "That's not enough for someone they were paying as much as me, or someone who has as much energy as I," he said later. The crowning blow was that finally CBS allowed him "time only to make your point but not to build your case." What he had discovered was that commercial television had money but not enough air time, while public television had air time but not enough money.

In 1987, he moved to PBS where he would earn a tenth of what he earned at CBS but would have ten times the amount of air time. He pays dearly for the increased air time, far beyond a decrease in salary. "I spend one half my time being a journalist and the other half being an entrepreneur," he said.

"I'm like the publisher of a small-town newspaper. I've got to worry about raising money, selling ads, dealing with my constituents."

But finally, on PBS he seems to have found work which is made to order for his talents and his values. He has done many highly praised documentaries, including *In Search of the Constitution*, about the history of the United States Constitution; *God and Politics*, about Southern Baptists; six hours of interviews with mythologist Joseph Campbell (later a book, *The Power of Myth*); and interviews with forty-two outstanding writers and intellectuals (later a book, *A World of Ideas*).

New York Times critic John O'Connor commented in 1988, "Needless to say, by any reasonable estimate, Mr. Moyers and his 'talking heads' are responsible for an inordinately hefty share of public TV's most memorable moments over the past two decades." And a little later that year, O'Connor paid the ultimate compliment in television journalism: "The much-vaunted Edward R. Morrow tradition of broadcasting excellence has decidedly passed into Moyers' hands."

When I walked into Moyers' office and heard his Texas drawl, I found myself reverting immediately to my own Texas drawl, which usually appears in the presence of another Texan. I commented on the large photograph of the University of Texas tower (I did not comment on the array of Emmys on top of a bookcase), and we were off on a run-through of similar interests, which I knew about from clippings I had gathered about him. We talked for a short time about the university, our training in religion, and his interest in buying a home in the Hill Country of Texas, where I own a ranch. I felt I had known him much longer than the few minutes we had been together, and it struck me that those he interviews must feel the same, not because of common interests, necessarily, but because of his warmth and rapt attention.

Oddly, while interviewing has been at the center of much of his professional life, Moyers was originally hesitant to see me to discuss the topic.

The introduction to Moyers was offered to me by Mrs. William Schuman, longtime fund-raiser for public television and wife of the composer, who called Jay Iselin, former president of WNET in New York, who in turn said I should

phone Moyers and say that he had recommended I call. I was
not prepared for Moyers' response: he said that he did not
know anything about interviewing. I responded that I could
probably pull out of him more than he might think he had to
say. Then he sprang another surprise: he said that he was not
sure that he wanted to analyze what he does. I said that this was
a totally different matter. I could certainly understand that,
and if this were true, he perhaps should not see me. He said
that I should get in touch with him later.

When the allotted time had passed, I wrote a letter stating, "I
certainly understand any hesitation you have about analyzing
what you do. If on further reflection you feel strongly about
that, we could focus not on your own interviewing but on your
general views of interviewing. Is that a viable way out, or does
it amount to the same thing?" He made a note in tiny
handwriting on my letter and returned it to me. He would see
me, he said, and invited me to ask any question I wanted. I
called and we made an appointment.

This is what he said on the topic he professed to know
nothing about:

■ What makes a good interview depends upon what kind
of interview.

If I'm doing a documentary, where I'm going from
person to person trying to carry on a story, a good
interview is that crystallizing moment that carries the
story forward. At the same time I'm interviewing you
about what's on your mind, in my mind is the story of
the whole that I am pursuing in the documentary. So a
good interview for the documentary becomes that
moment when the story, like a camera, comes into focus.
A documentary interview can be authentic in two ways:
it can confirm the story you have discovered in the
beginning, or it can move the story in a wholly
unexpected direction.

There is yet another kind of good interview, which is
totally unrelated to the documentary; it is the interview
in which the interview itself is the program. Like a
conversation with Archibald MacLeish, or with any of
the two-hundred-and-some people I have done over the

last ten or fifteen years. A good interview by that
definition is performance. It can be the mind revealing
itself in an arresting way, or it can be the presence of the
person who doesn't have that much to say but whose
witness in your living room becomes an experience you
could never have had otherwise. And irrespective of
what the person says, it's an experience to be enjoyed
because you're meeting someone for the first time.

I was out in Toledo some time ago to make a speech,
and a fellow came up to me afterward and said, "I want
to thank you, Mr. Moyers, for bringing Mortimer Adler
to Toledo, and not only bringing him to Toledo but
bringing him to my living room. I would never have met
Mortimer Adler except for that series of six great ideas
that you did with him."

A good interview is theater, circuit theater delivered
to the individual in his or her own home. That kind of
interview is not only what is said. It becomes a revelation
of character as well as of intellect. The interviewer has
to engage the subject at various levels: intellectual,
emotional, personal.

I do not get a good interview if I am hostile with the
person. Mike Wallace can, and there are different
interviews and different interviewers and different
techniques, but I am not after the hidden secret around
which the subject has organized his defenses, never to be
penetrated. Some people can penetrate those defenses
and get out that secret. I see that very rarely, by the way.

The important thing about an interview is that it is
collaborative and cooperative, and the person must have
something to say. And the interviewer has to help the
person to say what that person has on his or her mind
in a way that becomes as personal for the viewer at
home as our conversation is this very moment.

The best interview allows the viewer to eavesdrop
almost the way a child might eavesdrop behind a couch
on his older brother or sister courting in the parlor. Not
that you're overhearing secrets that are sacred or
embarrassing, but that you're hearing the intimacy of
really good conversation. Lovers are the best

conversationalists, because they want the other person to know how they feel, and what they think. If you can overhear a conversation between lovers, you're overhearing the most personal and authentic communication. A good interview makes you feel like you're witnessing something real.

The interviewer's job is to create an environment, as in a good conversation, in which the person eavesdropping doesn't feel guilty about eavesdropping, but feels delighted because he's invited, and is sharing a moment of true communication, a true encounter. There comes a moment when it's a religious experience to listen to somebody speak who speaks well, and to share that person's experience, mind, ideas, vision, or just confession. I think there's no better production value than a mind thinking in front of you—literally, in front of you.

I think TV does two things very well: sporting events and talking heads. And the craft of the interviewer is to create authentic theater and not imitative theater.

Mostly today people who have nothing to say get on TV. If you have something to say, you don't get on TV. We're in this celebrity worship, so that people who have nothing to say, but are well known, command the most air time. The philosopher, or historian, or good teacher, or a writer or a psychologist—someone who has something of value to say—has very little time to say it on TV.

An interviewer should do his homework: he has to know what the person means. In an hour-long conversation, I've got to be familiar with that person's writing, familiar enough to plumb his experience with my own curiosity, but at the same time, familiar enough to follow him if he suddenly leaps onto a ground that I hadn't anticipated. Time and time again—I don't want to seem immodest—but time and time again people like Hugh Trevor-Roper, Rebecca West, and others would say to my producer, "I've never talked to anybody who's read everything I've ever written." Well, obviously, I hadn't read everything, but I had studied enough to go with them on grounds that were foreign to me and still be at home there. That's craftsmanship. A good interviewer is a good student, above all.

I like journalism because I'm paid to be a student of the news, a student of events. One has to be a good student in order to ask a good question. I've had the longest-running adult education course I know of at somebody else's expense.

I think I'm a journalist mostly because from early days I have been genuinely curious about the world and curious about other people. I think I like the interview not because I like interviews, but because I like to know other people, and engage other people, and listen to other people. There are extemporaneous speakers, and there are extemporaneous listeners. I think I am a very good extemporaneous listener. There are crafts of the trade that enable one to be better at extemporaneous listening, but the appetite to listen extemporaneously, I think, comes with the equipment. It's built into the system that you bring into this world—the cultural inheritance, or the accidents and incidents of childhood.

Growing up in a Baptist Church made me conscious of other people. They would get up in front of the church and tell their stories, give their testimonies. That's a vivid part of my childhood experience. Even now I can see Lamar Smith and Dexter Riddle and all those men get up at the hour of testimony and tell their story. You get interested in other people's lives, not in some voyeuristic way, but in a political way—I mean that in the best sense of the term *political:* the sense of society, the sense of community, the sense of connection and relationship.

The most interesting question in the world to me is, What makes a life? I've always been curious about that. I will often get diverted, I will often detour unexpectedly from the course of a conversation by simply wanting to know what it was that made this person who this person is.

One must also have a sense of story. Southerners are

very good at that, because we are people of the oral
tradition and of the Bible, which is basically a series of
stories. And curiosity has to be connected to a sense of
story, an intuition for the dramatic—that is, the
unfolding of a tale that is a part of all of our lives.

Television discriminates against the inarticulate. And I
accept that; in the same way that a paraplegic cannot be
a swimmer, TV discriminates against the inarticulate.
But you can work at finding the story the inarticulate
has to tell and do it in such a way, edit it in such a way,
that even the inarticulate gets some of his or her story
out. That comes from a sense of drama, a sense of what
happens on a stage.

One of the ways of honing people's natural
endowment in conversation, or on TV, is to close out the
space between you and the subject, that artificial world
of TV, which is the camera and the lights and the
microphones. And there are ways you do that.

One is concentration. Look the person in the eye; get
the person to see you as the center of his or her universe
at that moment. You can lean forward like this, which
sometimes motivates the other person to lean forward.
Do anything you can do to get the individual to
concentrate on you instead of the lights and the camera.

You can learn how to make good notes that become
the road map in your lap or in your hands. But at the
same time you have to learn how to put your notes
down. You learn from experience that there are some
people for whom no road map is possible or desirable.

When you're doing an interview, you're at the same
time editing. In your own mind, you're living on several
levels in the interview: you're living on the level of
immediate encounter; you're living in the past tense of
that person's writings, that person's works and ideas; and
you also live in the future tense: How am I going to edit
this?

The person has said something to you that you need
to connect with something else that's been said in the
past. At the same time, there's this little machine that's

thinking ahead, "How am I going to edit this, to get either the story that I'm after, or the story that he has to tell, or the essense of this experience?"

And so you are at that moment not just an interviewer, not just a journalist, but you're a producer, an editor, a director, you're a playwright, you're an audience. You're always thinking how this is going to look. Not only "How am I going to make this happen, physically and honestly?" but "How will it appear to that viewer sitting in his living room?"

Once you get to know people, there is something in their lives that connects them all and I'm at ease with anybody. But why that is so I can't say. But you need a different set of journalistic skills to interview the shah of Iran than you do if you're interviewing your hometown schoolteachers. With the shah, I'm not Bill Moyers; I'm a journalist and his mental apparatus is different. I must find a way to make his apparatus work for my limited purpose. I'm comfortable personally with the shah, as I am with those schoolteachers, although I might enjoy the experience with the schoolteachers and might not enjoy the experience with the shah.

I don't like interviewing officials, because I know that there are certain things officials want to say and that's all they're going to say. I'm not interested in sparring with them, because the story is what's on their minds, not my confrontation with them.

Confrontation, or sparring, interviews I consider unbecoming. I just don't like to do them anymore, because the best interview for me is the interview where the person *wants* to talk, *wants* to share his ideas, *wants* to talk about her experiences, has some predictions and values and ideas that he or she is eager to communicate.

I once did an interview with Jimmy Carter when he was campaigning for the presidency—an hour on *Bill Moyers' Journal*. It was wonderful. We talked about "amazing grace," we talked about growing up in the South, we talked about all those things that connected him. Eighteen months later, when he was President, I did the first hour interview he did on TV, and it didn't go anywhere. There was an invisible shield between us, and I just couldn't get him off the official position. And the minute the interview was over and the lights were turned off, he put his arm around me and said, "I'm sorry I couldn't tell you the truth. It's different now that I'm President." I recognize that. Officials mustn't let the press hustle their priorities; otherwise, they shouldn't be in office. A President's agenda is different from his agenda as candidate, and is certainly different from my agenda as journalist.

The first knack of a good interviewer is to know whom to interview. I wasn't interested in interviewing Roy Cohn, but Mike Wallace was fascinated with Roy Cohn. We tend to reach for those people to interview about whom we're most interested, about whom we are curious. And so if you're lucky, you interview those people who create a genuine experience, a true encounter.

For me, the close-knittedness of a small town, the influence of a democratic church, the study of ethics and theology, traveling as a graduate student at the University of Edinburgh, my experiences in government, politics, publishing a paper, all of that creates a particular kind of person who encounters the kind of people I interview, or even causes me to seek out those people.

Everybody is the sum of his or her experiences and brings to his or her work that set of values, experiences, influence of persons, peak moments, that make life, and so nobody could do my kind of interviewing because nobody's me. And I couldn't do somebody else's kind of interviewing because I'm not that person.

Epilogue

DURING OUR INTERVIEWING for this book, we were often told by friends who the "best" interviewers were—and therefore whom we should interview. The odd thing was that the opinions, even within the limited number of people we know, varied greatly.

And then our friends would ask us, "Which interviewer is the best?" They often seemed frustrated with our replies.

After reading our book, you may come to our conclusion: "best" depends on the perspective of the judge. There is the boss of the interviewer (CBS makes a great deal of money from the interviewing of Mike Wallace); there is the viewer, the reader, or the listener (who may want to learn something, be entertained, or collect gossip); and there is the interviewee (Ken Auletta urged us to interview some of the people he had interviewed to get their perspective). How "good" the interviewer is depends on what is wanted by whom.

The bosses of these interviewers—television executives, magazine and newspaper editors, and book publishers—are in the business of making money. No money is made without an audience. Interviewers must have a forum; without it, the interviewer is never read, heard, or seen.

Viewers judge interviewers on the basis of what they like. Some people obviously liked Morton Downey, Jr.; others hated him. As you have read, Barbara Walters is fully aware of the different ways people perceive her (sometimes as too tough, sometimes as too cream puff).

We have not yet followed Ken Auletta's suggestion to interview the interviewees, but we did stumble upon some perspective from someone who is frequently interviewed. Obsessed with our work, we told a Boston physician sitting next to us on the Boston-LaGuardia air shuttle about the book. His basis of appraisal was this: "I can sure tell a good interviewer from a poor one. The good ones do something that makes it easy for me to talk. With the bad ones, I get nervous, don't know what they're after, want to help them out, and finally just clam up."

The people in this book please their bosses (they make money), they please readers, listeners, or viewers (they are popular), and, most important of all, they know how to get through to interviewees. As we wrote at the beginning of this book, these interviewers know how to turn on the tap. That, in a nutshell, is what puts them at the top of their profession.

Notes

Introduction

4   "My mail suggests": Quoted in Katherine Bouton, "Bill Moyers: The Quest for Quality TV," *Saturday Review*, February 1982, p. 20.

4   "I love the breathtaking way": Quoted in Richard Zoglin, "Star Power," *Time*, August 7, 1989, p. 46.

9   Mark Twain on interviewing: "An Encounter With an Interviewer," *The Unabridged Mark Twain* (Philadelphia: Running Press, 1976), pp. 411–12.

Confronting, Prosecuting

11   Mike Wallace on Vietnam War: Leslie Bennetts, "How Television Saw the News of 1968," *New York Times*, January 14, 1988, p. C30.

12   Tom Wicker on American press: *New York Times*, January 14, 1988.

12   Oriana Fallaci "cajoled, badgered, and charmed": *Current Biography* 1977 (New York: H. W. Wilson, 1977), p. 147.

13   "At the end": Peter J. Boyer, "'60 Minutes': A Hit Confronts the Odds," *New York Times*, September 13, 1987, p. 38.

Oriana Fallaci

16   Robert Scheer on Fallaci interview: "Playboy Interview: Oriani Fallaci," *Playboy*, November 1981, p. 78.

20   "Sometimes I blush": Quoted in "Oriana's World," *Newsweek*, August 17, 1964, p. 57.

Mike Wallace

33   "The executives at CBS": Mike Wallace and Gary Paul Gates, *Close Encounters: Mike Wallace's Own Story* (New York: Berkley Books, 1984), p. 485.

37–38   Early career of Mike Wallace: Ibid., pp. 5, 25, 350.

40   "What I did was": Quoted in Arthur Ungar, "300 Minutes With Mike Wallace at Sixty-seven," *Television Quarterly* 22, no. 1 (November 1986), p. 13.

40–41   Interview with Ronald Reagan: Wallace and Gates, *Close Encounters,* p. 216.

41   "Most of the interview": Ibid., p. 451.

43–44   My Lai interview: Ibid., p. 236.

Ted Koppel

47   Mike Wallace on Ted Koppel: Quoted in Arthur Ungar, "300 Minutes With Mike Wallace at Sixty-seven," p. 10.

47   "As much as anyone": John Corry, "'Koppel Report' on TV Evangelists," *New York Times,* May 12, 1988.

48   "I'm not very well organized": Quoted in Nancy Collins, "The Smartest Man on TV," *New York,* August 13, 1984, p. 22.

49   "I have never gotten":Quoted in Judith Adler Hennessee, "The Man Who Wouldn't Be King," *Esquire,* January 1984, p. 53.

49   "I've learned to listen": Quoted in Collins, "The Smartest Man on TV," p. 26.

50   "There was no question": Ibid., p. 28.

51   "In this industry": Quoted in Collins, "The Smartest Man on TV," p. 31.

52   "I'm just old enough": Quoted in Jonathan Alter with Renee Michael and Michael Lerner, "America's Q&A," *Newsweek,* June 15, 1987, p. 56

52   "I'm a registered independent": Quoted in Collins, "The Smartest Man on TV," p. 75.

55   "Ted needs any edge": Quoted in "Ted Koppel's Edge," *New York Times Magazine,* August 14, 1988, p. 16.

59   "judicious-to-delicious": Tom Shales, "I'm the National Interest," *Washington Post,* November 15, 1977, p. 4.

59   "Koppel interrupts": Wally Pfister, personal communication.

John Chancellor

62   On plans for teaching: *Contemporary Authors* New Revision Series (Detroit: Gale Research, 1979),

63   "I had money": Quoted in Henry F. Waters with Betsy Carter and Lucy Howard, "Hairstring Anchor," *Newsweek,* December 12, 1977.

63   "charming, eclectic, gentlemanly": Bob Williams, *New York Post Magazine,* July 30, 1961, p. 2.

Robert MacNeil

76   "I liked the money": Quoted in Gerry Nadel, "The MacNeil/ Lehrer Report," *TV Guide,* October 8, 1977, pp. 22–24.

77   "The answer we now know": Robert MacNeil, *The Right Place at the Right Time* (Boston: Little, Brown, 1982), p. 289.

77   "By a curious turn": Ibid., p. 288.

Roger Mudd

87   "the best Washington reporter": Desmond Smith, "The Third Men," *New York,* January 31, 1983, p. 31.

87   "conceived and undertaken": Charles Maritz, ed., *Current Biography Yearbook* 1981 (New York: H. W. Wilson, 1982), p. 313.

89   "a journalistic job": "The Selling of the Pentagon," *Variety,* March 3, 1971, p. 45.

89   "an act of choler": Peter J. Boyer, "NBC and Roger Mudd Said to Agree on Split," *New York Times,* January 29, 1987.

89   "One of the problems": Quoted in "The Unmuddling of Mudd," *Time,* July 14, 1980, p. 75.

90   "I *ran* the *Today* show": Quoted in Smith, "The Third Men," *New York,* January 31, 1983, p. 31.

90   "NBC News insiders": Smith, ibid.

90   "full circle": Eleanor A. Blair, "Roger Mudd's Switch," *New York Times,* June 20, 1988, p. C8.

90   "The imperturbability": *Current Biography Yearbook* 1981, p. 314.

93   "appeared vague": Ibid.

93–95   Kennedy interview: *CBS Reports* transcript, November 4, 1979.

96–97   Hart interview: Radio TV Reports, "NBC Reports Super Tuesday," March 13, 1984.

Nicholas Pileggi

102   "I went to a lot": Quoted in Carol E. Rinzler, "Pileggi on Record," *Cosmopolitan,* January 1986, p. 30.

102   "I would fly": Quoted in Joseph Barbato, "P.W. Interviews Nicholas Pileggi," *Publishers Weekly,* February 7, 1986, pp. 56–57.

102   "I don't think so": Ibid., p. 57.

102   "Not much. Crime reporters": Quoted in Rinzler, "Pileggi on Record," p. 34.

102   "Once I saw": Quoted in Barbato, "P.W. Interviews Nicholas Pileggi," p. 56.

104   Pileggi on career: Ibid.

Barbara Walters

119   Pryor interview: Barwall Productions, "Barbara Walters Special," December 2, 1986.

119   Hepburn interview: Barwall Productions, "Barbara Walters Special, June 2, 1981.

120–21   Townley on Walters, quoting Duffy, Lansbury, and White: "Does She Push Too Hard?: A Report Card on Barbara Walters," *TV Guide,* July 4–10, 1987.

125   "Yeah, I'm called too strident": Quoted in Barbara Gruzzuti Harrison, "Barbara Walters: Survivor," *McCall's,* January 1985, pp. 30–31.

125   "My Lord, I'm Lucky": *How to Talk to Practically Anybody About Practically Anything* (New York: Doubleday, 1970), p. xiii.

Marie Brenner

133   Characterizations of Brenner: Quoted in Diane Reischel, "Marie Brenner," *Dallas Morning News,* April 16, 1989, p. 2-E.

134   "the Tiger Lady": Jill Brooks, "Tiger Lady: Writer Marie Brenner," *Hamptons,* June 30, 1989.

134   "People shouldn't speak to Marie": Ibid.

134   "She knows how": Ibid.

Thomas B. Morgan

141   "Over time, deliberately": Thomas B. Morgan, *Self-Creations: Thirteen Impersonalities* (New York: Holt & Rinehart, 1959), p. 4.

141   "The answer is": Ibid., p. 2.

141   "Vanity is": Ibid., p. 8.

150   Rockefeller was quoted as saying: In Ibid., p. 128.

Diane Sawyer

154   "By the testimony": Harry F. Waters, George Hackett, and Mary Ford, "CBS's New Morning Star," *Newsweek,* March 14, 1983, pp. 74–76.

155   Sawyer on her life and career: "Brief Encounter," *Esquire,* July 1982, pp. 69–70; *Current Biography Yearbook* 1985.

156   Sawyer on Nixon: Leonard Zeidenberg, "The Class Act of Diane Sawyer," *Broadcasting,* November 22, 1982.

156   Sawyer at CBS: John Wesimann, "Is Diane Sawyer Tough Enough for *60 Minutes?" TV Guide,* October 20, 1984, pp. 6–11.

156   "Life is going to pass her by": Waters, Hackett, and Ford, "CBS's New Morning Star."

156   "I can't imagine": Ibid.

157   National Junior Miss contest: *Current Biography Yearbook* 1985.

158   the "ice princess": James Brady, "They Talk of Diane Sawyer, the 'Ice Princess' of *60 Minutes,*" *Parade,* September 21, 1986.

Dick Cavett

164   "I was president": Dick Cavett and Christopher Porterfield, *Eye on Cavett* (New York: Arbor House, 1983), p. 10.

164   "I did have this sense": Dick Cavett and Christopher Porterfield, *Cavett* (New York: Harcourt, Brace, Jovanovitch, 1974), p. 17.

164–66   Cavett on career: Cavett and Porterfield, *Eye on Cavett* and *Cavett*.

166   "It is remarkable": *Cavett*, p. 138.

166   "Now, as a highly paid ... performer": *Cavett*, p. 300.

166   "I loved the radio acting": *Cavett*, p. 123

166   "I would really love": *Cavett*, p. 123

166–67   On Broadway appearance: Carey Winfrey, "Dick Cavett: 'I Love It When the Ice Gets Thin,'" *New York Times Biographical Service*, January 1981, pp. 20–21.

167   "I would sometimes sight-read": *Cavett*, p. 173.

167–68   Cavett at CBS: *Eye on Cavett*, pp. 112, 114.

171   Bette Davis autobiography: *This 'n That* (New York: Putnam's, 1987), p. 73.

Ken Auletta

179   "Most of my work": *Contemporary Authors*, ed. by Frances C. Lochner and Ann Evory, rev. ed., 1974.

180   "Feeling close to people": Quoted in Linda Cateura, *Growing Up Italian* (New York: Morrow, 1987), pp. 168–77.

180   A reviewer of *The Underclass:* Charles Peters, *New York Times Book Review*, May 11, 1982.

Harrison Salisbury

193   *Times* critic on Salisbury: Thomas Griffith, "Back From Everywhere," *New York Times Book Review*, March 20, 1988, p. 11.

195   On losing the Putlizer Prize: *Current Biography Yearbook* 1982, p. 380.

Studs Terkel

208   Studs Terkel "understands": Peter S. Prescott, "Studs' Best Tapes," *Newsweek*, April 1, 1974, 78.

208   "a formidable gift": *Contemporary Authors*, ed. by Frances C. Lochner and Ann Evory, rev. ed. vol. 18.

208   "an uncanny flair": *Current Biography Yearbook* 1974, p. 405.

Gay Talese

214   "now considered classic": *Contemporary Authors.* rev. ed., vol. 9, p. 481.

215   "I became involved": Quoted in Ibid.

215   "I wasn't a student": *Chicago Tribune*, February 6, 1972.

215   "I don't know why": Quoted in *Contemporary Authors*, p. 484.

216   "After reading several books": *Thy Neighbor's Wife* (New York: Doubleday, 1980), pp. 600–603.

217   "That the marriage survived": Ibid., p. 622.

Phil Donahue

225   *Esquire* description of Donahue: William Brashler, "Blessed Are the Women of America, for Donahue Is Their Shepherd," *Esquire*, January 30, 1979, p. 42.

225   "He has the ability": Harry F. Waters, Frank Maier, and Cynthia Wilson, "The Talk of Television," *Newsweek*, October 19, 1979, pp. 76–82.

226   "He never shied": Brashler, "Blessed Are the Women."

227   "The man is smart": "Phil Donahue in New York," *TV Guide*, August 31, 1985, pp. 34–38.

227   "Get him going": Susan Dworkin, "Turning the Tables," *Woman's Day*, October 1986, p. 30.

227   "The money was good": Phil Donahue, *My Own Story* (New York: Simon & Schuster, 1979), p. 100.

228   "I'd like to be known": Quoted in Brashler, "Blessed Are the Women," p. 49.

228   "a shy, insecure ... child": *Current Biography Yearbook* 1980, p. 78.

228   He told a *Newsday* reporter: *Newsday*, June 30–July 6, 1985.

236   "Why does it work?": Roger Simon, "The Phil Donahue Phenomenon," *TV Guide*, May 7, 1978, pp. 25–30.

Susan Sheehan

244   "laughter, tears": Richard R. Lingeman [book review], *New York Times*, August 27, 1976.

Bill Moyers

250   "I know not many have done": *Current Biography Yearbook* 1976, p. 274.

251   "My mail suggests": Katherine Bouton, "Bill Moyers: The Question of Quality TV," *Saturday Review*, February 1982, p. 20.

251   "There will come a time": Ibid.

251   "That's not enough": *San Antonio Express-News*, April 13, 1987, p. 8-D.

251   "The crowning blow": Thomas Giffith, "The Decline of the Furrowed Brow," *Time*, April 7, 1986, p. 84.

253   "I spend one half my time": *San Antonio Express-News*, ibid.

254   "Needless to say": John J. O'Connor, "Talking Heads and the Public TV Pickle," *New York Times*, February 14, 1988.

254   "The much-vaunted ... Murrow tradition": John J. O'Connor, "Moyers, Campbell, and Life's Essence," *New York Times*, June 27, 1988.

Index

273